Seventh-day Adventist

CHURCH
MANUAL

Seventh-day Adventist

CHURCH MANUAL

Revised 2000
16th Edition

Review and Herald® Publishing Association
Hagerstown, Maryland 21740

Printed in U.S.A.

04 03 02 01 00   5 4 3 2 1

ISBN 0-8280-1597-X   hardcover
ISBN 0-8280-1598-8   paperback

Table Of Contents

CHAPTER 6

CHAPTER 9
Auxiliary Organizations of the Church and Their Officers ... 93

CHAPTER 10

CHAPTER 11

CHAPTER 12

CHAPTER 13

CHAPTER 14

Introduction

Historical Development of the
Seventh-day Adventist Church

In fulfillment of the divine plan, the Advent Movement began its prophetic journey toward the kingdom in the year 1844. Few in number, often with unhappy memories of having been cast out of their churches because they had accepted the Advent doctrine, the Movement's pioneers walked uncertainly at first. They were sure of the doctrines they held, but unsure as to the form of organization, if any, that they should adopt. Indeed, most of them so sharply remembered how strong, well-organized church bodies had used that strength to oppose the Advent truth, that they instinctively feared any centralized order and government. Nevertheless, certain pioneer leaders saw with increasing clarity that some kind of government was imperative if good order was to prevail and the Movement grow strong. Their conviction was greatly strengthened by messages coming from the pen of Ellen G. White.

The result was that in 1860 a church name, Seventh-day Adventist, was chosen and a legal body created to hold church property. This was followed, in 1861, by the organization of our first conference, Michigan. This involved the organizing of local churches, with the members signing a church covenant, and the organizing of the various churches into one united body to constitute what is now called a local conference. Action was also taken to give identifying papers to the ministers, thus protecting the churches against impostors who might seek to prey upon them.

In 1863 the General Conference was organized, thus gathering into one organization a number of local conferences which had been created by that time. This set the Advent Movement on a coordinated, organized course.

Historical Development of the *Church Manual*

As the General Conference met year by year, in session, actions were taken on various matters of church order in an endeavor to spell out the proper rules for different situations in church life. The 1882 General

Conference Session voted to have prepared "instructions to church officers, to be printed in the *Review and Herald* or in tract form."—*Review and Herald*, Dec. 26, 1882. This action revealed the growing realization that church order was imperative if church organization was to function effectively, and that uniformity in such order required its guiding principles to be put into printed form. Accordingly the articles were published. But at the 1883 General Conference Session, when it was proposed that these articles be placed in permanent form as a church manual, the idea was rejected. The brethren feared that it would possibly formalize the church and take from its ministers their freedom to deal with matters of church order as they might individually desire.

But this fear—doubtless reflecting the opposition that had existed twenty years before to any kind of church organization—evidently soon departed. The annual General Conference sessions continued to take actions on matters of church order. In other words, they slowly but surely were producing material for a church manual. At times certain prominent brethren sought to gather together in book or booklet form the generally accepted rules for church life. Perhaps the most impressive of such endeavors was a 184-page book by none other than the pioneer J. N. Loughborough, entitled, *The Church, Its Organization, Order and Discipline*, which was published in 1907. Elder Loughborough's book, though in a sense a personal undertaking, dealt with many of the topics now covered by the *Church Manual* and long held an honored place in the Movement.

Meanwhile the Movement continued to grow rapidly both at home and abroad. It was therefore in the best interests of the very order and proper uniformity that had long been our goal, that the General Conference Committee took action in 1931 to publish a church manual. J. L. McElhany, then vice-president of the General Conference for North America, and later president of the General Conference for fourteen years, was asked to prepare the manuscript. This manuscript was carefully examined by the General Conference Committee and then published in 1932. The opening sentence of the preface of that first edition observes that "it has become increasingly evident that a manual on church government is needed to set forth and preserve our denominational practices and polity." Note the word *preserve*. Here was no attempt at a late date to suddenly create a whole pattern of church government. Rather it was an endeavor first to *preserve* all the good actions taken through the years, and then to add such regulations as the church's increasing growth and complexity might require

See Chapter 1, *Authority of the Church and the Church Manual*, with respect to the role of the *Church Manual* in the Seventh-day Adventist Church.

Content of the *Church Manual*

The 2000 General Conference Session authorized the reclassification of some existing *Church Manual* material and approved the process for making modifications to such. The content of this *Church Manual*, as it is presented in chapters and sections within the chapters, is divided into two types of material. The main content of each chapter is of worldwide value and applicable to every church. Recognizing the need for some variations, additional material which is explanatory in nature appears as Notes at the end of some chapters and is given as guidance. The Notes have subheadings which correspond to chapter subheadings and correlate to specific page numbers.

Procedure for Changes in the *Church Manual*

Realizing increasingly how important it is that everything "be done decently and in order" in our worldwide work, and that actions on church government should not only express the mind but have the full authority of the church, the 1946 General Conference Session adopted the following procedure: "All changes or revisions of policy that are to be made in the *Manual* shall be authorized by the General Conference session."—*General Conference Report*, No. 8, p. 197 (June 14, 1946).

However, local conditions in different parts of the world sometimes call for special actions. Accordingly, the 1948 Autumn Council, which had taken action to submit suggested revisions of the *Church Manual* to the 1950 General Conference Session, also voted:

"That each division, including the North American Division of the world field, prepare a 'Supplement' to the new *Church Manual* not in any way modifying it but containing such additional matter as is applicable to the conditions and circumstances prevailing in the division; the manuscripts for these Supplements to be submitted to the General Conference Committee for endorsement before being printed."—*Autumn Council Actions*, 1948, p. 19.

Changes in or revisions of the *Church Manual*, the Notes excepted (see below), can be made only by action of a General Conference session in which delegates of the world body of believers are assembled and have a voice in making revisions. If revisions in the *Church Manual* are considered necessary by any of the constituent levels (see p. 26), such revisions should be submitted to the next constituent level for wider counsel and study. If approved, the suggested revisions are then submitted to the next constituent level for further evaluation. Any proposed revisions shall then be sent to the General Conference Church Manual Committee. This committee will consider all recommended amendments or revisions and, if approved, prepare them for presentation at an Annual Council and/or General Conference session.

If revisions to the Notes at the end of some chapters of the *Church Manual* are considered necessary by any of the constituent levels (see p. 26), such revisions should be submitted to the next constituent level for consideration. If approved, the suggested revisions should continue on through the next constituent levels for further evaluation until they are received by the Church Manual Committee. The Church Manual Committee will process the request and, if approved, the revisions will be acted upon by the General Conference Executive Committee at the final Annual Council of the quinquennium to coordinate them with the changes of the main content that the General Conference Executive Committee will recommend to the next General Conference session. However, the General Conference Executive Committee may address changes to the Notes at any Annual Council.

A new edition of the *Church Manual* is published after every General Conference session. It is recommended that leaders at all levels of the church should always work with the most recent edition of the *Church Manual*.

Clarification of Meaning

Churches should look to the local conference for advice pertaining to the operating of the church or on questions arising from the *Church Manual*. If mutual understanding or agreement is not reached, the matter should be referred to the union for clarification.

Use of the Term Conference, etc

Each organized Seventh-day Adventist church is a member of the sisterhood of churches known as a conference, which is a united organized body of churches in a state, country, or territory. Until full conference status is achieved (see General Conference *Working Policy*), other terminology such as mission, section, delegation, or field may be used to describe the collective organization of local churches. In the *Church Manual* the term *conference* or *union conference* may also apply to a mission or a union mission.

The Present Edition

This present edition incorporates all revisions and additions accepted up to and including the 2000 General Conference Session.

CHAPTER 1

Authority of the Church and the *Church Manual*

Church Authority in the Early Church

As Creator, Redeemer and Sustainer, Lord and King of all creation, God alone is the source and ground of authority for the church. He delegated authority to His prophets and apostles (2 Cor. 10:8). They, therefore, occupied a crucial and unique position in the transmission of the Word of God and the edification of the church (Eph. 2:20).

In the early church, the elders and bishops held great authority. One of their main functions was general pastoral care and oversight (Acts 20:17-28; Heb. 13:17; 1 Peter 5:1-3), with special tasks such as giving instruction in sound doctrine and refuting those who contradicted it (1 Tim. 3:1, 2; Titus 1:5, 9). Those who ruled well were to be "considered worthy of double honour" more particularly so if they labored in "preaching and teaching" (1 Tim. 5:17).

The church bore responsibility for purity in doctrine and practice. It was to "test the spirits to see whether they are of God" (1 John 4:1) or, in Paul's terms, to "test everything" and "to hold fast what is good" (1 Thess. 5:21). The same was true regarding the exercise of church discipline (Matt. 18: 15-17). The exercise of discipline ranged all the way from private and caring admonition (cf. Matt. 18:16; Gal. 6:1) to removal from church membership (Matt. 18:18; 1 Cor. 5:11, 13; 2 Cor. 2:5-11). The church had authority to settle the conditions of membership and the rules governing the church.

Church Authority in the Seventh-day Adventist Church

The 1946 General Conference Session action that all "changes or revisions of policy" in the *Church Manual* shall be "authorized by the General Conference session," reflects a conception of the authoritative status of General Conference sessions that has long been held. In the 1877 session this action was taken:

"*Resolved*, that the highest authority under God among Seventh-day Adventists is found in the will of the body of that people, as expressed in the decisions of the General Conference when acting within its proper jurisdiction; and that such decisions should be submitted to by all without exception, unless they can be shown to conflict with the word of God and the rights of individual conscience."—*Review and Herald*, vol. 50, No. 14, p. 106.

Ellen G. White wrote in 1909: "But, when, in a General Conference, the judgment of the brethren assembled from all parts of the field is exercised, private independence and private judgment must not be stubbornly maintained, but surrendered. Never should a laborer regard as a virtue the persistent maintenance of his position of independence, contrary to the decision of the general body."—*Testimonies*, vol. 9, p. 260.

Long before this—in 1875—Ellen G. White had written in the same vein: "The church of Christ is in constant peril. Satan is seeking to destroy the people of God, and one man's mind, one man's judgment, is not sufficient to be trusted. Christ would have His followers brought together in church capacity, observing order, having rules and discipline, and all subject one to another, esteeming others better than themselves."—*Testimonies*, vol. 3, p. 445

In these inspired words, in the 1877 General Conference action, and in the need for well-defined rules that are requisite to good order, is found a basis for this *Church Manual* and its rightful claim upon us all, both ministry and laity.

The content of the *Church Manual* is the expression of the Seventh-day Adventist Church's understanding of Christian life and church governance and discipline based on biblical principles. It expresses the authority of a duly assembled General Conference session. "God has ordained that the representatives of His church from all parts of the earth, when assembled in a General Conference, shall have authority."—*Testimonies*, vol. 9, p. 261.

CHAPTER 2

The Church of the Living God

To belong to the church of God is a unique and soul-satisfying privilege. It is the divine purpose to gather out a people from the far corners of the earth to bind them into one body, the body of Christ, the church, of which He is the living head. All who are children of God in Christ Jesus are members of this body, and in this relationship they may enjoy fellowship with each other, and fellowship also with their Lord and Master.

The church is referred to in the Scriptures by such expressions as "the church of God" (Acts 20:28), "the body of Christ" (Eph. 4:12), "the church of the living God" (1 Tim. 3:15), the last name being the term chosen for the title of this chapter.

The word *church* is used in the biblical record in at least two senses: a general sense applying to the church in all the world (Matt. 16:18; 1 Cor. 12:28), and also in a particular sense applying to the church in a city or a province. Observe in the following texts where local churches are mentioned: the church at Rome (Rom. 1:6, 7), the church at Corinth (1 Cor. 1:2), the church at Thessalonica (1 Thess. 1:1). Note also the reference made to provincial churches: the churches of Galatia (1 Cor. 16:1), the churches of Asia (1 Cor. 16:19), the churches of Syria and Cilicia (Acts 15:41).

Christ, being the head of the church and its living Lord, has a deep love for the members of His body. In the church He is to be glorified (Eph. 3:21); through the church He will reveal the "manifold wisdom of God" (Eph. 3:10). Day by day He nourishes the church (Eph. 5:29), and His longing desire is to make of it "a glorious church, not having spot, or wrinkle, or any such thing; but that it should be holy and without blemish" (Eph. 5:27).

No Wall of Partition

Christ sought by precept and example to teach the truth that with God there was to be no dividing wall between Israel and the other nations (John 4:4-42; 10:16; Luke 9:51-56; Matt. 15:21-28). The apostle Paul wrote, "The Gentiles are fellow heirs, members of the same body, and partakers of the promise in Christ Jesus through the gospel" (Eph. 3:6, RSV).

Nor was there to be among Christ's followers any preference of caste or nationality or race or color, for all are of one blood, and "Whosoever believeth in him should not perish, but have everlasting life." The elect of God are a universal brotherhood, a new humanity, "all one in Christ Jesus" (John 3:16; Gal. 3:28).

"Christ came to this earth with a message of mercy and forgiveness. He laid the foundation for a religion by which Jew and Gentile, black and white, free and bond, are linked together in one common brotherhood, recognized as equal in the sight of God. The Saviour has a boundless love for every human being."—*Testimonies*, vol. 7, p. 225.

"No distinction on account of nationality, race, or caste, is recognized by God. He is the Maker of all mankind. All men are of one family by creation, and all are one through redemption. Christ came to demolish every wall of partition, to throw open every compartment of the temple, that every soul may have free access to God. . . . In Christ there is neither Jew nor Greek, bond nor free. All are brought nigh by His precious blood."—*Christ's Object Lessons*, p. 386.

The Supreme Object of Christ's Regard

Those in His service who are called to leadership in the church are "to take care of the church" (1 Tim. 3:5); they are to "feed the church of God" (Acts 20:28); and upon the shoulders of some will rest "the care of all the churches," as was the experience of the beloved apostle to the Gentiles (2 Cor. 11:28). The following extracts from the Spirit of Prophecy illustrate the great love of Christ for His people gathered together into church fellowship.

"I testify to my brethren and sisters that the church of Christ, enfeebled and defective as it may be, is the only object on earth on which He bestows His supreme regard. While He extends to all the world His invitation to come to Him and be saved, He commissions His angels to render divine help to every soul that cometh to Him in repentance and contrition, and He comes personally by His Holy Spirit into the midst of His church. 'If Thou, Lord, shouldest mark iniquities, O Lord, who shall stand? But there is forgiveness with Thee, that Thou mayest be feared. I wait for the Lord, my soul doth wait, and in His word do I hope. My soul waiteth for the Lord more than they that watch for the morning. . . . Let Israel hope in the Lord: for with the Lord there is mercy, and with Him is plenteous redemption. And He shall redeem Israel from all his iniquities.'

"Ministers and all the church, let this be our language, from hearts that respond to the great goodness and love of God to us as a people and to us individually, 'Let Israel hope in the Lord from henceforth and forever.' 'Ye that stand in the house of the Lord, in the courts of the house of our God, praise the Lord; for the Lord is good: sing praises unto His name; for it is pleasant. For the Lord hath chosen Jacob unto Himself, and Israel for His peculiar treasure. For I know that the Lord is great, and that our Lord is above all gods.' Consider, my brethren and sisters, that the Lord has a people, a chosen people, His church, to be His own, His own fortress, which He holds in a sin-stricken, revolted world; and He intended that no authority should be known in it, no laws be acknowledged by it, but His own."— *Testimonies to Ministers,* pp. 15, 16.

The Opposition of the Enemy

"Satan has a large confederacy, his church. Christ calls them the synagogue of Satan because the members are the children of sin. The members of Satan's church have been constantly working to cast off the divine law, and confuse the distinction between good and evil. Satan is working with great power in and through the children of disobedience to exalt treason and apostasy as truth and loyalty. And at this time the power of his satanic inspiration is moving the living agencies to carry out the great rebellion against God that commenced in heaven."—*Testimonies to Ministers,* p. 16.

"At this time the church is to put on her beautiful garments—'Christ our righteousness.' There are clear, decided distinctions to be restored and exemplified to the world in holding aloft the commandments of God and the faith of Jesus. The beauty of holiness is to appear in its native luster in contrast with the deformity and darkness of the disloyal, those who have revolted from the law of God. Thus we acknowledge God, and recognize His law, the foundation of His government in heaven and throughout His earthly dominions. His authority should be kept distinct and plain before the world; and no laws are to be acknowledged that come in collision with the laws of Jehovah. If in defiance of God's arrangements the world be allowed to influence our decisions or our actions, the purpose of God is defeated. However specious the pretext, if the church waver here, there is written against her in the books of heaven a betrayal of the most sacred trusts, and treachery to the kingdom of Christ. The church is firmly and decidedly to hold her principles before the whole heavenly universe and the kingdoms of the world; steadfast fidelity in maintaining the honor and sacredness of the law of God will attract the notice and admiration of even the world, and many will, by the good works which they shall behold, be led to glorify our Father in heaven. The loyal and true bear the credentials of heaven, not of earthly potentates. All men shall know who are the disciples of Christ, chosen and faithful, and shall know them when crowned and glorified as those who honored God and whom He has honored, bringing them into possession of an eternal weight of glory. . . ."—*Testimonies to Ministers*, pp. 16, 17.

The Church Complete in Christ

"The Lord has provided His church with capabilities and blessings, that they may present to the world an image of His own sufficiency, and that His church may be complete in Him, a continual representation of another, even the eternal world, of laws that are higher than earthly laws. His church is to be a temple built after the divine similitude, and the angelic architect has brought his golden measuring rod from heaven, that every stone may be hewed and squared by the divine measurement and polished to shine as an emblem of heaven, radiating in all directions the bright, clear beams of the Sun of Righteousness. The church is to be fed with manna from heaven and to be kept under the sole guardianship of His grace. Clad in complete armor of light and righteousness, she enters upon her final conflict. The dross, the worthless material, will be consumed, and the influence of the truth testifies to the world of its sanctifying, ennobling character. . . .

"The Lord Jesus is making experiments on human hearts through the exhibition of His mercy and abundant grace. He is effecting transformations so amazing that Satan, with all his triumphant boasting, with all his confederacy of evil united against God and the laws of His government, stands viewing them as a fortress impregnable to his sophistries and delusions. They are to him an incomprehensible mystery. The angels of God, seraphim and cherubim, the powers commissioned to cooperate with human agencies, look on with astonishment and joy, that fallen men, once children of wrath, are through the training of Christ developing characters after the divine similitude, to be sons and daughters of God, to act an important part in the occupations and pleasures of heaven.

"To His church, Christ has given ample facilities, that He may receive a large revenue of glory from His redeemed, purchased possession. The church, being endowed with the righteousness of Christ, is His depository, in which the wealth of His mercy, His love, His grace, is to appear in full and final display. The declaration in His intercessory prayer, that the Father's love is as great toward us as toward Himself, the only-begotten Son, and that we shall be with Him where He is, forever one with Christ and the Father, is a marvel to the heavenly host, and it is their great joy. The gift of His Holy Spirit, rich, full, and abundant, is to be to His church as an encompassing wall of fire, which the powers of hell shall not prevail against. In their untainted purity and spotless perfection, Christ looks upon His people as the reward of all His suffering, His humiliation, and His love, and the supplement of His glory—Christ, the great center from which radiates all glory. 'Blessed are they which are called unto the marriage supper of the Lamb.'"—*Testimonies to Ministers*, pp. 15-19.

To the foregoing principles of the unity of Christ's church the Seventh-day Adventist Church is committed. By the peace and power which Christ's righteousness brings, the church is pledged to the conquest of every barrier which sin has erected between human beings.

CHAPTER 3

Fundamental Beliefs
of Seventh-day Adventists

Seventh-day Adventists accept the Bible as their only creed and hold certain fundamental beliefs to be the teaching of the Holy Scriptures. These beliefs, as set forth here, constitute the church's understanding and expression of the teaching of Scripture. Revision of these statements may be expected at a General Conference session when the church is led by the Holy Spirit to a fuller understanding of Bible truth or finds better language in which to express the teachings of God's Holy Word.

1. The Holy Scriptures

The Holy Scriptures, Old and New Testaments, are the written Word of God, given by divine inspiration through holy men of God who spoke and wrote as they were moved by the Holy Spirit. In this Word, God has committed to man the knowledge necessary for salvation. The Holy Scriptures are the infallible revelation of His will. They are the standard of character, the test of experience, the authoritative revealer of doctrines, and the trustworthy record of God's acts in history. (2 Peter 1:20, 21; 2 Tim. 3:16, 17; Ps. 119:105; Prov. 30:5, 6; Isa. 8:20; John 17:17; 1 Thess. 2:13; Heb. 4:12.)

2. The Trinity

There is one God: Father, Son, and Holy Spirit, a unity of three co-eternal Persons. God is immortal, all-powerful, all-knowing, above all, and ever present. He is infinite and beyond human comprehension, yet known through His self-revelation. He is forever worthy of worship, adoration, and service by the whole creation. (Deut. 6:4; Matt. 28:19; 2 Cor. 13:14; Eph. 4:4-6; 1 Peter 1:2; 1 Tim. 1:17; Rev. 14:7.)

3. The Father

God the eternal Father is the Creator, Source, Sustainer, and Sovereign of all creation. He is just and holy, merciful and gracious, slow to anger, and abounding in steadfast love and faithfulness. The qualities and powers exhibited in the Son and the Holy Spirit are also revelations of the Father. (Gen. 1:1; Rev. 4:11; 1 Cor. 15:28; John 3:16; 1 John 4:8; 1 Tim. 1:17; Ex. 34:6, 7; John 14:9.)

4. The Son

God the eternal Son became incarnate in Jesus Christ. Through Him all things were created, the character of God is revealed, the salvation of humanity is accomplished, and the world is judged. Forever truly God, He became also truly man, Jesus the Christ. He was conceived of the Holy Spirit and born of the virgin Mary. He lived and experienced temptation as a human being, but perfectly exemplified the righteousness and love of God. By His miracles He manifested God's power and was attested as God's promised Messiah. He suffered and died voluntarily on the cross for our sins and in our place, was raised from the dead, and ascended to minister in the heavenly sanctuary in our behalf. He will come again in glory for the final deliverance of His people and the restoration of all things. (John 1:1-3, 14; Col. 1:15-19; John 10:30; 14:9; Rom. 6:23; 2 Cor. 5:17-19; John 5:22; Luke 1:35; Phil. 2:5-11; Heb. 2:9-18; 1 Cor. 15:3, 4; Heb. 8:1, 2; John 14:1-3.)

5. The Holy Spirit

God the eternal Spirit was active with the Father and the Son in Creation, incarnation, and redemption. He inspired the writers of Scripture. He filled Christ's life with power. He draws and convicts human beings; and those who respond He renews and transforms into the image of God. Sent by the Father and the Son to be always with His children, He extends spiritual gifts to the church, empowers it to bear witness to Christ, and in harmony with the Scriptures leads it into all truth. (Gen. 1:1, 2; Luke 1:35; 4:18; Acts 10:38; 2 Peter 1:21; 2 Cor. 3:18; Eph. 4:11, 12; Acts 1:8; John 14:16-18, 26; 15:26, 27; 16:7-13.)

6. Creation

God is Creator of all things, and has revealed in Scripture the authentic account of His creative activity. In six days the Lord made "the heaven and the earth" and all living things upon the earth, and rested on the seventh day of that first week. Thus He established the Sabbath as a perpetual memorial of His completed creative work. The first man and woman were made in the image of God as the crowning work of Creation, given dominion over the world, and charged with responsibility to care for it. When the world was finished it was "very good," declaring the glory of God. (Gen. 1; 2; Ex. 20:8-11; Ps. 19:1-6; 33:6, 9; 104; Heb. 11:3.)

7. The Nature of Man

Man and woman were made in the image of God with individuality, the power and freedom to think and to do. Though created free beings, each is an indivisible unity of body, mind, and spirit, dependent upon God for life and breath and all else. When our first parents disobeyed God, they denied their dependence upon Him and fell from their high position under God. The image of God in them was marred and they became subject to death. Their descendants share this fallen nature and its consequences. They are born with weaknesses and tendencies to evil. But God in Christ reconciled the world to Himself and by His Spirit restores in penitent mortals the image of their Maker. Created for the glory of God, they are called to love Him and one another, and to care for their environment. (Gen. 1:26-28; 2:7; Ps. 8:4-8; Acts 17:24-28; Gen. 3; Ps. 51:5; Rom. 5:12-17; 2 Cor. 5:19, 20; Ps. 51:10; 1 John 4:7, 8, 11, 20; Gen. 2:15.)

8. The Great Controversy

All humanity is now involved in a great controversy between Christ and Satan regarding the character of God, His law, and His sovereignty over the universe. This conflict originated in heaven when a created being, endowed with freedom of choice, in self-exaltation became Satan, God's adversary, and led into rebellion a portion of the angels. He introduced the spirit of rebellion into this world when he led Adam and Eve into sin. This human sin resulted in the distortion of the image of God in humanity, the disordering of the created world, and its eventual devastation at the time of the worldwide flood. Observed by the whole creation, this world became the arena of the universal conflict, out of which the God of love will ultimately be vindicated. To assist His people in this controversy, Christ sends the Holy Spirit and the loyal angels to guide, protect, and sustain them in the way of salvation. (Rev. 12:4-9; Isa. 14:12-14; Eze. 28:12-18; Gen. 3; Rom. 1:19-32; 5:12-21; 8:19-22; Gen. 6-8; 2 Peter 3:6; 1 Cor. 4:9; Heb. 1:14.)

9. The Life, Death, and Resurrection of Christ   *Jesus justifies*

In Christ's life of perfect obedience to God's will, His suffering, death, and resurrection, God provided the only means of atonement for human sin, so that those who by faith accept this atonement may have eternal life, and the whole creation may better understand the infinite and holy love of the

Creator. This perfect atonement vindicates the righteousness of God's law and the graciousness of His character; for it both condemns our sin and provides for our forgiveness. The death of Christ is substitutionary and expiatory, reconciling and transforming. The resurrection of Christ proclaims God's triumph over the forces of evil, and for those who accept the atonement assures their final victory over sin and death. It declares the Lordship of Jesus Christ, before whom every knee in heaven and on earth will bow. (John 3:16; Isa. 53; 1 Peter 2:21, 22; 1 Cor. 15:3, 4, 20-22; 2 Cor. 5:14, 15, 19-21; Rom. 1:4; 3:25; 4:25; 8:3, 4; 1 John 2:2; 4:10; Col. 2:15; Phil. 2:6-11.)

10. The Experience of Salvation

In infinite love and mercy God made Christ, who knew no sin, to be sin for us, so that in Him we might be made the righteousness of God. Led by the Holy Spirit we sense our need, acknowledge our sinfulness, repent of our transgressions, and exercise faith in Jesus as Lord and Christ, as Substitute and Example. This faith which receives salvation comes through the divine power of the Word and is the gift of God's grace. Through Christ we are justified, adopted as God's sons and daughters, and delivered from the lordship of sin. Through the Spirit we are born again and sanctified; the Spirit renews our minds, writes God's law of love in our hearts, and we are given the power to live a holy life. Abiding in Him we become partakers of the divine nature and have the assurance of salvation now and in the judgment. (2 Cor. 5:17-21; John 3:16; Gal. 1:4; 4:4-7; Titus 3:3-7; John 16:8; Gal. 3:13, 14; 1 Peter 2:21, 22; Rom. 10:17; Luke 17:5; Mark 9:23, 24; Eph. 2:5-10; Rom. 3:21-26; Col. 1:13, 14; Rom. 8:14-17; Gal. 3:26; John 3:3-8; 1 Peter 1:23; Rom. 12:2; Heb. 8:7-12; Eze. 36:25-27; 2 Peter 1:3, 4; Rom. 8:1-4; 5:6-10.)

11. The Church

The church is the community of believers who confess Jesus Christ as Lord and Saviour. In continuity with the people of God in Old Testament times, we are called out from the world; and we join together for worship, for fellowship, for instruction in the Word, for the celebration of the Lord's Supper, for service to all mankind, and for the worldwide proclamation of the gospel. The church derives its authority from Christ, who is the incarnate Word, and from the Scriptures, which are the written Word. The church is God's family; adopted by Him as children, its members live on the basis of the new covenant. The church is the body of Christ, a community of faith of which Christ Himself is the Head. The church is the bride for whom Christ died that He might sanctify and cleanse her. At His return in triumph, He will present her to Himself a glorious church, the faithful of all the ages, the purchase of His blood, not having spot or wrinkle, but holy and without blemish. (Gen. 12:3; Acts 7:38; Eph. 4:11-15; 3:8-11; Matt. 28:19, 20; 16:13-20; 18:18; Eph. 2:19-22; 1:22, 23; 5:23-27; Col. 1:17, 18.)

12. The Remnant and Its Mission

The universal church is composed of all who truly believe in Christ, but in the last days, a time of widespread apostasy, a remnant has been called out to keep the commandments of God and the faith of Jesus. This remnant announces the arrival of the judgment hour, proclaims salvation through Christ, and heralds the approach of His second advent. This proclamation is symbolized by the three angels of Revelation 14; it coincides with the work of judgment in heaven and results in a work of repentance and reform on earth. Every believer is called to have a personal part in this worldwide witness. (Rev. 12:17; 14:6-12; 18:1-4; 2 Cor. 5:10; Jude 3, 14; 1 Peter 1:16-19; 2 Peter 3:10-14; Rev. 21:1-14.)

13. Unity in the Body of Christ

The church is one body with many members, called from every nation, kindred, tongue, and people. In Christ we are a new creation; distinctions of race, culture, learning, and nationality, and differences between high and low, rich and poor, male and female, must not be divisive among us. We are all equal in Christ, who by one Spirit has bonded us into one fellowship with Him and with one another; we are to serve and be served without partiality or reservation. Through the revelation of Jesus Christ in the Scriptures we share the same faith and hope, and reach out in one witness to all. This unity has its source in the oneness of the triune God, who has adopted us as His children. (Rom. 12:4, 5; 1 Cor. 12:12-14; Matt. 28:19, 20; Ps. 133:1; 2 Cor. 5:16, 17; Acts 17:26, 27; Gal. 3:27, 29; Col. 3:10-15; Eph. 4:14-16; 4:1-6; John 17:20-23.)

14. Baptism

By baptism we confess our faith in the death and resurrection of Jesus Christ, and testify of our death to sin and of our purpose to walk in newness of life. Thus we acknowledge Christ as Lord and Saviour, become His people, and are received as members by His church. Baptism is a symbol of our union with Christ, the forgiveness of our sins, and our reception of the Holy Spirit. It is by immersion in water and is contingent on an affirmation of faith in Jesus and evidence of repentance of sin. It follows instruction in the Holy Scriptures and acceptance of their teachings. (Rom. 6:1-6; Col. 2:12, 13; Acts 16:30-33; 22:16; 2:38; Matt. 28:19, 20.)

15. The Lord's Supper

The Lord's Supper is a participation in the emblems of the body and blood of Jesus as an expression of faith in Him, our Lord and Saviour. In this experience of communion Christ is present to meet and strengthen His people. As we partake, we joyfully proclaim the Lord's death until He comes again. Preparation for the Supper includes self-examination, repentance, and confession. The Master ordained the service of foot-washing to signify renewed cleansing, to express a willingness to serve one another in Christlike humility, and to unite our hearts in love. The communion service is open to all believing Christians. (1 Cor. 10:16, 17; 11:23-30; Matt. 26:17-30; Rev. 3:20; John 6:48-63; 13:1-17.)

16. Spiritual Gifts and Ministries

God bestows upon all members of His church in every age spiritual gifts which each member is to employ in loving ministry for the common good of the church and of humanity. Given by the agency of the Holy Spirit, who apportions to each member as He wills, the gifts provide all abilities and ministries needed by the church to fulfill its divinely ordained functions. According to the Scriptures, these gifts include such ministries as faith, healing, prophecy, proclamation, teaching, administration, reconciliation, compassion, and self-sacrificing service and charity for the help and encouragement of people. Some members are called of God and endowed by the Spirit for functions recognized by the church in pastoral, evangelistic, apostolic, and teaching ministries particularly needed to equip the members for service, to build up the church to spiritual maturity, and to foster unity of the faith and knowledge of God. When members employ these spiritual gifts as faithful stewards of God's varied grace, the church is protected from the destructive influence of false doctrine, grows with a growth that is from God, and is built up in faith and love. (Rom. 12:4-8; 1 Cor. 12:9-11, 27, 28; Eph. 4:8, 11-16; Acts 6:1-7; 1 Tim. 3:1-13; 1 Peter 4:10, 11.)

17. The Gift of Prophecy

One of the gifts of the Holy Spirit is prophecy. This gift is an identifying mark of the remnant church and was manifested in the ministry of Ellen G.

White. As the Lord's messenger, her writings are a continuing and authoritative source of truth which provide for the church comfort, guidance, instruction, and correction. They also make clear that the Bible is the standard by which all teaching and experience must be tested. (Joel 2:28, 29; Acts 2:14-21; Heb. 1:1-3; Rev. 12:17; 19:10.)

18. The Law of God

The great principles of God's law are embodied in the Ten Commandments and exemplified in the life of Christ. They express God's love, will, and purposes concerning human conduct and relationships and are binding upon all people in every age. These precepts are the basis of God's covenant with His people and the standard in God's judgment. Through the agency of the Holy Spirit they point out sin and awaken a sense of need for a Saviour. Salvation is all of grace and not of works, but its fruitage is obedience to the Commandments. This obedience develops Christian character and results in a sense of well-being. It is an evidence of our love for the Lord and our concern for our fellow men. The obedience of faith demonstrates the power of Christ to transform lives, and therefore strengthens Christian witness. (Ex. 20:1-17; Ps. 40:7, 8; Matt. 22:36-40; Deut. 28:1-14; Matt. 5:17-20; Heb. 8:8-10; John 15:7-10; Eph. 2:8-10; 1 John 5:3; Rom. 8:3, 4; Ps. 19:7-14.)

19. The Sabbath

The beneficent Creator, after the six days of Creation, rested on the seventh day and instituted the Sabbath for all people as a memorial of Creation. The fourth commandment of God's unchangeable law requires the observance of this seventh-day Sabbath as the day of rest, worship, and ministry in harmony with the teaching and practice of Jesus, the Lord of the Sabbath. The Sabbath is a day of delightful communion with God and one another. It is a symbol of our redemption in Christ, a sign of our sanctification, a token of our allegiance, and a foretaste of our eternal future in God's kingdom. The Sabbath is God's perpetual sign of His eternal covenant between Him and His people. Joyful observance of this holy time from evening to evening, sunset to sunset, is a celebration of God's creative and redemptive acts. (Gen. 2:1-3; Ex. 20:8-11; Luke 4:16; Isa. 56:5, 6; 58:13, 14; Matt. 12:1-12; Ex. 31:13-17; Eze. 20:12, 20; Deut. 5:12-15; Heb. 4:1-11; Lev. 23:32; Mark 1:32.)

20. Stewardship

We are God's stewards, entrusted by Him with time and opportunities, abilities and possessions, and the blessings of the earth and its resources. We are responsible to Him for their proper use. We acknowledge God's ownership by faithful service to Him and our fellow men, and by returning tithes and giving offerings for the proclamation of His gospel and the support and growth of His church. Stewardship is a privilege given to us by God for nurture in love and the victory over selfishness and covetousness. The steward rejoices in the blessings that come to others as a result of his faithfulness. (Gen. 1:26-28; 2:15; 1 Chron. 29:14; Haggai 1:3-11; Mal. 3:8-12; 1 Cor. 9:9-14; Matt. 23:23; 2 Cor. 8:1-15; Rom. 15:26, 27.)

21. Christian Behavior

We are called to be a godly people who think, feel, and act in harmony with the principles of heaven. For the Spirit to recreate in us the character of our Lord we involve ourselves only in those things which will produce Christlike purity, health, and joy in our lives. This means that our amusement and entertainment should meet the highest standards of Christian taste and beauty. While recognizing cultural differences, our dress is to be simple, modest, and neat, befitting those whose true beauty does not consist of outward adornment but in the imperishable ornament of a gentle and quiet spirit. It also means that because our bodies are the temples of the Holy Spirit, we are to care for them intelligently. Along with adequate exercise and rest, we are to adopt the most healthful diet possible and abstain from the unclean foods identified in the Scriptures. Since alcoholic beverages, tobacco, and the irresponsible use of drugs and narcotics are harmful to our bodies, we are to abstain from them as well. Instead, we are to engage in whatever brings our thoughts and bodies into the discipline of Christ, who desires our wholesomeness, joy, and goodness. (Rom. 12:1, 2; 1 John 2:6; Eph. 5:1-21, Phil. 4:8; 2 Cor. 10:5; 6:14-7:1; 1 Peter 3:1-4; 1 Cor. 6:19, 20; 10:31; Lev. 11:1-47; 3 John 2.)

22. Marriage and the Family

Marriage was divinely established in Eden and affirmed by Jesus to be a lifelong union between a man and a woman in loving companionship. For the Christian a marriage commitment is to God as well as to the spouse, and should be entered into only between partners who share a common faith. Mutual love, honor, respect, and responsibility are the fabric of this relationship, which is to reflect the love, sanctity, closeness, and permanence of the relationship between Christ and His church. Regarding divorce, Jesus taught that the person who divorces a spouse, except for fornication, and marries another, commits adultery. Although some family relationships may fall short of the ideal, marriage partners who fully commit themselves to each other in Christ may achieve loving unity through the guidance of the Spirit and the nurture of the church. God blesses the family and intends that its members shall assist each other toward complete maturity. Parents are to bring up their children to love and obey the Lord. By their example and their words they are to teach them that Christ is a loving disciplinarian, ever tender and caring, who wants them to become members of His body, the family of God. Increasing family closeness is one of the earmarks of the final gospel message. (Gen. 2:18-25; Matt. 19:3-9; John 2:1-11; 2 Cor. 6:14; Eph. 5:21-33; Matt. 5:31, 32; Mark 10:11, 12; Luke 16:18; 1 Cor. 7:10, 11; Ex. 20:12; Eph. 6:1-4; Deut. 6:5-9; Prov. 22:6; Mal. 4:5, 6.)

23. *Christ's Ministry in the Heavenly Sanctuary*

There is a sanctuary in heaven, the true tabernacle which the Lord set up and not man. In it Christ ministers on our behalf, making available to believers the benefits of His atoning sacrifice offered once for all on the cross. He was inaugurated as our great High Priest and began His intercessory ministry at the time of His ascension. In 1844, at the end of the prophetic period of 2300 days, He entered the second and last phase of His atoning ministry. It is a work of investigative judgment which is part of the ultimate disposition of all sin, typified by the cleansing of the ancient Hebrew sanctuary on the Day of Atonement. In that typical service the sanctuary was cleansed with the blood of animal sacrifices, but the heavenly things are purified with the perfect sacrifice of the blood of Jesus. The investigative judgment reveals to heavenly intelligences who among the dead are asleep in Christ and therefore, in Him, are deemed worthy to have part in the first resurrection. It also makes manifest who among the living are abiding in Christ, keeping the commandments of God and the faith of Jesus, and in Him, therefore, are ready for translation into His everlasting kingdom. This judgment vindicates the justice of God in saving those who believe in Jesus. It declares that those who have remained loyal to God shall receive the kingdom. The completion of this ministry of Christ will mark the close of human probation before the Second Advent. (Heb. 8:1-5; 4:14-16; 9:11-28; 10:19-22; 1:3; 2:16, 17; Dan. 7:9-27; 8:13, 14; 9:24-27; Num. 14:34; Eze. 4:6; Lev. 16; Rev. 14:6, 7; 20:12; 14:12; 22:12.)

24. The Second Coming of Christ

The second coming of Christ is the blessed hope of the church, the grand climax of the gospel. The Saviour's coming will be literal, personal, visible, and worldwide. When He returns, the righteous dead will be resurrected, and together with the righteous living will be glorified and taken to heaven, but the unrighteous will die. The almost complete fulfillment of most lines of prophecy, together with the present condition of the world, indicates that Christ's coming is imminent. The time of that event has not been revealed, and we are therefore exhorted to be ready at all times. (Titus 2:13; Heb. 9:28; John 14:1-3; Acts 1:9-11; Matt. 24:14; Rev. 1:7; Matt. 24:43, 44; 1 Thess. 4:13-18; 1 Cor. 15:51-54; 2 Thess. 1:7-10; 2:8; Rev. 14:14-20; 19:11-21; Matt. 24; Mark 13; Luke 21; 2 Tim. 3:1-5; 1 Thess. 5:1-6.)

25. Death and Resurrection

The wages of sin is death. But God, who alone is immortal, will grant eternal life to His redeemed. Until that day death is an unconscious state for all people. When Christ, who is our life, appears, the resurrected righteous and the living righteous will be glorified and caught up to meet their Lord. The second resurrection, the resurrection of the unrighteous, will take place a thousand years later. (Rom. 6:23; 1 Tim. 6:15, 16; Eccl. 9:5, 6; Ps. 146:3, 4; John 11:11-14; Col. 3:4; 1 Cor. 15:51-54; 1 Thess. 4:13-17; John 5:28, 29; Rev. 20:1-10.)

26. The Millennium and the End of Sin

The millennium is the thousand-year reign of Christ with His saints in heaven between the first and second resurrections. During this time the wicked dead will be judged; the earth will be utterly desolate, without living human inhabitants, but occupied by Satan and his angels. At its close Christ with His saints and the Holy City will descend from heaven to earth. The unrighteous dead will then be resurrected, and with Satan and his angels will surround the city; but fire from God will consume them and cleanse the earth. The universe will thus be freed of sin and sinners forever. (Rev. 20; 1 Cor. 6:2, 3; Jer. 4:23-26; Rev. 21:1-5; Mal. 4:1; Eze. 28:18, 19.)

27. The New Earth

On the new earth, in which righteousness dwells, God will provide an eternal home for the redeemed and a perfect environment for everlasting life, love, joy, and learning in His presence. For here God Himself will dwell with His people, and suffering and death will have passed away. The great controversy will be ended, and sin will be no more. All things, animate and inanimate, will declare that God is love; and He shall reign forever. Amen. (2 Peter 3:13; Isa. 35; 65:17-25; Matt. 5:5; Rev. 21:1-7; 22:1-5; 11:15.)

CHAPTER 4

Organization Founded on Divine Principles

Correct organization is of God; it is based on divine principles. "System and order are manifest in all the works of God throughout the universe."— *Testimonies to Ministers*, p. 26. The myriads of stars that speed through space move in perfect order. In the structure of every plant that grows and in every living creature we have a marvelous demonstration of order and system.

In heaven there is absolute, faultless organization. "Angels work harmoniously. Perfect order characterizes all their movements."— *Testimonies to Ministers,* p. 28. "Order is the law of heaven, and it should be the law of God's people on the earth."—*Testimonies to Ministers*, p. 26.

Biblical Basis for Organization

When God called the children of Israel out of Egypt and chose them as His peculiar people, He provided for them an impressive system of organization to govern their conduct in both civil and religious matters. "The government of Israel," we are told by the messenger of the Lord, "was characterized by the most thorough organization, wonderful alike for its completeness and its simplicity. The order so strikingly displayed in the perfection and arrangement of all God's created works was manifest in the Hebrew economy. God was the center of authority and government, the sovereign of Israel. Moses stood as their visible leader, by God's appointment, to administer the laws in His name. From the elders of the tribes a council of seventy was afterward chosen to assist Moses in the general affairs of the nation. Next came the priests, who consulted the Lord in the sanctuary. Chiefs, or princes, ruled over the tribes. Under these were 'captains over thousands, and captains over hundreds, and captains over fifties, and captains over tens,' and, lastly, officers who might be employed for special duties."—*Patriarchs and Prophets*, p. 374.

When we consider the New Testament church we find the same perfection in its organization. It could not be otherwise, for it is of divine origin. Christ Himself, who formed the church, "set the members every one

21

of them in the body, as it hath pleased him" (1 Cor. 12:18). It was He who endowed them with gifts and talents adequate for the functions devolving upon them and organized them into a living, working body, of which He is the head.

"For as we have many members in one body, and all members have not the same office: so we, being many, are one body in Christ, and every one members one of another" (Rom. 12:4, 5).

"And he [Christ] is the head of the body, the church: who is the beginning, the firstborn from the dead; that in all things he might have the preeminence" (Col. 1:18).

"Now there are diversities of gifts, but the same Spirit. And there are differences of administrations, but the same Lord." "For as the body is one, and hath many members, and all the members of that one body, being many, are one body: so also is Christ." "Now ye are the body of Christ, and members in particular. And God hath set some in the church, first apostles, secondarily prophets, thirdly teachers, after that miracles, then gifts of healings, helps, governments, diversities of tongues" (1 Cor. 12:4, 5, 12, 27, 28).

Vital Importance of Organization

Just as there can be no living, active human body unless its members are organically united and functioning together under central control, so there can be no living, growing, prospering church unless its members are organized into a united body, all performing their God-given duties and functions under the direction of a divinely constituted authority.

Without organization no institution or movement can prosper. A nation without organized government would soon be in chaos. A business enterprise without organization would fail; so would it be with the church: without organization it would disintegrate and perish.

For the sake of her healthy development and for the accomplishment of her glorious task of carrying the gospel of salvation to all the world, Christ gave to His church a simple but effective system of organization. Success in her endeavors to achieve her mission depends on loyal adherence to this divine pattern.

"Some have advanced the thought that as we near the close of time, every child of God will act independently of any religious organization. But I have been instructed by the Lord that in this work there is no such thing as every man's being independent. The stars of heaven are all under law, each influencing the other to do the will of God, yielding their common obedience to the law that controls their action. And in order that the Lord's work may advance healthfully and solidly, His people must draw together."—*Testimonies to Ministers*, p. 489.

"Oh, how Satan would rejoice if he could succeed in his efforts to get in among this people and disorganize the work at a time when thorough organization is essential and will be the greatest power to keep out spurious uprisings and to refute claims not endorsed by the word of God! We want to hold the lines evenly, that there shall be no breaking down of the system of organization and order that has been built up by wise, careful labor. License must not be given to disorderly elements that desire to control the work at this time."—*Testimonies to Ministers*, p. 489.

Divine Purpose in Organization

"As our numbers increased, it was evident that without some form of organization there would be great confusion, and the work would not be carried forward successfully. To provide for the support of the ministry, for carrying the work in new fields, for protecting both the churches and the ministry from unworthy members, for holding church property, for the publication of the truth through the press, and for many other objects, organization was indispensable."—*Testimonies to Ministers*, p. 26.

"In our work we must consider the relation that each worker sustains to the other workers connected with the cause of God. We must remember that others as well as ourselves have a work to do in connection with this cause. We must not bar the mind against counsel. In our plans for the carrying forward of the work, our mind must blend with other minds.

"Let us cherish a spirit of confidence in the wisdom of our brethren. We must be willing to take advice and caution from our fellow laborers. Connected with the service of God, we must individually realize that we are parts of a great whole. We must seek wisdom from God, learning what it means to have a waiting, watching spirit, and to go to our Saviour when tired and depressed."—*Testimonies to Ministers*, p. 500.

"As members of the visible church, and workers in the vineyard of the Lord, all professed Christians should do their utmost to preserve peace, harmony, and love in the church. Mark the prayer of Christ: 'That they all may be one; as Thou, Father, art in Me, and I in Thee, that they also may be one in Us: that the world may believe that Thou hast sent Me.' The unity of the church is the convincing evidence that God has sent Jesus into the world as its Redeemer."—*Testimonies*, vol. 5, pp. 619, 620.

"'By the cords of tender love and sympathy the Lord linked all men to Himself. Of us He says, Ye "are laborers together with God: ye are God's husbandry, ye are God's building." This relationship we should recognize. If we are bound up with Christ, we shall constantly manifest Christlike sympathy and forbearance toward those who are striving with all their God-given ability to bear their burdens, even as we endeavor to bear our appointed burdens.'"—*Testimonies to Ministers*, p. 495.

CHAPTER 5

The Form of Organization in the Seventh-day Adventist Church

The Saviour's commission to the church to carry the gospel to all the world (Matt. 28:19, 20; Mark 16:15) meant not only preaching the message but ensuring the welfare of those who accepted that message. This involved shepherding as well as housing the flock, and also meeting problems of relationship. Such a situation called for organization.

At first the apostles constituted a council that directed the activities of the infant church from Jerusalem (Acts 6:2; 8:14). When the company in that city became so large that the administration of its practical affairs became a problem, deacons were appointed to look after the business of the church (Acts 6:2-4).

Later, other congregations grew up, not only in Asia, but also in Europe, and this called for further steps in the matter of organization. We find that, in Asia Minor, elders were ordained "in every church" (Acts 14:23). It seems clear also from the divine record that the extension of the work throughout the various provinces of the Roman Empire called for the organization of churches into what might be called conferences which, it seems, included the churches in a specific province, such as "the churches of Galatia" (Gal. 1:2). Thus step by step the early church was organized. As the needs arose God guided and directed the leaders of His work so that, in counsel with the church, a form of organization was developed which safeguarded the interests of the work of God as it extended to every land.

Forms of Church Government

There are four generally recognized forms of church government. These may be summarized as follows:

1. Episcopal—the form of church government by bishops, usually with three orders of ministers, as bishops, priests, and deacons.

2. Papal—the form of church government in which the supreme authority is vested in the Pope. From him the church is governed by cardinals, archbishops, bishops, and priests. The local church or individual member has no authority in church administration.

3. Independent—the form of church polity that makes the local church congregation supreme and final within its own domain. This is usually referred to as congregationalism.

4. Representative—the form of church government which recognizes that authority in the church rests in the church membership, with executive responsibility delegated to representative bodies and officers for the governing of the church. This form of church government recognizes also the equality of the ordination of the entire ministry. The representative form of church government is that which prevails in the Seventh-day Adventist Church.

Four Constituent Levels in the Seventh-day Adventist Organization

Among Seventh-day Adventists there are four constituent levels leading from the individual believer to the worldwide organization of the work of the church:

1. The local church, a united organized body of individual believers.

2. The local conference or local field/mission, a united organized body of churches in a state, province, or territory. (See p. *xxii*.)

3. The union conference or union mission, a united body of conferences, missions, or fields within a larger territory.

4. The General Conference, the largest unit of organization, embraces all unions in all parts of the world. Divisions are sections of the General Conference, with administrative responsibility assigned to them in designated geographical areas.

"Every member of the church has a voice in choosing officers of the church. The church chooses the officers of the state conferences. Delegates chosen by the state conferences choose the officers of the union conferences, and delegates chosen by the union conferences choose the officers of the General Conference. By this arrangement every conference, every institution, every church, and every individual, either directly or through representatives, has a voice in the election of the men who bear the chief responsibilities in the General Conference."—*Testimonies*, vol. 8, pp. 236, 237.

The Church's Institutions

Within these four constituent levels the church operates a variety of institutions. Seventh-day Adventists see in the gospel commission and the example of the Lord and His apostles the responsibility of followers of Christ to serve the whole person. In their world outreach they have therefore followed the pattern of their beginnings in the development of educational, health-care, publishing, and other institutions.

In Seventh-day Adventist theology and philosophy of church operations, such institutions have been from their inception integral parts of the church, direct instruments in the carrying out of its divine commission. Therefore, the Seventh-day Adventist Church makes use of its denominationally owned and operated institutions such as health care institutions,* publishing houses, health food industries, and educational institutions as integral parts to fulfill health, literature, and teaching ministries; therefore, they are indispensable to and inseparable from the total ministry of the church in carrying the gospel to all the world.

The multiple units of the world church, whether congregations, conferences, health-care institutions, publishing houses, schools, or other organizations, all find their organizational unity in the General Conference of Seventh-day Adventists in which they have representation. Through them the world church reaches out in the name of Christ to meet the needs of a distraught world.

General Conference the Highest Authority

The General Conference in session, and the Executive Committee between sessions, is the highest organization in the administration of the church's worldwide work, and is authorized by its constitution to create subordinate organizations to promote specific interests in various sections of the world; it is therefore understood that all subordinate organizations and institutions throughout the world will recognize the General Conference as the highest authority, under God, among Seventh-day Adventists. When differences arise in or between organizations and institutions, appeal to the next higher organization is proper until it reaches the General Conference in session, or the Executive Committee at the Annual Council. During the interim between these sessions the Executive Committee shall constitute the body of final authority on all questions where a difference of viewpoint may develop. The committee's decision may be reviewed at a session of the General Conference or at an Annual Council of the Executive Committee.

"I have often been instructed by the Lord that no man's judgment should be surrendered to the judgment of any other one man. Never should the

---

* For North American Division, see *Church Manual*, NAD Supplement, p. 215.

mind of one man or the minds of a few men be regarded as sufficient in wisdom and power to control the work and to say what plans shall be followed. But when, in a General Conference, the judgment of the brethren assembled from all parts of the field is exercised, private independence and private judgment must not be stubbornly maintained, but surrendered. Never should a laborer regard as a virtue the persistent maintenance of his position of independence, contrary to the decision of the general body.

"At times, when a small group of men entrusted with the general management of the work have, in the name of the General Conference, sought to carry out unwise plans and to restrict God's work, I have said that I could no longer regard the voice of the General Conference, represented by these few men, as the voice of God. But this is not saying that the decisions of a General Conference composed of an assembly of duly appointed, representative men from all parts of the field should not be respected. God has ordained that the representatives of His church from all parts of the earth, when assembled in a General Conference, shall have authority. The error that some are in danger of committing is in giving to the mind and judgment of one man, or of a small group of men, the full measure of authority and influence that God has vested in His church in the judgment and voice of the General Conference assembled to plan for the prosperity and advancement of His work.

"When this power, which God has placed in the church, is accredited wholly to one man, and he is invested with the authority to be judgment for other minds, then the true Bible order is changed. Satan's efforts upon such a man's mind would be most subtle and sometimes well-nigh overpowering, for the enemy would hope that through his mind he could affect many others. Let us give to the highest organized authority in the church that which we are prone to give to one man or a small group of men."— *Testimonies*, vol. 9, pp. 260, 261.

Authority of the Church and the Church Manual—(See Chapter 1.)

CHAPTER 6

Church Membership

Membership on a Spiritual Basis

The serious, solemn obligations of church membership should be impressed on everyone who applies for admittance to the church. All should be faithfully taught what it means to become a member of the body of Christ. Only those giving evidence of having experienced the new birth, and who are enjoying a spiritual experience in the Lord Jesus, are prepared for acceptance into church membership. Thorough instruction in the fundamental teachings and related practices of the church should be given to every candidate for church membership before being baptized and received into church fellowship. Each person seeking admittance to the church should be informed of the principles for which the church stands.

This is a spiritual relationship. It can be entered into only by those who are converted. Only in this way can the purity and spiritual caliber of the church be maintained. It is the duty of every minister to instruct those who accept the principles of the truth, that they may enter the church on a sound, spiritual basis. While there is no stated age for baptism, it is recommended that very young children who express a desire to be baptized should be encouraged and entered into an instruction program that may lead to baptism.

"The members of the church, those whom He has called out of darkness into His marvelous light, are to show forth His glory. The church is the repository of the riches of the grace of Christ; and through the church will eventually be made manifest, even to 'the principalities and powers in heavenly places,' the final and full display of the love of God."—*The Acts of the Apostles*, p. 9.

Baptism a Gospel Requirement

The New Testament establishes baptism as the rite for admission to the church. "Go ye therefore, and teach all nations, baptizing them in the name of the Father, and of the Son, and of the Holy Ghost: teaching them to observe all things whatsoever I have commanded you: and, lo, I am with you alway, even unto the end of the world. Amen" (Matt. 28:19, 20).

"Then Peter said unto them, Repent, and be baptized every one of you in the name of Jesus Christ for the remission of sins, and ye shall receive the gift of the Holy Ghost" (Acts 2:38).

Baptism a Prerequisite to Church Membership—"Christ has made baptism the sign of entrance to His spiritual kingdom. He has made this a positive condition with which all must comply who wish to be acknowledged as under the authority of the Father, the Son, and the Holy Spirit. Before man can find a home in the church, before passing the threshold of God's spiritual kingdom, he is to receive the impress of the divine name, 'The Lord our Righteousness.' Jeremiah 23:6.

"Baptism is a most solemn renunciation of the world. Those who are baptized in the threefold name of the Father, the Son, and the Holy Spirit, at the very entrance of their Christian life declare publicly that they have forsaken the service of Satan and have become members of the royal family, children of the heavenly King. They have obeyed the command: 'Come out from among them, and be ye separate, . . . and touch not the unclean thing.' And to them is fulfilled the promise: 'I will receive you, and will be a Father unto you, and ye shall be My sons and daughters, saith the Lord Almighty.' 2 Corinthians 6:17, 18. . . .

"The principles of the Christian life should be made plain to those who have newly come to the truth. None can depend upon their profession of faith as proof that they have a saving connection with Christ. We are not only to say, 'I believe,' but to practice the truth. It is by conformity to the will of God in our words, our deportment, our character, that we prove our connection with Him."—*Testimonies*, vol. 6, pp. 91, 92.

Mode of Baptism—Seventh-day Adventists believe in baptism by immersion and accept into membership only those who have been baptized in this manner. Those who acknowledge their lost state as sinners, sincerely repent of their sins, and experience conversion, may, after proper instruction, be accepted as candidates for baptism and church membership.

Ministers Thoroughly to Instruct Candidates Previous to Baptism—A minister should not present any candidate for baptism and church membership until he can satisfy the church by a public examination that the candidate has been well instructed and is ready to take such a step. (See pp. 31-34.) In churches where frequent baptisms might reduce the significance of a public examination, an alternative plan should be observed. The minister's work is not completed until he has thoroughly instructed the candidates, and they are familiar with and committed to all fundamental beliefs and related practices of the church and are prepared to assume the responsibilities of church membership. Churches should insist on the application of this as a guiding principle in the reception of new members. Churches, through the church board, should insist that candidates be instructed individually and, in addition, wherever possible, that they be taught in a baptismal class.

"The test of discipleship is not brought to bear as closely as it should be upon those who present themselves for baptism. It should be understood whether they are simply taking the name of Seventh-day Adventists, or whether they are taking their stand on the Lord's side, to come out from the world and be separate, and touch not the unclean thing. Before baptism there should be a thorough inquiry as to the experience of the candidates. Let this inquiry be made, not in a cold and distant way, but kindly, tenderly, pointing the new converts to the Lamb of God that taketh away the sin of the world. Bring the requirements of the gospel to bear upon the candidates for baptism."—*Testimonies*, vol. 6, pp. 95, 96.

"When they give evidence that they fully understand their position, they are to be accepted."—*Testimonies to Ministers*, p. 128.

Public Examination—The church has a right to know concerning the faith and attitude of every individual applying for church membership. It is proper for a public examination of all candidates to be held prior to their baptism, preferably in the presence of the church. If this should prove to be impracticable, then it should be before the church board or a committee appointed by the church board, such as the board of elders whose report should then be rendered to the church prior to the baptism. In using the alternative mentioned under the preceding section, opportunity should be given for candidates to give public expression of their desire to unite with the church and to be identified with and by the church.

Baptismal Covenant—A summary of doctrinal beliefs, prepared especially for the instruction of candidates for baptism, together with Baptismal Vow and Certificate of Baptism and Commitment have been adopted by the denomination as a baptismal covenant. A printed copy of this covenant, with the Certificate of Baptism and Commitment properly completed, should be furnished to all those who are accepted for church membership by baptism. In the case of those received on profession of faith, an appropriate certificate will also be given.

This summary of doctrinal beliefs is especially prepared for the instruction of candidates for baptism. Each candidate should be thoroughly familiar with the teachings contained in this summary and with the duties enjoined upon believers and by practice demonstrate a willing acceptance of all the doctrines taught by Seventh-day Adventists and the principles of conduct which are the outward expression of these teachings, for it is "by their fruits ye shall know them."

Prospective members of the Seventh-day Adventist Church, before baptism or acceptance on profession of faith, should be carefully instructed from the Scriptures in the fundamental beliefs of the church as presented in chapter 3 (see p. 9) of this *Church Manual*. In order to assist evangelists, pastors, and others in giving such instruction and making it Scripture-based and practical, a specially prepared summary appears as an appendix on pages 209-213 of this *Church Manual* and in the *Minister's Handbook*.

Baptismal Vow and Baptism

Baptismal Vow—Candidates for baptism or those being received into fellowship by profession of faith shall affirm their acceptance of the doctrinal beliefs of the Seventh-day Adventist Church in the presence of the church or other properly appointed body. (See p. 31.) The minister or elder should address the following questions to the candidate(s), whose reply may be by verbal assent or by raising the hand.

Vow

1. Do you believe there is one God: Father, Son, and Holy Spirit, a unity of three coeternal Persons?

2. Do you accept the death of Jesus Christ on Calvary as the atoning sacrifice for your sins and believe that by God's grace through faith in His shed blood you are saved from sin and its penalty?

3. Do you accept Jesus Christ as your Lord and personal Saviour believing that God, in Christ, has forgiven your sins and given you a new heart, and do you renounce the sinful ways of the world?

4. Do you accept by faith the righteousness of Christ, your Intercessor in the heavenly sanctuary, and accept His promise of transforming grace and power to live a loving, Christ-centered life in your home and before the world?

5. Do you believe that the Bible is God's inspired Word, the only rule of faith and practice for the Christian? Do you covenant to spend time regularly in prayer and Bible study?

6. Do you accept the Ten Commandments as a transcript of the character of God and a revelation of His will? Is it your purpose by the power of the indwelling Christ to keep this law, including the fourth commandment, which requires the observance of the seventh day of the week as the Sabbath of the Lord and the memorial of Creation?

7. Do you look forward to the soon coming of Jesus and the blessed hope when "this mortal shall . . . put on immortality"? As you prepare to

meet the Lord, will you witness to His loving salvation by using your talents in personal soul-winning endeavor to help others to be ready for His glorious appearing?

8. Do you accept the biblical teaching of spiritual gifts and believe that the gift of prophecy is one of the identifying marks of the remnant church?

9. Do you believe in church organization? Is it your purpose to worship God and to support the church through your tithes and offerings and by your personal effort and influence?

10. Do you believe that your body is the temple of the Holy Spirit; and will you honor God by caring for it, avoiding the use of that which is harmful; abstaining from all unclean foods; from the use, manufacture, or sale of alcoholic beverages; the use, manufacture, or sale of tobacco in any of its forms for human consumption; and from the misuse of or trafficking in narcotics or other drugs?

11. Do you know and understand the fundamental Bible principles as taught by the Seventh-day Adventist Church? Do you purpose, by the grace of God, to fulfill His will by ordering your life in harmony with these principles?

12. Do you accept the New Testament teaching of baptism by immersion and desire to be so baptized as a public expression of faith in Christ and His forgiveness of your sins?

13. Do you accept and believe that the Seventh-day Adventist Church is the remnant church of Bible prophecy and that people of every nation, race, and language are invited and accepted into its fellowship? Do you desire to be a member of this local congregation of the world church?

Certificate of Baptism and Commitment—A space will be provided for the new member to sign the certificate as an affirmation of this commitment. Following the baptism, a Certificate of Baptism and Commitment will be presented to the candidate as a covenant document. The commitment will read as follows:

Commitment

1. I believe there is one God: Father, Son, and Holy Spirit, a unity of three coeternal Persons.

2. I accept the death of Jesus Christ on Calvary as the atoning sacrifice for my sins and believe that by God's grace through faith in His shed blood I am saved from sin and its penalty.

3. I accept Jesus Christ as my Lord and personal Saviour and believe that God, in Christ, has forgiven my sins and given me a new heart, and I

renounce the sinful ways of the world.

4. I accept by faith the righteousness of Christ, my Intercessor in the heavenly sanctuary, and accept His promise of transforming grace and power to live a loving, Christ-centered life in my home and before the world.

5. I believe that the Bible is God's inspired Word, the only rule of faith and practice for the Christian. I covenant to spend time regularly in prayer and Bible study.

6. I accept the Ten Commandments as a transcript of the character of God and a revelation of His will. It is my purpose by the power of the indwelling Christ to keep this law, including the fourth commandment, which requires the observance of the seventh day of the week as the Sabbath of the Lord and the memorial of Creation.

7. I look forward to the soon coming of Jesus and the blessed hope when "this mortal shall . . . put on immortality." As I prepare to meet the Lord, I will witness to His loving salvation by using my talents in personal soul-winning endeavor to help others to be ready for His glorious appearing.

8. I accept the biblical teaching of spiritual gifts and believe that the gift of prophecy is one of the identifying marks of the remnant church.

9. I believe in church organization. It is my purpose to worship God and to support the church through my tithes and offerings and by my personal effort and influence.

10. I believe that my body is the temple of the Holy Spirit; and I will honor God by caring for it, avoiding the use of that which is harmful; abstaining from all unclean foods; from the use, manufacture, or sale of alcoholic beverages; the use, manufacture, or sale of tobacco in any of its forms for human consumption; and from the misuse of or trafficking in narcotics or other drugs.

11. I know and understand the fundamental Bible principles as taught by the Seventh-day Adventist Church. I purpose, by the grace of God, to fulfill His will by ordering my life in harmony with these principles.

12. I accept the New Testament teaching of baptism by immersion and desire to be so baptized as a public expression of faith in Christ and His forgiveness of my sins.

13. I accept and believe that the Seventh-day Adventist Church is the remnant church of Bible prophecy and that people of every nation, race, and language are invited and accepted into its fellowship. I desire to be a member of this local congregation of the world church.

Welcoming Candidates—After the candidates have, in the presence of the church membership or other properly appointed body, answered the questions of the vow in the affirmative, or assurance has been given to the church that such answers have already been given, the church body should be asked to vote on their acceptance into the church, subject to baptism, which ordinance should not be unduly delayed.

Receiving Members Who Are Not Known—In preparing for the baptism of his converts, an evangelist should invite the pastor or elder to visit his baptismal classes and become acquainted with his converts. Such contacts will enable the church to be better prepared to receive the new members into church fellowship. This general procedure should not apply in the case of isolated believers who wish to unite with the conference/ mission/field church.

Baptismal Ceremony—At this ceremony the deacons should make the necessary preparation and assist the male candidates into and out of the water. (See p. 55.) The deaconesses should assist all female candidates. (See p. 56.) Care should be exercised to see that proper attire is provided for the candidates. Robes of suitable heavy material are preferable. If such are not available, the candidates should dress in such a manner that they will be modestly attired. The baptismal ceremony should be followed by extending the right hand of fellowship and the giving of a few words of welcome by the pastor or elder in behalf of the entire church.

Regular Standing

All church members are considered to be in regular standing unless they are under church discipline. (See pp. 182-185.)

Transferring Members

Transferring Church Members—When a church member moves to a different area, the clerk of the church holding the membership record should write to the secretary of the relevant conference/mission/field requesting that a pastor in the new locality make a pastoral visit to the individual. This pastoral intervention may facilitate the transfer process.

The clerk of the church holding the membership record should also notify the member of the intention to give the member's new address to a pastor in the new locality.

A church member who moves from one locality to another for a period of longer than six months, should make immediate application for a letter of transfer to a church near his/her new place of residence. In the case of a member locating in an isolated area with no church within a reasonable distance, the customary plan is to make application to join the conference/

mission/field church. Such a letter of transfer is valid for six months from date of issue, and unless acted upon within that time is void.

Method of Granting Letters of Transfer—Application for a letter should be made to the clerk of the church with which the member desires to unite. The clerk then sends the request to the clerk of the church from which the member desires to be transferred. On receiving this, the clerk brings the request to the pastor, if he is an ordained minister, or to the church elder, who in turn lays the request before the church board. After due consideration the board recommends to the church, favorably or otherwise, concerning the application. (See p. 36 below and pp. 37, 38, 40, 41, 57, 190, 202.) The pastor or elder then brings the recommendation to the attention of the church, announcing that this is the first reading. Final action is taken the following week, when the request is again presented and a vote of the church is taken. The purpose of allowing one week's interval is to give any member opportunity to object to the granting of the letter for any valid reason. This objection should not ordinarily be publicly stated, but be lodged with the pastor or elder, whose duty it is to call the church board to consider the objection. The objector should be given opportunity to appear before the board to present the objections. If they are not based on valid grounds, the person raising objection should be admonished to withdraw them. On the other hand, if they are based on valid grounds, it is the duty of the church board to institute such investigation as may be needed. In such case the final action on granting the letter by the church is deferred until the matter has been satisfactorily settled.

If the difficulties involve personal relationships every effort should be made to effect reconciliation. If public offenses are involved, disciplinary measures may be called for. If there is some spiritual lapse, efforts should be made to restore the member in question.

Clerk to Prepare Letter—When the church has granted the letter of transfer, the church clerk fills out the regular form used for this purpose and forwards it to the clerk of the church which the member proposes to join. The clerk of this church passes the letter to the pastor or church elder, who presents it first to the church board for recommendation, after which the request is presented to the church at its next regular service. It is then held over for one week, when final action is taken by vote accepting the person into membership. The clerk of the receiving church then adds the member's name and date of admittance to the church membership record. The clerk also fills out the return portion of the church letter, certifying that the member has been accepted, and sends it back to the clerk of the church from which the member was transferred. (See p. 57.)

Membership During Interval of Transfer—Under no circumstances shall the clerk of the church granting the letter remove the member's name from the church roll until the return portion of the letter has been received, certifying that the member has been voted into the fellowship of the receiving church. To follow any other plan is to deprive the person of church membership during the interval of transfer and is a procedure which should never be followed. The clerk, the elder, the minister, and the conference/mission/field president are all responsible for seeing that the above plan is uniformly adhered to in all the churches.

The Receiving of Members Disturbed by World Conditions—On account of world conditions there may be instances of persons concerning whom no communication can be sent to or received from the church where their membership is recorded. In such cases the church where they are residing, in counsel with the local conference/mission/field, should satisfy themselves as to the standing of these individuals, and then receive them upon profession of faith. If later the way opens to communicate with their former church, a letter should be sent by the receiving church giving information of what has been done.

Counted in Statistical Reports—At the end of the quarter and of the year, when church statistical reports are made up, all members to whom letters have been granted, but whose return certificates have not been received, are to be counted in the membership of the church granting the letters. When the return certificate has been received, certifying that the member has been accepted by the receiving church, the name is then removed from the list of the granting church and is not included in the next quarterly statistical report. The receiving church will place the name on its roll and the member will be included in its next quarterly report.

If Member Is Not Accepted—The church to which the letter of transfer is addressed is under obligation to receive the member, unless it knows a good and sufficient reason why it should not extend the privilege of membership. In case it does not receive the member, the church clerk should return the letter to the granting church, with a full explanation of the reasons. The person's membership then rests just where it was before the request for transfer was made, namely, with the granting church. The member should cooperate with the church in clearing up any questions that arise out of the refusal of the objecting church to accept the individual into membership.

No Letters to Members Under Discipline—In no case should a church vote a letter of transfer to a member who is under discipline. To do so would be a violation of the spirit of the golden rule.

Church Letters Granted Only to Those in Regular Standing—Church letters are granted only to members who are in regular standing. Qualifying statements on church letters are out of order. If a member who has moved to a new location has grown cold and indifferent, the church elder may, to be clear in the matter of granting a letter of transfer, take up the question with the elder of the church in the community to which the member has moved, before a transfer is granted.

Not to Vote Letter Without Member's Approval—In no case should a church vote a letter of transfer contrary to the desire or request of the member in question, nor should any church accept into membership a member by a letter granted under such circumstances.

Church membership is the personal relationship of an individual to the body of Christ. The church should recognize this relationship and avoid any course which might be construed as arbitrary.

On the other hand, the member is under obligation to recognize the welfare of the church and to make every effort to relieve the church of the problems incident to absentee members. When one moves from the area in which church membership is held, it is the individual's duty to cheerfully cooperate in this matter by requesting a letter of transfer.

In the case of a church expelled from the sisterhood of churches by the action of a conference/mission session, it is necessary in order to safeguard the church membership of loyal members to transfer all members of an expelled church to the conference/mission/field church on a provisional basis, except those who refuse to be thus transferred. Such individual memberships will be considered removed upon the expulsion of the church. The conference/mission/field church is empowered then to issue letters of transfer to loyal members as requested and to deal with other memberships as may be necessary. (See pp. 199-205.)

Church Boards Cannot Grant Letters—A church board does not have authority to vote letters of transfer or to receive members from other churches by letter. Their powers in this matter are limited to making recommendations to the church. Action on all transfers of membership, favorable or otherwise, should be taken by the church. (See pp. 35, 52.) The clerk has no authority to remove or add names to the church roll except following a vote of the church. When a member dies, no action is necessary to remove the name, the clerk simply records the date of death.

Conference/Mission/Field Church

Isolated members should unite with the conference/mission/field church, which is a body organized for the benefit of scattered believers who are otherwise without church privileges. Aged and infirm members who live adjacent to a local church organization should be members of the local church. It is the duty and responsibility of the local church to minister to such members. Such should not be transferred to the conference/mission/field church, which is not designed to function in place of the local church. Although conference/mission/field officers are the officers of their field churches, they should hold their membership in the church in the locality in which they reside. The conference/mission/field church is not intended to provide a church home for conference/mission/field workers. Ministers and workers should unite with the local churches in the community in which they reside.

The conference/mission/field president shall be the presiding elder of his conference/mission/field church and the work normally carried by the church clerk and the church treasurer shall be handled by the secretary-treasurer of the conference/mission/field. Any business normally conducted by a local church and its board shall, in the conference/mission/field church for which in the nature of the case there is no board, be conducted by the conference/mission/field committee. They shall also appoint the delegates from the conference/mission church to attend their respective sessions.

Organized Companies

Where a number of isolated believers reside in proximity to one another, a company of believers may be organized for fellowship and worship with the objective of growing into an organized church.

Such a group of believers may be organized as a company by approval of the conference/mission/field committee and may subsequently be dissolved by action of the conference/mission/field committee. When a conference/mission/field committee approves the organization of a company, such organization may be effected by the district pastor or by some other minister appointed by the conference/mission/field committee, who, in counsel with the local members, shall appoint from the baptized membership of the company a leader and a treasurer.

All other appointments such as Sabbath School officers, Personal Ministries officers, and Adventist Youth Society officers should be made by vote of the baptized members of the company at a meeting presided over by the district leader or by such person as may be authorized by the conference/mission/field committee.

The leader of such a company shall not be ordained to that office and shall not have the authority to perform those functions that are vested in an elder of the church. However, where exceptional circumstances warrant, the conference/mission/field committee may appoint a person of church experience and leadership ability to serve as elder of that company.

The treasurer of the company shall keep careful record of all money received and disbursed. He/She shall send promptly, at the time established by the conference/mission/field, all tithes and offerings, other than funds collected for local purposes, to the conference/mission/field treasurer, who is also the treasurer of the conference/mission/field church.

Since all baptized members of an organized company are members of the conference/mission/field church, the company does not possess the right to administer church discipline. All such matters must be referred to the conference/mission/field committee, which constitutes the board of the conference/mission/field church, the president being the elder of that church.

Such a company of believers should grow and eventually develop to the point that would call for a regular church organization. The company leadership should therefore promote and foster all the church campaigns and activities that are usually carried forward by regular churches, thus preparing the members for the wider responsibilities that are associated with full church organization.

Queries Concerning Receiving and Removing Members

Receiving Members on Profession of Faith—There are four circumstances in which individuals who have accepted the Seventh-day Adventist message may be accepted into the local church by profession of faith:

1.   A committed Christian coming from another Christian communion who has already been baptized by immersion as practiced by the Seventh-day Adventist Church. (See p. 30.)

2.   A member of the Seventh-day Adventist Church who, because of world conditions, is unable to secure a letter of transfer from his/her home church. (See p. 37.)

3.   A member of the Seventh-day Adventist Church whose request for membership transfer has received no response of any kind from the church where he/she is a member. In this case the assistance of the conference/ mission/field shall be sought. In case the requesting church is located in another conference/mission/field, the assistance of both conferences/ missions/fields should be sought.

4.   An individual who has been a member, but whose membership has

been misplaced or has been withdrawn because he/she was a missing member, yet who in reality has remained faithful to his/her Christian commitment.

Great care should be exercised in receiving members if they have formerly been members of some other church in the denomination. Instances are not lacking of persons removed from membership in one church, later presenting themselves to other churches for membership on profession of faith. When a person applies for membership on profession of faith, earnest inquiries should be made concerning the applicant's former experience. The church officers should seek the advice and help of the conference/mission/field president. Sufficient time should be taken to extend the investigation as far as needed to reveal all the facts.

When persons apply for membership on profession of faith, and it is found that they are still members of another church in the denomination, no steps should be taken to receive them into membership until the church holding the membership grants their letters of transfer. If, after following the process of transfer (see p. 35), a church refuses to grant a letter of transfer, the member may appeal to the local conference/mission/field committee if it is considered that the letter has been unjustly denied. The church where membership is held, or the local conference/mission/field committee, is the proper organization to decide whether the past conduct has been such that the applicant is entitled to a church letter of transfer. Following such a course will result in a higher appreciation of the sacredness of church membership and in wrongs being made right where this is called for. No church has the right to withhold transfer unless the person is under discipline.

When an individual whose membership has been removed seeks readmission to church membership, such readmission is normally preceded by rebaptism. (See p. 189.)

Removing Names—Names should be removed from the list only on a vote of the church, by granting letters of transfer, or by removing from church membership, except in the case of deceased members. (See p. 57.)

No Retired Membership List—Each church should have but one membership list. Under no circumstances should the practice of keeping a retired list be followed. The church record should contain the names of all members. Names should be added to this list only on the vote of the church after the individual concerned has requested membership by profession of faith or baptism or letter.

Rebaptism

Although the church does not insist on the rebaptism of those coming to us from other religious communions who have already been baptized by immersion and who have lived consistent Christian lives in harmony with the light they then had, it is recognized that rebaptism is desirable.

Of Converts From Other Religious Communions—"This is a subject which each individual must conscientiously take his position upon in the fear of God. This subject should be carefully presented in the spirit of tenderness and love. Then the duty of urging belongs to no one but God; give God a chance to work with His Holy Spirit upon the minds, so that the individual will be perfectly convinced and satisfied in regard to this advanced step. A spirit of controversy and contention should never be allowed to come in and prevail on this subject. Do not take the Lord's work out of His hands into your own hands. Those who have conscientiously taken their position upon the commandments of God, will, if rightly dealt with, accept all essential truth. But it needs wisdom to deal with human minds. Some will be longer in seeing and understanding some kindred truths than others, especially will this be the case in regard to the subject of rebaptism, but there is a divine hand that is leading them—a divine spirit impressing their hearts, and they will know what they ought to do and do it."—*Evangelism*, pp. 373, 374.

Of Church Members and Former Seventh-day Adventists—When members have fallen away in apostasy and have lived in such a manner that the faith and principles of the church have been publicly violated, they should, in case of reconversion and application for church membership, enter the church as in the beginning, by baptism. (See pp. 189, 197.)

"The Lord calls for a decided reformation. And when a soul is truly reconverted, let him be rebaptized. Let him renew his covenant with God, and God will renew His covenant with him."—*Evangelism*, p. 375.

If members who have moved away from their home church, have grown cold or indifferent and have even given up the faith, but still retain their names on their home church books but then regain their Christian experience and desire to be rebaptized, the pastor or elder of the church with which they now associate should, before baptizing them communicate with the church where their membership is held, notifying it of the revived spiritual standing of the member in question, and make the necessary adjustments in the matter of membership. To avoid any confusion, such a person should not be taken into the membership of the receiving church without this step being taken.

CHAPTER 7

Church Officers and Their Duties

Choosing officers for the church or conference/mission/field is an important matter. The prosperity of the work depends largely upon its leadership. The greatest care should be exercised in calling men and women into positions of sacred responsibility. The following qualifications should be earnestly sought in those who are nominated for church office.

Their Qualifications

Moral Fitness—"Moreover thou shalt provide out of all the people able men, such as fear God, men of truth, hating covetousness; and place such over them, to be rulers of thousands, and rulers of hundreds, rulers of fifties, and rulers of tens" (Ex. 18:21).

"Wherefore, brethren, look ye out among you seven men of honest report, full of the Holy Ghost and wisdom, whom we may appoint over this business" (Acts 6:3).

"Moreover he must have a good report of them which are without; lest he fall into reproach and the snare of the devil" (1 Tim. 3:7).

"And the things that thou hast heard of me among many witnesses, the same commit thou to faithful men, who shall be able to teach others also" (2 Tim. 2:2).

Religious Fitness—"This is a true saying, If a man desire the office of a bishop, he desireth a good work. A bishop [elder] then must be blameless, the husband of one wife, vigilant, sober, of good behaviour, given to hospitality, apt to teach; not given to wine, no striker, not greedy of filthy lucre; but patient, not a brawler, not covetous; one that ruleth well his own house, having his children in subjection with all gravity; (for if a man know not how to rule his own house, how shall he take care of the church of God?) not a novice, lest being lifted up with pride he fall into the condemnation of the devil. Moreover he must have a good report of them which are without; lest he fall into reproach and the snare of the devil. Likewise must the deacons be grave, not doubletongued, not given to much wine, not greedy of filthy lucre; holding the mystery of the faith in a pure conscience. And let these also first be proved; then let them use the office of a deacon, being found blameless. Even so must their wives be grave, not slanderers, sober, faithful in all things. Let the deacons be husbands of one wife, ruling their children and their own houses well. For they that have used the office of a deacon well purchase to themselves a good degree, and great boldness in the faith which is in Christ Jesus" (1 Tim. 3:1-13).

"Let no man despise thy youth; but be thou an example of the believers, in word, in conversation, in charity, in spirit, in faith, in purity. Till I come, give attendance to reading, to exhortation, to doctrine. . . . Take heed unto thyself, and unto the doctrine; continue in them: for in doing this thou shalt both save thyself, and them that hear thee" (1 Tim. 4:12-16).

"For this cause left I thee in Crete, that thou shouldest set in order the things that are wanting, and ordain elders in every city, as I had appointed thee: if any be blameless, the husband of one wife, having faithful children not accused of riot or unruly. For a bishop must be blameless, as the steward of God; not selfwilled, not soon angry, not given to wine, no striker, not given to filthy lucre; but a lover of hospitality, a lover of good men, sober, just, holy, temperate; holding fast the faithful word as he hath been taught, that he may be able by sound doctrine both to exhort and to convince the gainsayers. For there are many unruly and vain talkers and deceivers, specially they of the circumcision: whose mouths must be stopped, who subvert whole houses, teaching things which they ought not, for filthy lucre's sake" (Titus 1:5-11).

"But speak thou the things which become sound doctrine. . . . In all things shewing thyself a pattern of good works: in doctrine shewing uncorruptness, gravity, sincerity, sound speech, that cannot be condemned; that he that is of the contrary part may be ashamed, having no evil thing to say of you" (Titus 2:1, 7, 8).

The Church Must be Guarded and Fed—The apostle Paul in his administrative work called together "the elders of the church" (Acts 20:17). He then counseled them: "Take heed therefore unto yourselves, and to all the flock, over the which the Holy Ghost hath made you overseers, to feed the church of God, which he hath purchased with his own blood. For I know this, that after my departing shall grievous wolves enter in among you, not sparing the flock. Also of your own selves shall men arise, speaking perverse things, to draw away disciples after them. Therefore watch, and remember, that by the space of three years I ceased not to warn every one night and day with tears" (Acts 20:28-31).

"The elders which are among you I exhort, who am also an elder, and a witness of the sufferings of Christ, and also a partaker of the glory that shall be revealed: feed the flock of God which is among you, taking the oversight thereof, not by constraint, but willingly; not for filthy lucre, but of a ready mind; neither as being lords over God's heritage, but being ensamples to the flock" (1 Peter 5:1-3).

Respect and Deference Due to Ministers and Officers of the Church—"And, we beseech you, brethren, to know them which labour among you, and are over you in the Lord, and admonish you; and to esteem them very highly in love for their work's sake. And be at peace among yourselves" (1 Thess. 5:12, 13).

"Let the elders that rule well be counted worthy of double honour, especially they who labour in the word and doctrine" (1 Tim. 5:17).

"Remember them which have the rule over you, who have spoken unto you the word of God: whose faith follow, considering the end of their conversation." "Obey them that have the rule over you, and submit yourselves: for they watch for your souls, as they that must give account, that they may do it with joy, and not with grief: for that is unprofitable for you" (Heb. 13:7, 17).

"The Thessalonian believers were greatly annoyed by men coming among them with fanatical ideas and doctrines. Some were 'disorderly, working not at all, but . . . busybodies.' The church had been properly organized, and officers had been appointed to act as ministers and deacons. But there were some, self-willed and impetuous, who refused to be subordinate to those who held positions of authority in the church. They claimed not only the right of private judgment, but that of publicly urging their views upon the church. In view of this, Paul called the attention of the Thessalonians to the respect and deference due to those who had been chosen to occupy positions of authority in the church."—*The Acts of the Apostles*, pp. 261, 262.

"Many do not realize the sacredness of church relationship and are loath to submit to restraint and discipline. Their course of action shows that they exalt their own judgment above that of the united church, and they are not careful to guard themselves lest they encourage a spirit of opposition to its voice. Those who hold responsible positions in the church may have faults in common with other people and may err in their decisions; but notwithstanding this, the church of Christ on earth has given to them an authority that cannot be lightly esteemed."—*Testimonies*, vol. 4, p. 17.

Not to be Hurried Into Office—"In many places we meet men who have been hurried into responsible positions as elders of the church when they are not qualified for such a position. They have not proper government over themselves. Their influence is not good. The church is in trouble continually in consequence of the defective character of the leader. Hands have been laid too suddenly upon these men."—*Testimonies*, vol. 4, pp. 406, 407.

"The apostle Paul writes to Titus: 'Set in order the things that are wanting, and ordain elders in every city, as I had appointed thee: if any be blameless, the husband of one wife, having faithful children not accused of riot, or unruly. For a bishop [elder] must be blameless, as the steward of God.' It would be well for all our ministers to give heed to these words and not to hurry men into office without due consideration and much prayer that God would designate by His Holy Spirit whom He will accept.

"Said the inspired apostle: 'Lay hands suddenly on no man.' In some of our churches the work of organizing and of ordaining elders has been premature; the Bible rule has been disregarded, and consequently grievous trouble has been brought upon the church. There should not be so great haste in electing leaders as to ordain men who are in no way fitted for responsible work . . . ."—*Testimonies*, vol. 5, p. 617.

Those Opposed to Unity Not Suitable for Office—"There have of late arisen among us men who profess to be the servants of Christ, but whose work is opposed to that unity which our Lord established in the church. They have original plans and methods of labor. They desire to introduce changes into the church to suit their ideas of progress and imagine that grand results are thus to be secured. These men need to be learners rather than teachers in the school of Christ. They are ever restless, aspiring to accomplish some great work, to do something that will bring honor to themselves. They need to learn that most profitable of all lessons, humility and faith in Jesus. . . .

"Teachers of the truth, missionaries, officers in the church, can do a good work for the Master if they will but purify their own souls by obeying the truth. . . . As members of the body of Christ all believers are animated by the same spirit and the same hope. Divisions in the church dishonor the religion of Christ before the world and give occasion to the enemies of truth to justify their course. Paul's instructions were not written alone for the church in his day. God designed that they should be sent down to us."—*Testimonies*, vol. 5, pp. 238, 239.

Unsafe to Choose Those Who Refuse to Cooperate With Others—"God has placed in the church, as His appointed helpers, men of varied talents, that through the combined wisdom of many the mind of the Spirit may be met. Men who move in accordance with their own strong traits of character, refusing to yoke up with others who have had a long experience in the work of God, will become blinded by self-confidence, unable to discern between the false and the true. It is not safe for such ones to be chosen as leaders in the church; for they would follow their own judgment and plans, regardless of the judgment of their brethren. It is easy for the enemy to work through those who, themselves needing counsel at every step, undertake the guardianship of souls in their own strength, without having learned the lowliness of Christ."—*The Acts of the Apostles*, p. 279. (See p. 53.)

Membership Required for Election

Seventh-day Adventist church members in regular standing are eligible for election to leadership positions in the local church where they hold membership. (See pp. 144, 146.) Exceptions may be made for the following:

1. Students who are members in regular standing but who, for purposes of education, live away from their normal home and regularly attend a church in the area of their temporary residence.

2. A conference/mission/field employee assigned by the conference/mission/field as pastor/leader for two or more congregations. (See p. 137.)

3. A local elder who, when necessary and with the recommendation of the conference/mission/field committee, may be elected to serve in more than one church. (See p. 51.)

Other exceptions may be considered by the conference/mission/field committee.

Term of Office

The term of office for officers of the church and auxiliary organizations shall be one year, except where the local church in a business meeting votes to have elections every two years in order to facilitate continuity and development of spiritual gifts and eliminate the work involved in having yearly elections. While it is not advisable for one person to serve indefinitely in a particular position, officers may be reelected.

The Church Elder

The Office an Important One—In the work and organization of the church, if a pastor has not been provided by the conference/mission/field, the office of elder ranks as the highest and most important. In the preceding paragraphs the moral and religious fitness of elders as well as other church officers has been set forth.

A Religious Leader of the Church—The local elder must be one recognized by the church as a strong religious and spiritual leader, and must have a good reputation "with them that are without." In the absence of a pastor, the elder is the religious leader of the church and by precept and example must continually seek to lead the church into a deeper and fuller Christian experience.

Capable of Ministering the Word—The elder should be capable of conducting services of the church. It is not always possible for the conference/mission/field to supply ministerial help for all the churches; consequently the elder must be prepared to minister in word and doctrine. However, the elder should not be chosen primarily because of social position, or because of speaking ability, but rather because of a consecrated life and leadership ability. This should be taken into consideration by the nominating committee in preparing its report at the time of the church election.

Term of Office—Like all other church officers, the elder is elected for a one or two year term as determined by the local church. (See p. 47.) It is not advisable for one person to serve indefinitely, but the elder may be reelected. The church is under no obligation, however, to reelect, but may choose another for eldership whenever a change seems advisable. Upon the election of a new elder, the former elder no longer functions as elder, but may be elected to any other church office.

Ordination of Local Elder—Election to the office of elder does not in itself qualify one as an elder. Ordination is required before an elder has authority to function in that office. During the interim between election and ordination, the elected elder may function as church leader but not administer the ordinances of the church.

The ordination service is only performed by an ordained minister with credentials from the local conference/mission/field. It may be a courtesy to invite a visiting ordained minister to assist in the ordination. However, only on the specific request of the local conference/mission/field officers would a visiting ordained minister or a retired ordained minister conduct the ordination.

The sacred rite of ordination should be simply performed in the presence of the church and may include a brief outline of the office of elder, the qualities required, and the principal duties the elder will be authorized to perform for the church. After the exhortation, the minister, assisted by other ordained ministers and/or local ordained elders who are participating in the service, will ordain the elder by prayer and the laying on of hands. (See p. 200.) Having once been ordained as a church elder, ordination is not required again upon reelection to office as an elder, or upon election as elder of another church, provided that regular standing in the church has been maintained. One who has been ordained as elder is thereby qualified to serve subsequently in the deaconate office.

Training and Equipping of Local Elders—The Ministerial Association, in cooperation with the departments, promotes the training and equipping of local church elders. However, the pastor has the primary responsibility for training the local elder. (See Notes, #1, p. 63.)

Work of Church Elder Is Local—The authority and work of an ordained local elder are confined to the church in which the election has been made. It is not permissible for a conference/mission/field committee by vote to confer on a local church elder the status which is granted to an ordained minister to serve other churches as elder. If there exists the need for such service, the conference/mission/field committee may recommend to the church or churches requiring the services of the elder of another church that they elect and invite the elder of the nearby church to serve them also. Thus by election one individual may, when necessary, serve more than one church at a time. When such an arrangement is made it should be in counsel with the conference/mission/field committee. However, this authority is inherent in the church and not in the conference/mission/field committee. The only way one may be qualified for serving the church at large is by ordination to the gospel ministry. (See p. 49 below.)

To Foster All Lines of Church Work—Under the pastor and in the absence of a pastor, the local elder is a spiritual leader of the church and is responsible for fostering all departments and activities of the work. The elder should maintain a mutually helpful relationship with all other church officers.

Relationship to the Ordained Minister—In a case where the conference/mission/field committee assigns an ordained minister to labor as a pastor of a church, he should be considered as the ranking officer, and the local elder as his assistant. Their work is closely related; they should therefore work together harmoniously. The minister should not gather to himself all lines of responsibility, but should share these with the local elder and other officers. The minister serving the church regularly as pastor acts as the chairman of the church board. (See pp. 83, 137.) There may be circumstances, however, when it would be advisable for the elder to act in this capacity. The pastoral work of the church should be shared by both. The elder should, in counsel with the minister, assist in the pastoral responsibility, which includes visiting the church members, ministering to the sick, arranging or leading out in anointing services and child dedications, and encouraging those who are disheartened. Too much emphasis cannot be placed on this part of an elder's work, who as an undershepherd should exercise a constant vigilance over the flock. If the appointed pastor is a licensed minister, the local church or churches that he serves should elect him as an elder. (See p. 137.)

Because the pastor is appointed to the position in the local church by the conference/mission/field, he serves the church as a conference/mission/field worker, and is responsible to the conference/mission/field committee, yet he maintains a sympathetic and cooperative relation to and works in harmony with all the plans and policies of the local church. The elder having been elected by the local church is naturally responsible to that body, and also to its board. (See p. 49.)

Conduct of Church Services—Under the pastor, or in the absence of a pastor, the elder is responsible for the services of the church and must either conduct them or arrange for someone to do so. The communion services must always be conducted by an ordained minister or by the elder. Only ordained ministers or ordained elders holding office are qualified to do this.

The pastor usually serves as chairman of the business meeting, and in his absence the elder shall officiate as chairperson.

The Baptismal Service—In the absence of an ordained pastor, the elder shall request the president of the conference/mission/field to arrange for the administration of the rite of baptism to those desiring to unite with the church. (See pp. 32-35.) A local church elder should not officiate in the baptismal service without first obtaining permission from the conference/mission/field president.

The Marriage Ceremony—In the marriage ceremony the charge, vows, and declaration of marriage are given only by an ordained minister except in those areas where division committees have taken action to approve that selected licensed or commissioned ministers who have been ordained as local elders may perform the marriage ceremony. (See pp. 137, 138.) Either an ordained minister, licensed or commissioned minister, or a local elder may officiate in delivering the sermonette, offering the prayer, or in giving the blessing. (See Notes, #2, p. 63.)

To Cooperate With the Conference/Mission/Field—The pastor, elder(s), and all church officers should cooperate with the conference/mission/field officers and departmental directors in carrying out local, union, division, and General Conference plans. They should inform the church of all regular and special offerings, and should promote all the programs and activities of the church.

The elder should work very closely with the church treasurer and see that all conference/mission/field funds are remitted promptly to the conference/mission/field treasurer at the time established by the conference/mission/field. The elder should give personal attention to seeing that the church clerk's report is sent promptly to the conference/mission/field secretary at the close of each quarter.

The elder should regard all correspondence from the conference/mission/field office as important. Letters calling for announcements to the church should be presented at the proper time.

The first elder, in the absence of and in cooperation with the pastor, should see that delegates to conference/mission sessions are elected and that the names of such delegates are sent to the conference/mission office by the clerk.

The elder should give counsel and help to officers in the church to measure up to their responsibilities in cooperating with the conference/mission/field in carrying out plans and policies, and in seeing that reports are accurately and promptly forwarded.

To Foster Worldwide Work—Another important feature of the elder's work is to foster world mission work. This should be done by making a careful study of the worldwide work and presenting its needs to the church. The elder should encourage members to take a personal part in both supporting and working for the cause of missions. A kindly, tactful attitude on the part of the elder will do much to encourage liberality on the part of the church members both in the regular church services and in the Sabbath School.

To Foster Tithing—As one who faithfully returns tithe, the elder can do much to encourage the church members to return a faithful tithe. (See pp. 153-155, 211.) Anyone who fails to set an example in this important matter should not be elected to the position of elder or to any other church office. Tithing can be fostered by public presentation of the scriptural privilege and responsibility of stewardship and by personal labor with the members. Such labor should be carried on in a tactful and helpful manner. The elder should regard all financial matters pertaining to church members as confidential and should not place such information in the hands of unauthorized persons.

To Distribute Responsibility—In the distribution of duties pertaining to church activities, care should be taken not to lay too much responsibility upon willing workers, while others with perhaps lesser talents are passed by. The election of one individual to several offices is to be discouraged unless circumstances make it necessary. The elder especially should be left free from other burdens to perform effectually the many duties of this sacred office. It may be advisable in some cases to ask the elder to lead the outreach (missionary) work of the church, but even this should be avoided if other talent is available.

First Elder—In churches with a large membership it is advisable to choose more than one elder. The burdens of office may be too great for one person, and should be shared by as many as are required to do the work. In such event one of them should be designated as "first elder." The work should be divided among the elders in harmony with their experience and ability.

Elder Not a Delegate Ex Officio—In order to serve as a delegate to the conference/mission session, the elder must be elected as a delegate by the church. An elder is not a delegate ex officio.

Limitation of Authority—An elder does not have the authority to receive or dismiss church members. This is done only by vote of the church. The elder and the church board may recommend that the church vote to receive or dismiss members. (See pp. 34, 35, 38.)

Church Leaders

Occasionally in newly organized churches, and sometimes in older ones, there is no one possessing the necessary experience and qualifications to serve as elder. Under such circumstances the church should elect a person to be known as "leader." In the absence of a minister the leader is responsible for the services of the church, including the business meetings. The leader must either conduct these or arrange for someone else to do so. A church leader may not preside at any of the church ordinances, administer baptism, conduct the Lord's Supper, perform the marriage ceremony, or preside at business meetings when members are disciplined. A request should be made to the conference/mission/field president for an ordained minister to preside at such meetings.

The Deacon

The office of deacon is described in the New Testament (1 Tim. 3:8-13) where the Greek word *diakonos* is used from which the English "deacon" is derived. The Greek word is variously interpreted as "servant, minister, writer, attendant" and in Christian circles acquired the specialized meaning now attached to "deacon." Scripture clearly endorses the office in the New Testament church: "They that have used the office of a deacon well purchase to themselves a good degree, and great boldness in the faith which is in Christ Jesus" (1 Tim. 3:13). On this authority, the church elects some of its members to serve in eminently practical ways, caring for several aspects of church services, as well as for church property.

The deacon is elected to office, serving for a term of one or two years as determined by the local church. (See p. 47.)

Importance of the Office—In the account of the choosing of the men who came to be known as the seven deacons of the apostolic church, as recorded in Acts 6:1-8, we are told that they were chosen and ordained to attend to the "business" of the church.

But the call to the office of deacon included more than caring for the business of the fast-growing Christian community. The deacons were engaged in an important part of the Lord's work, demanding qualifications but slightly less exacting than those of an elder. (See 1 Tim. 3:8-13.) "The fact that these brethren had been ordained for the special work of looking after the needs of the poor, did not exclude them from teaching the faith. On the contrary, they were fully qualified to instruct others in the truth, and they engaged in the work with great earnestness and success."—*The Acts of the Apostles*, p. 90. Stephen, the first Christian martyr, and Philip, afterward called "the evangelist," were among the first seven deacons chosen in the Christian church (Acts 6:5, 6; 8:5-26; 21:8).

This inspired arrangement resulted in great progress in the building up of the work of the early church. "The appointment of the seven to take the oversight of special lines of work, proved a great blessing to the church. These officers gave careful consideration to individual needs as well as to the general financial interests of the church, and by their prudent management and their godly example they were an important aid to their fellow officers in binding together the various interests of the church into a united whole."—*The Acts of the Apostles*, p. 89.

The appointment of deacons in the present-day church through election by the church brings similar blessings in church administration by relieving pastors, elders, and other officers of duties that may well be performed by deacons. "The time and strength of those who in the providence of God have been placed in leading positions of responsibility in the church, should be spent in dealing with the weightier matters demanding special wisdom and largeness of heart. It is not in the order of God that such men should be appealed to for the adjustment of minor matters that others are well qualified to handle."—*The Acts of the Apostles*, p. 93.

Board of Deacons—Where a church has a sufficient number of deacons to warrant the formation of a board of deacons it is well to organize such a board, with the head deacon as chairman and with another deacon serving as secretary. Such a body affords a well-ordered means of distributing responsibility and coordinates deacon contributions to the well-being of the church. It also provides a training ground where younger men, rightly recruited as deacons, may be instructed in their duties. The head deacon is a member of the church board.

Deacons Must be Ordained—A newly elected deacon cannot fill his office until he has been set apart by an ordained minister who holds current credentials from the conference/mission/field.

The sacred rite of ordination should be simply performed in the presence of the church by an ordained minister, and may consist of a brief reference to the office of deacon, the qualities required of such a servant of the church, and the principal duties he will be authorized to perform for the church. After a short exhortation to faithfulness in service, the minister, assisted by an elder where appropriate, ordains the deacon by prayer and the laying on of hands. (See p. 200.) If he has been once ordained as deacon, and has maintained his membership, it is not necessary for him to be ordained again even though he has transferred to another church. When the term for which he was elected expires, he must be reelected if he is to continue to serve as deacon. Should one who has been ordained as elder be elected as deacon of a church, it is not necessary for him to be ordained as deacon; his ordination as elder covers this office.

Deacons Not Authorized to Preside—The deacon is not authorized to preside at any of the ordinances of the church, nor can he perform the marriage ceremony. He may not preside at any of the business meetings of the church, neither may he officiate at the reception or transfer of members. Where a church has no one authorized to perform such duties, the church shall contact the conference/mission/field for assistance.

The Duties of Deacons—The work of the deacons involves a wide range of practical services for the church including:

    1. *Assistance at Services and Meetings*—At church services, the

deacons are usually responsible for welcoming members and visitors as they enter the church, and for assisting them, where necessary, to find seats. They also stand ready to cooperate with pastor and elders for the smooth functioning of the meetings conducted in the church.

2. *Visitation of Members*—An important duty belonging to deacons is that of visiting church members in their homes. (See p. 56.) In many churches this is arranged by a distribution of membership by districts, assigning a deacon to each district, with the expectation that he will visit each home at least once a quarter.

3. *Preparation for Baptismal Services*—The deacons should do their part in making the necessary preparations for this service; there should be no confusion or delay. (See p. 35.) (See Notes, #3, p. 63.)

4. *Assistance at the Communion Service*—At the celebration of the ordinance of foot-washing, the deacons or deaconesses provide everything that is needed for the service, such as: towels, basins, water (at a comfortable temperature as the occasion may require), buckets, et cetera. After the service they should see that the vessels and linen used are washed and returned to their proper place.

Following the Lord's Supper, great care should be exercised in disposing of any bread or wine left over after all have partaken of these emblems. Any wine remaining that was blessed, is to be poured out. Any of the bread remaining which was blessed should be burned.

5. *The Care of the Sick and the Poor*—Another important responsibility of deacons is the care of the sick, relieving the poor, and aiding the unfortunate. Money should be provided for this work from the church fund for the needy. The treasurer, on recommendation from the church board, will pass over to the deacons or deaconesses whatever may be needed for use in needy cases. This work is the particular charge of the deacons and the deaconesses, but the church is to be kept fully acquainted with the needs, in order to enlist the membership's support.

6. *Care and Maintenance of Church Property*—In some churches, where the responsibility for the care and maintenance of the church property is not assigned to a building committee, the deacons have this responsibility. (See Notes, #4, p. 63.)

The Deaconess

Deaconesses were included in the official staff of the early Christian churches. "I commend to you our sister Phoebe, a deaconess of the church at Cenchreae, that you may receive her in the Lord as befits the saints, and help her in whatever she may require from you, for she has been a helper of many and of myself as well" (Rom. 16:1, 2, RSV).

The deaconess is elected to office, serving for a term of one or two years as determined by the local church. (See p. 47.) It does not follow that the wife of a man chosen as deacon thereby becomes a deaconess, nor is it incumbent upon a church to choose the wife of a deacon as deaconess because her husband is a deacon. The deaconess is to be chosen from the standpoint of consecration and other qualifications that fit her to discharge the duties of the office. The church may arrange for a suitable service of induction for the deaconess by an ordained minister holding current credentials.

The Duties of Deaconesses—Deaconesses serve the church in a wide variety of important activities including:

1. *Assistance at Baptisms*—Deaconesses assist at the baptismal services, ensuring that female candidates are cared for both before and after the ceremony. They also give such counsel and help as may be necessary regarding suitable garments for baptism. Robes of suitable material should be provided. Where robes are used, the deaconesses should see that they are laundered and carefully set aside for future use. (See p. 35.)

2. *Arrangements for the Communion Service*—The deaconesses assist in the ordinance of foot-washing, giving special aid to women visitors or those who have newly joined the church. It is the duty of the deaconesses to arrange everything needed for this service, such as seeing that the table linen, towels, et cetera, used in the celebration of ordinances, are laundered and carefully stored. (See p. 76.)

The deaconesses make arrangements for the communion table including: preparing the bread and wine, arranging the ordinance table, pouring the wine, placing the plates of unleavened bread, and covering the table with the linen provided for that purpose. All these matters should be cared for before the service begins.

3. *The Care of the Sick and the Poor*—Deaconesses are to do their part in caring for the sick, the needy, and the unfortunate, cooperating with the deacons in this work. (See p. 55.)

Board of Deaconesses—Where several deaconesses have been elected, a board of deaconesses should be formed, with the head deaconess serving as chairperson and another as secretary. This board is authorized to assign duties to individual deaconesses, and cooperates closely with the board of deacons, especially in welcoming members and visitors and in home visitation. (See pp. 54, 55.)

The Church Clerk

An Important Office—The clerk of the church has one of the important church offices, upon the proper administration of which much of the efficient functioning of the church depends. Like all other church officers, the church clerk is elected for a one or two year term as determined by the local church (see p. 47); but because of the important and specialized functions of this office, it is wise to choose one who can be reelected to repeated terms to provide continuity in record keeping and reporting. In large churches assistant clerks may be elected as needed. The clerk serves as the secretary of all the business meetings of the church and should keep a correct record of all such meetings. If for any reason the clerk must be absent from any meeting, arrangements should be made for the assistant to be present to take the minutes of the proceedings. (See Notes, #5, p. 64.)

No Names Added or Removed Without Vote of the Church—There must always be a vote of the church to add or remove a name from the church membership roll, except in the case of the death of a member. No name is to be added or removed on the action of the church board alone. The clerk has no authority to add or remove names from the church list without a vote of the church. When a member dies the clerk should, at an early date, record the date of the death opposite the name in the membership book. (See p. 41.)

Transferring Members—The church clerk handles the correspondence between individual members and churches in the transferring of church membership. (See pp. 35-38.)

Corresponding With Members—The clerk should endeavor to keep in touch with absent members by correspondence. (See Notes, #6, p. 64.)

Delegates' Credentials for Conference/Mission Session—The clerk, on authorization of the church board, issues credentials for all delegates elected to represent the church at any session of the local conference/mission and sends them promptly to the conference/mission secretary. All blanks for records, reports, credentials, church letters, et cetera, are provided by the conference/mission/field office. (See pp. 148, 149.)

Reports to be Furnished Promptly—It is the duty of the church clerk to furnish promptly certain reports. Some of these are annual, while others are quarterly. It is essential that they be sent to the conference/mission/field secretary within the time specified as these reports are important for the accuracy of reports prepared by other organizations of the world church. The information required for these reports is to be secured from the treasurer, the Personal Ministries secretary, the deacon, the Sabbath School secretary, the Adventist Youth Society secretary, the church school teacher, and from the clerk's own records. (See Notes, #7, p. 64.)

Church Records—The church clerk is the keeper of the church records. These should be carefully preserved. All records and account books of the various church officers are the property of the church; they are to be surrendered to the newly elected clerk at the expiration of the term of office, or to the church at any time during the term on request of the pastor or elder.

The Church Treasurer

A Sacred Work—The treasurer is called to an important task and is elected as are other officers for a one or two year term as determined by the local church. (See p. 47.) In large churches it may be deemed advisable to elect assistant treasurers as needed.

The treasurer can greatly encourage faithfulness in the returning of tithe and deepen the spirit of liberality on the part of the church members. A word of counsel given in the spirit of the Master will help the brother or sister to render faithfully to God His own in tithes and offerings, even in a time of financial stringency.

Church Treasurer the Custodian of All Church Funds—The church treasurer is the custodian of all church funds. These funds are (1) conference/mission/field funds, (2) local church funds, and (3) funds belonging to the auxiliary organizations of the local church.

All funds (conference/mission/field, local church, and local church auxiliary) are deposited by the treasurer in a bank or financial institution account in the name of the church, unless the local conference/mission/field authorizes another system. This is a separate bank account which is not to be combined with any personal account. Surplus church funds may be deposited in savings accounts upon authorization of the church board. Where large balances are carried for building or special projects, the church board may authorize separate bank accounts. Such accounts, however, shall be operated by the treasurer.

Conference/Mission/Field Funds—Conference/Mission/Field funds, which include tithe, all regular mission funds, and all funds for special conference/mission/field projects and institutions, are trust funds. At the close of each month, or more often if requested by the conference/mission/

field, the church treasurer shall send to the conference/mission/field treasurer the entire amount of conference/mission/field funds received during that period of time. The church may not borrow, use, or withhold such conference/mission/field funds for any purpose.

Sabbath School Funds—All Sabbath School offerings for missions are to be passed over to the church treasurer by the Sabbath School secretary-treasurer weekly, the church treasurer keeping a careful record of all such offerings. These mission funds are transmitted to the conference/mission/field office as outlined on pages 58-62 of this *Church Manual*. Sabbath School expense funds are to be passed over to the church treasurer weekly, to be held in trust, subject to the orders of the Sabbath School Council (see p. 96), to meet the routine expenses of the Sabbath School.

Adventist Youth Society Funds—Adventist Youth Society (AYS) funds have to do with both the Adventist Youth (AY) and the Adventist Junior Youth (AJY) Societies, and the funds of each society shall be kept separately on the church treasurer's books. Society offerings to missions and general church work or to conference/mission/field enterprises shall be handed to the church treasurer as soon as possible after they are received, to be forwarded to the conference/mission/field treasurer. All funds contributed to society expense shall be given promptly to the church treasurer, to be held in trust for the society.

The expense funds of the AY Society shall be disbursed by the church treasurer on the order of the Adventist Youth Society Committee. (See pp. 102, 103.) Expense funds of the AJY Society shall be disbursed on the order of the AJY Society leader.

Local Church Funds—Local church funds include such funds as church expense, church building and repair funds, and the church fund for the poor and needy. These funds belong to the local church and are disbursed by the treasurer only by authorization of the church board or church business meetings. However, the church treasurer shall pay from the church expense funds all bills for local church expense authorized by the church board, such as rentals, janitor, water, light, fuel, insurance, paving assessments, et cetera. The treasurer should be careful to secure receipts for all bills paid.

Funds of Auxiliary Organizations—Auxiliary organization funds include such funds as church outreach programs, welfare, family life, Adventist Youth Society, Dorcas Society, Sabbath School expense, and that portion of the health ministries funds belonging to the church, and may include church school funds. All money received by and for these organizations is turned over promptly to the church treasurer by the secretary of the organization or by the deacons. These funds belong to the auxiliary organizations of the church. They may be disbursed only by order of the auxiliary organization to which they belong.

The treasurer shall give receipts for all funds received including those deposited by any of the subsidiary organizations of the church. On receiving money from the church treasurer, the secretary of such organization shall give a proper receipt to the treasurer.

Safeguarding the Purpose of Funds—When an offering is taken for worldwide missions or for any general or local enterprise, all money placed in the offering plate (unless otherwise indicated by the donor) shall be counted as part of that particular offering. It is of the utmost importance that all offerings and gifts contributed by individuals to the church for a specific fund or purpose be used for that purpose. Neither the church treasurer nor the church board has the authority to divert any funds from the objective for which they were given.

The funds of auxiliary organizations, a considerable proportion of which often represents donations given for specific purposes, are raised for that special part of the church's work for which the auxiliary organization is established. Such funds are held in trust by the church treasurer and they too may not be borrowed or in any way diverted by the treasurer or the church board from the objective for which they were raised.

When an auxiliary organization is discontinued, the church in regular business session may take action indicating the disposition of any remaining balance of funds in the account of such auxiliary organization.

Money for Personal Literature Orders—Money for personal orders of literature, books, pamphlets, magazines, and subscriptions for periodicals is cared for by the church treasurer in areas where a local Adventist Book Center does not exist. (See Notes, #8, p. 64.)

Proper Method for Payment of Money by Members—The treasurer should urge that all money paid in by church members, other than the regular church collection, be placed in the tithe and offering envelopes, instructing each member to list the various items and amounts on the envelope as indicated, and to make sure that the money enclosed equals the total shown. Members should sign their name and give their address, and place the envelope on the offering plate or hand it to the treasurer, who should preserve such envelopes to serve as vouchers until all accounts are checked by the conference/mission/field auditor.

The members who return their tithes and offerings by check or postal notes should, wherever legally possible, make such checks or notes payable to the church, rather than to any individual.

Receipts to Church Members—Receipts should be issued promptly for all money received, no matter how small the amount, and a strict account of all receipts and payments should be kept by the church treasurer. All general offerings not in the envelopes should be counted by the treasurer in the presence of another church officer, preferably a deacon, and a receipt given to such officer.

Proper Method of Remitting Funds to the Conference/Mission/ Field—In sending remittances to the conference/mission/field treasurer, all checks, bank drafts, or money orders should be made payable to the organization wherever legally possible and not to any individual. The duplicate sheet from the church treasurer's book should be enclosed with the remittance. Remittance blanks are furnished by the conference/mission/field.

Preservation of Financial Documents—Financial documents, vouchers, or receipted bills should be secured for all funds received and disbursed in accordance with the system authorized by the local conference/mission/field.

Books Should be Audited—The conference/mission/field treasurer, or some other individual appointed by the conference/mission/field committee, audits the church financial records, usually each year. The church treasurer's books and other financial records relating to the work of the church treasurer, the church school treasurer, and the treasurer of any other organization, may be called for and inspected at any time by the conference/ mission/field auditor or by the pastor, district leader, leading church elder, or by any others authorized by the church board, but should not be made available to unauthorized persons. (See p. 160.)

Reports of all funds received and disbursed should be presented at the regular business meetings of the church. A copy of these reports should be given to the leading church officers.

When the number of individuals returning tithe in the church is reported, the wife and minor children who are non-wage earners but are members of the church should be counted in this group, in addition to the head of the family when the individual is known to be faithful in this respect.

Relations With Members Confidential—The treasurer should always remember that relations with individual members are strictly confidential. The treasurer should be careful never to comment on the tithe returned by any member or of the income or anything concerning it, except to those who share the responsibility of the work. Great harm may be caused by failure to observe this rule.

Interest Coordinator

It is important that the many interests developed through the church's missionary outreach be cared for promptly. To this end, an interest coordinator, who may be an elder, should be elected at the time of the election of church officers. (See p. 47.) This person is a member of the church board and the Personal Ministries Council and works directly with the pastor and chairperson of that council. The duties involved in this office include:

1. To keep an organized list of all interests received by the church from every source such as Community Services, Ingathering, public evangelism, Bible studies, lay preaching and witnessing contacts, outreach (missionary) magazines, Sabbath School evangelism, literature evangelism, temperance and health evangelism, radio-television, and church outreach (missionary) literature.

2. To assist the pastor and chairperson of the Personal Ministries Council in the enlistment and recruitment of qualified laity for follow-up service.

3. To render to the church board a monthly report on the number of interests received and the number followed up. When an interest is sufficiently developed, it should be shared with the pastor.

A Church Officer Removed from Church Membership

When a church officer is removed from membership in the church and is subsequently readmitted to church membership, this action does not reinstate the individual to the former office.

Induction Service

All newly elected officers of the local church may be included in a service of induction conducted by a minister holding a current license or credential. (See p. 122.) If no minister is available, an ordained elder of the local church may conduct the induction service.

Notes

These notes contain explanatory material regarding how a local church may proceed in a particular matter. A local church may adopt alternate ways of handling such items. Such alternative methods should be in harmony with generally accepted principles of Seventh-day Adventist Church organization and operation.

1. *Training and Equipping of Local Elders*—(See p. 49.)—While the pastor has the primary responsibility for training local elders, conferences/missions/fields are encouraged to schedule periodic meetings designed for training them. In order to support a pastor-elder team relationship it is recommended that pastors also attend these meetings. Leaders of companies who function in the place of local elders should also be invited to attend.

2. *The Marriage Ceremony*—(See p. 50.)—In some countries or states a minister must be legally appointed and registered in order to conduct the marriage service. In many lands the minister may perform the ceremony in the church, but the marriage contract is legally signed by the district registrar, who usually sits in the vestry and listens to the approved form of marriage declaration. In still other lands, the minister cannot perform the ceremony at all, for it is recognized as a state responsibility and is looked upon as a civil contract. In such cases our members usually retire to the home or place of worship, where a special service is conducted by a minister, to seek the blessing of the Lord upon the couple. (See pp. 172-174, 191-198.)

3. *Preparation for Baptismal Services*—(See p. 55.)—The deacons should assist at baptismal services, ensuring that the baptism site is prepared, and that male candidates are cared for both before and after the ceremony.

4. *Care and Maintenance of Church Property*—(See p. 55.)—It is the deacons' duty to see that the building is kept clean and in repair, and that the grounds upon which the church stands are kept clean and made attractive. This also includes ensuring that the janitorial work is done. In large churches it is often necessary to employ a janitor. The deacons should recommend a suitable person to the church board, which takes action by vote

to employ such help, or the church board may authorize the deacons to employ a janitor. Church board authorization should be obtained for all major repair expenses. All bills for repairs, as well as for water, light, fuel, et cetera, are referred to the church treasurer for payment.

5. *An Important Office*—(See p. 57.)—These minutes should be recorded in the Church Record book, or in another appropriate record system adopted by the church, giving the time and date of meeting, number attending, and a report of all actions taken. The clerk should also make a list of any committees appointed at such meetings, giving to the chairperson a list of the members of each committee, together with its terms of reference and an outline of work it is asked to do. The Church Record book may be secured from the Adventist Book Center or, in some countries, from the publishing house.

This Church Record book contains a place for recording the church membership, giving the columns necessary to show how and when members are received or removed. This record must be kept chronologically, and supporting data for each entry should also be recorded in the section where minutes of membership actions are kept. The church membership record must be accurately and currently maintained in order to show the official standing of the membership.

6. *Corresponding With Members*—(See p. 57.)—The church clerk should correspond with absent members and should pass on to them interesting items of church progress, encouraging them, in turn, to report their own Christian activities each quarter. It is desirable for the clerk to write to them frequently.

7. *Reports to be Furnished Promptly*—(See p. 57.)—Every item of information called for in the blanks should be supplied. Special attention should be given to the transfer of members, and members received or removed for various causes, as indicated by the blank. The conference/mission/field secretary must report quarterly to the union conference/mission secretary, and the union conference/mission secretary must report to the division, and the division secretary to the General Conference office, relative to these important items; any omission or delay in the report seriously affects the work all along the way. Faithful attention to the details specified in the report blanks greatly assists in keeping accurate records of the worldwide work of the church.

8. *Money for Personal Literature Orders*—(See p. 60.)—In areas where a local Adventist Book Center does not exist, church members may

place their money for personal orders of literature, books, pamphlets, magazines, and subscriptions for periodicals in an envelope, with the order form properly filled out, and hand it to the Personal Ministries secretary. The treasurer then remits both order and payment for all such literature to the conference/mission/field Adventist Book Center, or to the publishing house according to the system adopted by the conference/mission/field. At the close of each quarter the Personal Ministries secretary will make a report to the church, at its quarterly business meeting, of the standing of its account with the Adventist Book Center and/or publishing house and shall provide a copy for the church treasurer. (See pp. 94, 124.)

CHAPTER 8

The Services and Meetings of the Church

General Principles

Spiritual Worship—"Although God dwells not in temples made with hands, yet He honors with His presence the assemblies of His people. He has promised that when they come together to seek Him, to acknowledge their sins, and to pray for one another, He will meet with them by His Spirit. But those who assemble to worship Him should put away every evil thing. Unless they worship Him in spirit and truth and in the beauty of holiness, their coming together will be of no avail. Of such the Lord declares, 'This people draweth nigh unto Me with their mouth, and honoreth Me with their lips; but their heart is far from Me.' Matthew 15: 8, 9. Those who worship God must worship Him 'in spirit and in truth: for the Father seeketh such to worship Him.' John 4:23."— *Prophets and Kings*, p. 50.

The Purpose of the Services and Meetings of the Church—The experience of a Christian is one of spiritual rebirth, joyful reconciliation, faithful mission, and humble obedience to God (2 Cor. 5:17; Phil. 2:5-8). Whatever a Christian does, or participates in, including the services and meetings of the church, is a testimony of this new life in Christ and a sharing of its fruits in the Spirit. The purpose of the services and meetings of the church is to worship God for His creative work and for all the benefits of His salvation; to understand His Word, His teachings, and His purposes; to fellowship with one another in faith and love; to witness about one's personal faith in Christ's atoning sacrifice at the cross; and to learn how to fulfill the gospel commission of making disciples in all the world (Matt. 28:19, 20).

Reverence for the House of Worship—"To the humble, believing soul, the house of God on earth is the gate of heaven. The song of praise, the prayer, the words spoken by Christ's representatives, are God's appointed agencies to prepare a people for the church above, for that loftier worship into which there can enter nothing that defileth.

"From the sacredness which was attached to the earthly sanctuary, Christians may learn how they should regard the place where the Lord meets with His people. . . . God Himself gave the order of His service, exalting it high above everything of a temporal nature.

"The house is the sanctuary for the family, and the closet or the grove the most retired place for individual worship; but the church is the sanctuary for the congregation. There should be rules in regard to the time, the place, and the manner of worshiping. Nothing that is sacred, nothing that pertains to the worship of God, should be treated with carelessness or indifference. In order that men may do their best work in showing forth the praises of God, their associations must be such as will keep the sacred distinct from the common, in their minds. Those who have broad ideas, noble thoughts and aspirations, are those who have associations that strengthen all thoughts of divine things. Happy are those who have a sanctuary, be it high or low, in the city or among the rugged mountain caves, in the lowly cabin or in the wilderness. If it is the best they can secure for the Master, He will hallow the place with His presence, and it will be holy unto the Lord of hosts."—*Testimonies*, vol. 5, pp. 491, 492.

Children to be Taught Reverence—"Parents, elevate the standard of Christianity in the minds of your children; help them to weave Jesus into their experience; teach them to have the highest reverence for the house of God and to understand that when they enter the Lord's house it should be with hearts that are softened and subdued by such thoughts as these: 'God is here; this is His house. I must have pure thoughts and the holiest motives. I must have no pride, envy, jealousy, evil surmising, hatred, or deception in my heart, for I am coming into the presence of the holy God. This is the place where God meets with and blesses His people. The high and holy One who inhabiteth eternity looks upon me, searches my heart, and reads the most secret thoughts and acts of my life.'"—*Testimonies*, vol. 5, p. 494.

Decorum and Quietness in the Place of Worship—"When the worshipers enter the place of meeting, they should do so with decorum, passing quietly to their seats. . . . Common talking, whispering, and laughing should not be permitted in the house of worship, either before or after the service. Ardent, active piety should characterize the worshipers.

"If some have to wait a few minutes before the meeting begins, let them maintain a true spirit of devotion by silent meditation, keeping the heart uplifted to God in prayer that the service may be of special benefit to their own hearts and lead to the conviction and conversion of other souls. They should remember that heavenly messengers are in the house. We all lose much sweet communion with God by our restlessness, by not encouraging moments of reflection and prayer. The spiritual condition needs to be often reviewed and the mind and heart drawn toward the Sun of Righteousness. If when the people come into the house of worship, they have genuine reverence for the Lord and bear in mind that they are in His presence, there will be a sweet eloquence in silence. The whispering and laughing and talking which might be without sin in a common business place should find no sanction in the house where God is worshiped. The mind should be prepared to hear the word of God, that it may have due weight and suitably impress the heart."—*Testimonies*, vol. 5, p. 492.

Arrangements for Church Meetings—Each church should arrange its services and meetings as seems necessary. Those most essential to the worship, study, and activity of the church are the Sabbath worship service, the communion service, the prayer meeting, the Sabbath School, the young people's meeting, and the church outreach (missionary) meeting. Sessions for proper attention to the business affairs of the church are also essential.

Hospitality—A spirit of hospitality should be cultivated in every church. Nothing is so deadening to the spiritual life of a church as a cold, formal atmosphere that drives out hospitality and Christian fellowship. Members should cultivate this essential element of Christian life and experience. Especially should this be so in connection with the worship of God. Every visitor who worships with us should be cordially received and made to feel welcome. It is the duty of the church officers to arrange for someone to give special attention to welcoming the visitors who attend the services of the church. "Be not forgetful to entertain strangers: for thereby some have entertained angels unawares" (Heb. 13:2).

Unauthorized Speakers in Our Churches—Under no circumstances should a minister, elder, or other church officer invite strangers or any unauthorized persons to conduct services in our churches. Individuals who have been removed from the ministry, or who have been dismissed from church fellowship in other places, or designing persons who have no authority from the church, should not be permitted with plausible words to gain admittance to our pulpits. Great care should be exercised to prevent this. Each one worthy of the confidence of our churches will be able to identify himself or herself by producing proper credentials. There may be times when it is proper for our congregations to be addressed by government officials or by civic leaders. All others should be excluded from the pulpit unless permission be granted from the conference/mission/field office. It is the duty of every elder, minister, and conference/mission/field president to see that this rule is carried out. (See pp. 137, 140, 205-207.)

Place of Music in Worship

Place of Music in Worship—"Music can be a great power for good, yet we do not make the most of this branch of worship. The singing is generally done from impulse or to meet special cases, and at other times those who sing are left to blunder along, and the music loses its proper effect upon the minds of those present. Music should have beauty, pathos, and power. Let the voices be lifted in songs of praise and devotion. Call to your aid, if practicable, instrumental music, and let the glorious harmony ascend to God, an acceptable offering."—*Testimonies*, vol. 4, p. 71.

Sing With the Spirit and the Understanding—"In their efforts to reach the people, the Lord's messengers are not to follow the ways of the world. In the meetings that are held, they are not to depend on worldly singers and theatrical display to awaken an interest. How can those who have no interest in the word of God, who have never read His word with a sincere desire to understand its truths, be expected to sing with the spirit and the understanding? How can their hearts be in harmony with the words of sacred song? How can the heavenly choir join in music that is only a form? . . .

"In the meetings held let a number be chosen to take part in the song service. And let the singing be accompanied with musical instruments skillfully handled. We are not to oppose the use of instrumental music in our work. This part of the service is to be carefully conducted, for it is the praise of God in song.

"The singing is not always to be done by a few. As often as possible, let the entire congregation join."—*Testimonies*, vol. 9, pp. 143, 144.

Selecting Choir Leaders—Great care should be used in selecting the choir leaders or those who have charge of the music in the services of the church. Only those who are known to be thoroughly consecrated should be chosen for this part of the church work. Untold harm may be done by selecting unconsecrated leaders. Those lacking in judgment as to the selection of proper and appropriate music for divine worship should not be chosen. Secular music or that of a doubtful or questionable nature should never be introduced into our services.

Choir leaders should work in close collaboration with the minister or church elder in order that the special musical selections harmonize with the theme of the sermon. The choir leader is under the direction of the pastor or elders of the church and does not work independently of them. The choir leader should counsel with them, not only as to the music to be rendered, but also concerning the selection of singers and musicians. The choir leader is not an ex officio member of the church board.

Membership of Church Choirs—Sacred music is an important part of public worship. The church needs to exercise care in the selecting of choir members who will rightly represent the principles of the church. Choir members occupy a conspicuous place in the services of the church. Their singing ability is only one of the qualifications they should have. They should be members of the church, or the Sabbath School, or the Adventist Youth Society who, in their personal appearance and manner of dress, conform to the standards of the church, setting an example in modesty and decorum. People of uncertain consecration or questionable character, or those not appropriately dressed, should not be permitted to participate in the musical features of the services. Any plan concerning the wearing of choir robes is optional on the part of the church.

The organization of children's choirs is to be encouraged as an effective means of spiritual nurture, bonding to the church family, and outreach.

Sabbath Services

The Sabbath School—The Sabbath School has rightly been called the church at study. It is one of the most important services held in connection with our church work. Sabbath by Sabbath the greater part of our membership and thousands of interested friends meet in Sabbath School to study God's Word systematically. All members of the church should be encouraged to attend Sabbath School and also to bring visitors. Each Sabbath School should endeavor to provide appropriate age-level programs for everyone. Materials and resources have been developed to assist in this important task and are available from the field/mission/conference/union/ division. The usual length of time for holding this service is one hour and ten minutes. This, however, does not prevent any local field from adopting a longer or shorter period if it is so desired. In arranging the program, care should be taken to provide at least thirty minutes for the Bible study.

The Worship Service—The Sabbath worship service is the most important of all the meetings of the church. Here the members gather week by week to unite in worshiping God in a spirit of praise and thanksgiving, to hear the Word of God, to gather strength and grace to fight the battles of life, and to learn God's will for them in soul-winning service. Reverence, simplicity, and promptness should characterize the whole service.

Sacredness of the Sabbath Worship Hour—The worship of God is the highest, holiest experience possible to humans, and the greatest care should be exercised in planning for this service.

"Is it not your duty to put some skill and study and planning into the matter of conducting religious meetings—how they shall be conducted so as to do the greatest amount of good, and leave the very best impression upon all who attend?"—E. G. White in *Review and Herald*, April 14, 1885, p. 225.

"Our God is a tender, merciful Father. His service should not be looked upon as a heart-saddening, distressing exercise. It should be a pleasure to worship the Lord and to take part in His work. . . . Christ and Him crucified should be the theme of contemplation, of conversation, and of our most joyful emotion. . . . as we express our gratitude we are approximating to the worship of the heavenly hosts. 'Whoso offereth praise glorifieth' God. Psalm 50:23. Let us with reverent joy come before our Creator, with 'thanksgiving, and the voice of melody.' Isaiah 51:3."—*Steps to Christ*, pp. 103, 104.

The Form of Service—The Sabbath morning service has two main divisions: the congregational response in praise and adoration, expressed in song, prayer, and gifts, and the message from the Word of God. (See Notes #1, p. 87)

We do not prescribe a set form or order for public worship. A short order of service is usually better suited to the real spirit of worship. Long preliminaries should be avoided. The opening exercises should not, under any circumstances, consume time required for worship and for the preaching of the Word of God. (For suggested forms of service, see Notes, #2, p. 88.)

Announcements—Thoughtful consideration should be given to the length and character of the announcements during the Sabbath service. If they deal with matters not specifically related to Sabbath worship or the work of the church, ministers and church officers should be careful to exclude them, maintaining even in this respect a proper spirit of worship and Sabbath observance. Many of our larger churches issue printed bulletins giving the order of service and also the announcements for the week. Where this is done, there is little or no need for oral announcements. Where no such printed provision is made, many churches find it desirable to make the announcements before the actual service begins. (See Notes, #2, p. 88.)

Proper consideration must also be given to the various departments of the church for the promotion of the interests for which they are responsible, but great care should be exercised when making appointments for their presentations, to safeguard the time needed for preaching the message from the Word of God.

Public Prayer—"Christ impressed upon His disciples the idea that their prayers should be short, expressing just what they wanted, and no more. . . .

One or two minutes is long enough for any ordinary prayer."—*Testimonies*, vol. 2, p. 581.

"When you pray, be brief, come right to the point. Do not preach the Lord a sermon in your long prayers."—*Testimonies*, vol. 5, p. 201.

"Let those who pray and those who speak pronounce their words properly and speak in clear, distinct, even tones. Prayer, if properly offered, is a power for good. It is one of the means used by the Lord to communicate to the people the precious treasures of truth. But prayer is not what it should be, because of the defective voices of those who utter it. Satan rejoices when the prayers offered to God are almost inaudible. Let God's people learn how to speak and pray in a way that will properly represent the great truths they possess. Let the testimonies borne and the prayers offered be clear and distinct. Thus God will be glorified."—*Testimonies*, vol. 6, p. 382.

The Communion Service

In the Seventh-day Adventist Church the communion service customarily is celebrated once per quarter. The service includes the ordinance of foot-washing and the Lord's Supper. It should be a most sacred and joyous occasion to the congregation, as well as to the minister or elder. Conducting the communion service is undoubtedly one of the most sacred duties that a minister or elder is called upon to perform. Jesus, the great Redeemer of this world, is holy. The angels declare: "Holy, holy, holy, Lord God Almighty, which was, and is, and is to come." Therefore, since Jesus is holy, the symbols that represent His body and His blood are also holy. Since the Lord Himself selected the deeply meaningful symbols of the unleavened bread and unfermented fruit of the vine and used the simplest of means for washing the disciples' feet, there should be great reluctance to introduce alternative symbols and means (except under truly emergency conditions) lest the original significance of the service be lost. Likewise in the order of service and the traditional roles played by the ministers, elders, deacons, and deaconesses in the communion service, there should be caution lest substitution and innovation contribute to a tendency to make common that which is sacred. Individualism and independence of action and practice could become an expression of unconcern for church unity and fellowship on this most blessed and sacred occasion. Desire for change could neutralize the element of remembrance in this service instituted by our Lord Himself as He entered upon His passion.

The service of the Lord's Supper is just as holy today as it was when instituted by Jesus Christ. Jesus is still present when this sacred ordinance is celebrated. We read, "It is at these, His own appointments, that Christ meets His people, and energizes them by His presence."—*The Desire of Ages*, p. 656.

Ordinance of Foot-Washing—"Now, having washed the disciples' feet, He said, 'I have given you an example, that ye should do as I have done to you.' In these words Christ was not merely enjoining the practice of hospitality. More was meant than the washing of the feet of guests to remove the dust of travel. Christ was here instituting a religious service. By the act of our Lord this . . . ceremony was made a consecrated ordinance. It was to be observed by the disciples, that they might ever keep in mind His lessons, of humility and service.

"This ordinance is Christ's appointed preparation for the sacramental service. While pride, variance, and strife for supremacy are cherished, the heart cannot enter into fellowship with Christ. We are not prepared to receive the communion of His body and His blood. Therefore it was that Jesus appointed the memorial of His humiliation to be first observed."— *The Desire of Ages*, p. 650.

In the act of washing the disciples' feet, Christ performed a deeper cleansing, that of washing from the heart the stain of sin. The communicant senses an unworthiness to accept the sacred emblems before experiencing the cleansing that makes one "clean every whit" (John 13:10). Jesus desired to wash away "alienation, jealousy, and pride from their hearts. . . . Pride and self-seeking create dissension and hatred, but all this Jesus washed away. . . . Looking upon them, Jesus could say, 'Ye are clean.'"—*The Desire of Ages*, p. 646.

The spiritual experience that lies at the heart of foot-washing lifts it from being a common custom to being a sacred ordinance. It conveys a message of forgiveness, acceptance, assurance, and solidarity, primarily from Christ to the believer, but also between the believers themselves. This message is expressed in an atmosphere of humility.

Unleavened Bread and Unfermented Wine—"Christ is still at the table on which the paschal supper has been spread. The unleavened cakes used at the Passover season are before Him. The Passover wine, untouched by fermentation, is on the table. These emblems Christ employs to represent His own unblemished sacrifice. Nothing corrupted by fermentation, the symbol of sin and death, could represent the 'Lamb without blemish and without spot.' 1 Peter 1:19."—*The Desire of Ages*, p. 653.

Neither the wine nor the bread contained elements of fermentation as on the evening of the first day of the Hebrew Passover all leaven, or fermentation, had been removed from their dwellings (Ex. 12:15, 19; 13:7).

Therefore, only unfermented grape juice and unleavened bread are appropriate for use in the communion service; so great care must be exercised in providing these elements. In those more isolated areas of the world where grape or raisin juice or concentrate is not available, the conference/mission/field office will provide advice or assistance.

A Memorial of the Crucifixion—"By partaking of the Lord's Supper, the broken bread and the fruit of the vine, we show forth the Lord's death until He comes. The scenes of His sufferings and death are thus brought fresh to our minds."—*Early Writings*, p. 217.

"As we receive the bread and wine symbolizing Christ's broken body and spilled blood, we in imagination join in the scene of Communion in the upper chamber. We seem to be passing through the garden consecrated by the agony of Him who bore the sins of the world. We witness the struggle by which our reconciliation with God was obtained. Christ is set forth crucified among us."—*The Desire of Ages*, p. 661.

A Proclamation of the Second Coming—"The Communion service points to Christ's second coming. It was designed to keep this hope vivid in the minds of the disciples. Whenever they met together to commemorate His death, they recounted how 'He took the cup, and gave thanks, and gave it to them, saying, Drink ye all of it; for this is My blood of the new testament, which is shed for many for the remission of sins. But I say unto you, I will not drink henceforth of this fruit of the vine, until that day when I drink it new with you in My Father's kingdom.' In their tribulation they found comfort in the hope of their Lord's return. Unspeakably precious to them was the thought, 'As often as ye eat this bread, and drink this cup, ye do show the Lord's death till He come.' 1 Cor. 11:26."—*The Desire of Ages*, p. 659.

Announcing the Communion Service—The communion service may appropriately be included as part of any Christian worship service. However, to give proper emphasis and make communion available to the greatest possible number of members, usually it is part of the Sabbath worship service, preferably on the next to the last Sabbath of each quarter.

On the preceding Sabbath an announcement should be made of the service calling attention to the importance of the forthcoming communion, so that all members may prepare their hearts and make sure that unresolved differences are put right with one another. When they come to the table of the Lord the following week, the service then can bring the blessing intended. Those who were not present for the announcement should be notified and invited to attend.

*Conducting the Communion Service—Length of Service—*Time is not the most significant factor in planning the communion service. However, attendance can be improved and the spiritual impact increased by:

1.   Eliminating all extraneous items from the worship service on this high day.

2.   Avoiding delays before and after the foot-washing.

3.   Having the deaconesses arrange the emblems on the communion table well beforehand.

Preliminaries—The introductory portion of the service should include only very brief announcements, hymn, prayer, offering, and a short sermon before separating for the washing of feet and then returning for the Lord's supper which follows. More worshipers will be encouraged to stay for the entire service if the early part of the service has been brief.

Foot-washing—Each church should have a plan for meeting the needs of its members for the foot-washing service. (See Notes, #3, p. 89.)

Bread and Wine—Following the foot-washing, the congregation comes together once again to partake of the bread and the wine. (See Notes, #4, p. 89.)

Celebration—The service may close with a musical feature or congregational singing followed by dismissal. However it closes, it should end on a high note. Communion should always be a solemn experience but never a somber one. Wrongs have been righted, sins have been forgiven, and faith has been reaffirmed; it is a time for celebration. Let the music be bright and joyous.

An offering for the poor is often taken as the congregation leaves. After the service the deacons and deaconesses clear the table, collect glasses, and dispose of any bread or wine left over by burning or burying the bread and pouring the wine on the ground.

Who May Participate—The Seventh-day Adventist Church practices open communion. All who have committed their lives to the Saviour may participate. Children learn the significance of the service by observing others participate. After receiving formal instruction in baptismal classes and making their commitment to Jesus in baptism, they are thereby prepared to partake in the service themselves.

"Christ's example forbids exclusiveness at the Lord's Supper. It is true that open sin excludes the guilty. This the Holy Spirit plainly teaches. 1 Cor. 5:11. But beyond this none are to pass judgment. God has not left it with men to say who shall present themselves on these occasions. For who can read the heart? Who can distinguish the tares from the wheat? 'Let a man examine himself, and so let him eat of that bread, and drink of that cup.' For 'whosoever shall eat this bread, and drink this cup of the Lord, unworthily, shall be guilty of the body and blood of the Lord.' 'He that eateth and drinketh unworthily, eateth and drinketh damnation to himself, not discerning the Lord's body.' 1 Cor. 11:28, 27, 29.

"When believers assemble to celebrate the ordinances, there are present messengers unseen by human eyes. There may be a Judas in the company, and if so, messengers from the prince of darkness are there, for they attend all who refuse to be controlled by the Holy Spirit. Heavenly angels also are present. These unseen visitants are present on every such occasion. There may come into the company persons who are not in heart servants of truth and holiness, but who may wish to take part in the service. They should not be forbidden. There are witnesses present who were present when Jesus washed the feet of the disciples and of Judas. More than human eyes beheld the scene."—*The Desire of Ages*, p. 656.

Every Member Should Attend—"None should exclude themselves from the Communion because some who are unworthy may be present. Every disciple is called upon to participate publicly, and thus bear witness that he accepts Christ as a personal Saviour. It is at these, His own appointments, that Christ meets His people, and energizes them by His presence. Hearts and hands that are unworthy may even administer the ordinance, yet Christ is there to minister to His children. All who come with their faith fixed upon Him will be greatly blessed. All who neglect these seasons of divine privilege will suffer loss. Of them it may appropriately be said, 'Ye are not all clean.'"—*The Desire of Ages*, p. 656

Who May Conduct Communion Service—The communion service is to be conducted by an ordained minister or a church elder. Deacons, although ordained, cannot conduct the service, but they can assist by passing the bread and wine to the members.

Communion for the Sick—If any members are ill or cannot for any other reason leave the home to attend the communion service in the house of worship, a special service in the home may be held for them. This service can be conducted only by an ordained minister or a church elder, who may be accompanied and assisted by deacons or deaconesses who assist in the regular service.

The Prayer Meeting

"The prayer meetings should be the most interesting gatherings that are held, but these are frequently poorly managed. Many attend preaching, but neglect the prayer meeting. Here, again, thought is required. Wisdom should be sought of God, and plans should be laid to conduct the meetings so that they will be interesting and attractive. The people hunger for the bread of life. If they find it at the prayer meeting they will go there to receive it.

"Long, prosy talks and prayers are out of place anywhere, and especially in the social meeting. Those who are forward and ever ready to speak are allowed to crowd out the testimony of the timid and retiring. Those who are most superficial generally have the most to say. Their prayers are long and mechanical. They weary the angels and the people who listen to them. Our prayers should be short and right to the point. Let the long, tiresome petitions be left for the closet, if any have such to offer. Let the Spirit of God into your hearts, and it will sweep away all dry formality."—*Testimonies*, vol. 4, pp. 70, 71.

The weekly prayer meeting is of so great importance that more than ordinary efforts should be made to assure its success. The meetings should begin on time, even though but two or three persons are present. There should be a short Scripture study or presentation from the *Testimonies*. Fifteen or twenty minutes are sufficient. Then give the members time for prayer and testimony. Vary the plan of the service from week to week. Have a season of prayer following the study one time; the next time, follow the study by testimonies, closing with a season of prayer and a song.

If the members are unable to assemble at the usual place for prayer meeting, cottage meetings can be conducted with great benefit to all who attend.

Adventist Youth Society*

The Adventist Youth Society is the action and fellowship organization for senior youth in the local church. Under the leadership of an elected Youth leader, young people are to work together in the development of a strong youth ministry which includes spiritual, mental, and physical development for each individual, Christian social interaction, and an active witnessing program which supports the general soul-winning plans of the local church. It should be the goal of the Adventist Youth Society to involve all young people in meaningful activities which will tie them closer to the church and train them for useful service.

Regular meetings of the youth should be scheduled each week. It is recommended that these meetings be held Friday evening or Sabbath

---

*This is an accepted abbreviated name for the full official name "Seventh-day Adventist Youth Society."

afternoon. Such meetings may be held in homes of responsible church members or as larger public meetings in the church. Since the youth program should not be isolated from the rest of the church, the public Adventist Youth Society meetings should be open to the entire church membership. Ideally, they should be planned and operated, however, by the youth themselves. In smaller churches the youth program of necessity must have a family-involvement approach. (See Notes, #5, p. 90.)

It is important that the youth program in the local church be coordinated with the work of all departments that provide ministry for children and youth. To encourage this cooperation and coordination, the Personal Ministries leader, Health Ministries leader, leader of the youth Sabbath School division, school principal, Pathfinder Club director, Adventurer Club director, and other leaders as needed are members of the Adventist Youth Ministries Committee, which is an umbrella organization in the local church responsible for planning the youth ministry program. (See p. 102.) (See Notes, #6, p. 90.)

While a successful youth ministry program in the local church includes a strong youth Sabbath School, there must be a specific time and place for more interaction, fellowship, recreation, witnessing outreach, and leadership training, which are all a part of the concepts to be fostered in the Adventist Youth Society.

Adventist Junior Youth Society

The purpose of the Adventist Junior Youth Society is similar to that of the organization for the Adventist Youth Society for senior youth. Its purpose is to build character, provide social interaction, give leadership training, and involve the junior youth in Christian service. In those countries where there are Adventist church schools, the Adventist Junior Youth Society is usually a part of the school spiritual curriculum. (See Notes, #7, p. 90.)

Pathfinder Club

The Pathfinder Club provides a specialized program needed for junior youth and in some areas has replaced the Adventist Junior Youth Society in the local church. Where there are both there must be close coordination and cooperation between the Pathfinder Club and the Adventist Junior Youth Society. Pathfinders will meet according to conference/mission/field departmental policy.

Adventurer Club

The Adventurer Club provides a specialized program suited to the rapidly developing primary/early school-age children in the local church. It is designed to strengthen parental involvement in early childhood development. Its meetings and other activities are to be carried out in accordance with local conference/mission/field policies as outlined in the club manuals and in coordination with other youth-related and family-related organizations of the local church.

Church Outreach (Missionary) Meetings

The Saviour's commission lays upon the church the task of heralding the gospel to all the world. This also places upon each individual member the responsibility of giving the message of salvation to as many others as possible. The Saviour "gave authority to His servants, and to every man his work." He appointed a meeting with His eleven disciples after His resurrection for the purpose of giving them counsel and encouragement, and at that time He gave the gospel commission to the disciples and to the assembled church, numbering more than five hundred brethren. That was the first outreach (missionary) meeting of the Christian church; it was certainly not to be the last.

As a permanent and definite part of the services of the Christian church, the outreach (missionary) meeting bears the divine endorsement for all time. Through the Spirit of Prophecy we are told: "God has committed to our hands a most sacred work, and *we need to meet together* to receive instruction, that we may be fitted to perform this work."—*Testimonies*, vol. 6, p. 32. (Italics supplied.)

Times of Meetings—The first Sabbath of the month is generally recognized as Church Outreach (Missionary) Sabbath. The worship service of this Sabbath is focused on lay evangelism, but other departments besides the Personal Ministries Department may also have opportunity on these special days to present their interests. This will be done, however, by careful counsel with the departments concerned. (See Notes, #8, p. 90.)

Supplying Literature on the Sabbath—It is generally recognized that the Sabbath affords the most opportune time for the Personal Ministries secretary to place literature in the hands of the members. Methods that are objectionable and that would tend to divert the attention of the congregation from true worship and reverence should be avoided on the Sabbath.

Business Meetings

Church business meetings duly called by the pastor, or the church board in consultation with the pastor, may be held monthly or quarterly according to the needs of the church. Members in regular standing on the roll of the church conducting the business meeting may attend and vote. Votes by proxy or letter shall not be accepted. In order to maintain a spirit of close cooperation between the local church and the conference/mission/field, the church shall secure counsel from the conference/mission/field officers on all major matters. The officers (president, secretary, treasurer) of the conference/mission/field to which the church belongs may attend without vote (unless granted by the church) any church business meeting within the conference/mission/field territory. A duly called business meeting of the church is a meeting that has been called at the regular Sabbath worship service, together with proper announcements as to the time and place of the meeting. At such meetings, at which the pastor will preside (or will arrange for the local elder to preside), full information should be given to the congregation regarding the work of the church. At the close of the year, reports should be rendered covering the activities of the church for the entire year and, based on those reports, the church should approve a full plan of action for the next year. When possible, reports and the next year's plan of action should be presented in writing. (See Notes, #9, p. 91.)

The Church Board and Its Meetings

Definition and Function—The church board is composed of the principal officers of the church. It has a number of important responsibilities, but its chief concern is the spiritual nurture of the church and the work of planning and fostering evangelism in all of its phases.

The great commission of Jesus makes evangelism, proclaiming the good news of the gospel, the primary function of the church (Matt. 28:18-20). It is therefore also the primary function of the church board to serve as the chief committee of the local church. When the board devotes its first interests and highest energies to every-member evangelism, most church problems are alleviated or prevented. A strong, positive influence is felt in the spiritual life and growth of the membership.

Included in church board responsibilities are:

1. Spiritual nurture.
2. Evangelism in all of its phases.
3. Maintenance of doctrinal purity.

4. Upholding Christian standards.
5. Recommending changes in church membership.
6. Church finances.
7. Protection and care of church properties.
8. Coordination of church departments.

The board is elected by the church membership at the time of the regular election of church officers. (See p. 47.)

Membership—The following church officers should be included in the church board membership:

Elder(s)
Head deacon
Head deaconess
Treasurer
Clerk
Personal Ministries leader
Personal Ministries secretary
Community Services and/or Dorcas leader
Sabbath School superintendent
Family Ministries leader
Women's Ministries leader
Children's Ministries coordinator
Education secretary
Home and School Association leader
Adventist Youth Society leader
Pathfinder Club director
Adventurer Club director
Interest coordinator
Communication Committee chairperson or Communication secretary
Health Ministries leader
Stewardship leader
Religious Liberty leader

In many cases two or more of these offices are carried by one individual. Additional members of the board may be elected by the church if desired. The minister appointed by the local field to serve the church as its pastor is always a member of the church board.

Officers—The chairman of the church board is the minister appointed to serve the church as pastor. If the pastor prefers not to act in this capacity or is unable to be present, he may arrange for the church elder to preside as chairman on a pro tem basis. The church clerk serves as secretary of the board and is responsible for preserving the minutes of the meetings.

Meetings—Because the work of the church board is vital to the life, health, and growth of the church, it needs to meet at least once each month. In larger churches more frequent meetings may be needed. It is well to fix the monthly meeting time for the same week and the same day each month. (Example: The first Monday of each month.)

The church board meeting is announced at the regular Sabbath worship service. Every effort should be made to have all board members present at each meeting.

Each church should determine at one of its regularly called business meetings the number of church board members who must be present at a church board meeting to constitute a quorum. Votes by proxy or letter shall not be accepted.

Work of the Board—1. Planning evangelism in all of its phases. Since evangelism is the primary work of the church, the first item on the agenda of each church board meeting is to relate directly to the evangelization of the outreach (missionary) territory of the church. In addition, once each quarter of the year the entire church board meeting can well be devoted to plans for evangelism. The board will study local field committee recommendations for evangelistic programs and methods. It will determine how these can best be implemented by the church. The pastor and the church board will initiate and develop plans for public evangelistic campaigns.

2. Coordinating outreach programs of departments. The church board is responsible for coordinating the work of all church departments. This includes the outreach programs of Personal Ministries, Sabbath School, Children's Ministries, Youth, Health Ministries, and Education. Each of these departments develops its plans for outreach within its own sphere. To avoid conflict in timing and competition in securing volunteer helpers, and to achieve maximum beneficial results, coordination is essential. Before completing and announcing plans for any program, each department should submit its plans to the church board for approval. The departments also report to the church board on the progress and results of their outreach programs. The church board may suggest to the departments how their programs can contribute to the preparation, conduct, and follow-up of a

public evangelistic campaign.

3.   Encouraging and helping the Personal Ministries Department of the church to enlist all church members and children in some form of personal outreach (missionary) service. Training classes should be conducted in various lines of outreach ministry.

4.   Cooperating with the Interest coordinator of the church to ensure that every reported interest in the message, aroused through whatever source, is personally and promptly followed up by an assigned layperson.

5.   Encouraging each department to report at least quarterly to the church board and to the church membership at business meetings and/or in Sabbath day meetings.

6.   The details of church business should be considered by the board, and the treasurer should report the state of church finance on a regular basis. The church roll should be studied, and inquiry should be made into the spiritual standing of all members, and provision made for visiting the sick, discouraged, and any backslidden member. The other officers should report concerning the work for which they are responsible.

Committees of the Board—The church board should permit no other business to interfere with planning for evangelism. Should other business be too time-consuming, the board may appoint committees to care for specific areas of church business such as finance or church building projects. Such committees will then make recommendations to the church board. In this way the resources of the board are conserved for its primary task—evangelism. (See Notes, #10, p. 92.)

School Board Meetings

In churches which have a church school the work is usually supervised by a church school board. A chairperson is elected who presides over the meetings of this board. A secretary is chosen to keep the records of board meetings and actions. This board should hold its meetings at regular times. Special meetings may be called by the chairperson when the need arises. Some churches prefer to have the church board, or a subcommittee of the church board, serve also as the school board.

Home and School Association

The Home and School Association is organized by the local church to coordinate the activities of the school, home, and church. It is recommended that meetings be conducted on a monthly basis. Attention should be given to the education of parents, as well as to assisting the school to obtain needed resources such as room parents, books, teaching materials, and equipment.

Materials to assist the Home and School leaders are available through the Department of Education.

Notes

These notes contain explanatory material regarding how a local church may proceed in a particular matter. A local church may adopt alternate ways of handling such items. Such alternative methods should be in harmony with generally accepted principles of Seventh-day Adventist Church organization and operation.

1. **The Form of Service** (See p. 72.)—As the ministers come to the rostrum and kneel, the congregation should, with bowed heads, implore the presence and blessing of God. A worshipful hush prepares the way for the opening hymn and the exercises which follow.

The two main divisions of the worship service are:

a. The congregational response in praise and adoration, expressed in song, prayer, and gifts.

b. The message from the Word of God. The one who brings the message and breaks the bread of life should fully sense the sacredness of this work and should be thoroughly prepared. Then, too, the one leading the worshipers into the presence of God through the medium of the pastoral prayer is performing perhaps the holiest exercise of the whole service and, with a sense of awe, should humbly realize its importance. It is customary to kneel, facing the congregation, and the congregation in turn should face the rostrum and, as far as practicable, kneel. The prayer should be brief but should include adoration, thanks, and mention of the personal needs of the worshipers, as well as of the great world field.

Special music or a devotional hymn is appropriate immediately before the sermon. Then comes what should be one of the most important parts of the worship hour—the spiritual feeding of the flock of God. Blessed results to the glory of God always follow when a congregation is truly fed and feels that "God has visited His people."

The offering is a vital part of the worship hour. While we are counseled to "worship the Lord in the beauty of holiness," we are also exhorted to "bring an offering, and come into his courts" (Ps. 96:9, 8). So the presentation of our gifts to God quite naturally finds its place as a part of the worship service.

The elder, particularly if he is a licensed minister, collaborates with the regular pastor in planning the order of the service. If the church has no regular pastor, the elder is in charge of the service and should either conduct it or arrange for someone to do so. From time to time a meeting for testimony and praise may be conducted, or the time may be given to certain members to relate their experiences in outreach (missionary) work.

2. *The Form of Service*—(See p. 72.)—Following are two suggested forms of service:

Longer Order of Worship

Organ Prelude
Announcements
Choir and Ministers Enter
Doxology
Invocation
Scripture Reading
Hymn of Praise
Prayer
Anthem or Special Music
Offering
Hymn of Consecration
Sermon
Hymn
Benediction
Congregation Standing or Seated for a Few Moments of Silent
        Prayer
Organ Postlude

Shorter Order of Worship

Announcements
Hymn
Prayer
Offering
Hymn or Special Music
Sermon
Hymn
Benediction
Congregation Standing or Seated for Silent Prayer

3.   *Foot-washing*—(See p. 76.)—Men and women should be provided separate areas for the foot-washing. Where stairs or distance is a problem, special arrangements should be made for the disabled. In places where it is socially acceptable and where clothing is such that there would be no immodesty, separate arrangements may be made for husband and wife or parents and baptized children to share with each other in the foot-washing ceremony. To encourage shy or sensitive people who may view the selecting of a foot-washing partner as an embarrassing experience, church leaders should be designated whose responsibility during the foot-washing is to help such persons find partners.

4.   *Bread and Wine*—(See p. 76.)—A hymn may be sung during the reassembly of the congregation as the officiating ministers or elders take their places at the table on which the bread and wine have been placed, and the deacons and deaconesses take their places. The covering over the bread is removed. A suitable passage of Scripture may be read such as 1 Corinthians 11:23, 24; Matthew 26:26; Mark 14:22; or Luke 22:19, or a brief sermon may be given at this point in the service rather than earlier. This can be especially effective if the sermon emphasizes the meaning of the bread and wine so its message is still fresh in the minds of participants as the emblems are being distributed. Those officiating normally kneel while the blessing is asked on the bread. The congregation may kneel or remain seated. Most of the bread to be served is usually broken ahead of time, with a small portion left on each plate for the elders or pastors to break. The minister and elders hand the plates containing the bread to the deacons, then the deacons serve the congregation. During this time there may be a choice of special music, testimonies, a summary of the sermon, selected readings, congregational singing, or meditative organ or piano music.

Each person should retain his/her portion of the bread until the officiating minister or elder has been served. When everyone has been seated, the leader invites all to partake of the bread together. Silent prayers are offered as the bread is eaten.

The minister then reads a suitable passage such as 1 Corinthians 11: 25, 26; Matthew 26:27-29; Mark 14:23-25; or Luke 22:20. Leaders kneel as the prayer is given over the wine. Again, deacons serve the congregation. Activities such as those suggested during the passing of the bread may be continued at this time. After the officiating ministers or elders have been served, all worshipers partake of the wine together.

An optional method is for the bread to be blessed and broken; then the bread and wine are placed on the same tray and passed to the congregation. The worshiper takes both from the tray at the same time. The bread is eaten, followed by silent prayer. Then after prayer over the wine, it is taken, followed by silent prayer. Where pews or seats are equipped with racks to hold the wine glasses, the collection of glasses is unnecessary until after the service.

5. *Adventist Youth Society*—(See p. 78)—Resource materials to help the local church Adventist Youth Society leadership are available from the division, union, and local conference/mission/field Youth departments. Included in these resource materials is *Youth Ministry Accent*, a quarterly journal published by the General Conference Youth Department. There are also many leaflets available covering a broad spectrum of topics to help in youth ministry. These may be secured from the conference/mission/field Youth departments and Adventist Book Centers.

6. *Adventist Youth Society*—(See p. 78.)—The Adventist Youth Society plan of organization is briefly outlined in Chapter 9, *Auxiliary Organizations of the Church and Their Officers*. Detailed information is available from the conference/mission/field Youth director. It is essential that each church study its own youth and family profile, resources, personnel, facilities, and school relationships, developing the best youth ministry in keeping with these factors. In some places another term for "society," such as "fellowship" or "action," may be selected, but the name "Adventist Youth" should always be used to clearly identify the organization.

7. *Adventist Junior Youth Society*—(See p. 79.)—Each classroom is considered a separate society, with the teacher as the leader and students elected as society officers. Where there is no church school, the junior youth membership should be integrated into the overall youth program with a family-involvement approach.

8. *Times of Meetings*—(See p. 80.)—In order to strengthen and develop the outreach (missionary) spirit among our members, auxiliary Personal Ministries meetings might be conducted in one or more of the following ways:

a.   The ten-minute weekly Personal Ministries meeting held each Sabbath, usually following the close of the Sabbath School and just preceding the preaching service.

b.   A midweek meeting combined with the weekly prayer meeting. On this occasion, the first part of the service may be given to a devotional message, followed by a season of prayer, remembering that worship is vital in spiritual growth and preparation for service. The remainder of the meeting time may then be devoted to a training period for lay evangelistic service.

Instruction in soul-winning methods is presented and the members are given opportunity to present for general discussion problems they have met in lay evangelism.

　　c.　Personal Ministries meetings at various times, as best suited to local conditions. The Personal Ministries Council should carefully plan to make the Personal Ministries services of the church occasions for spiritual revival and practical training, and see that they are conducted with the same regularity and continuity as other meetings of the church.

　　9.　*Business Meetings*—(See p. 81.)—Reports may comprise the following activities:

　　a.　A report from the clerk showing the present membership of the church and the number of members received and those transferred to other churches. Note also should be made, giving the number but not necessarily the names, of those who may have had to be removed from fellowship during the year, as well as those who have died. A brief statement of the decisions of the church board in its meetings would naturally be of interest to all members of the church

　　b.　A report from the Personal Ministries leader, giving a statement of outreach (missionary) activities, including Community Services activities, together with any plans for future work. This should be followed by a report from the Personal Ministries secretary.

　　c.　A report from the treasurer, showing the amount of tithe received and sent to the conference/mission/field treasurer; also a full statement of mission offerings received and forwarded; and a statement showing local church funds received and disbursed.

　　d.　A report from the deacons and deaconesses concerning visits to the members, their activities in behalf of the poor, and any other features that come under their supervision.

　　e.　A report from the secretary of the young people's society outlining the activities in outreach (missionary) and other lines by the youth of the church.

　　f.　A report from the Sabbath School secretary, giving the membership and other matters pertaining to the Sabbath School.

　　g.　A report from the treasurer as to the financial status of the church school, with details as to its needs in equipment and other matters.

　　h.　A report from the principal or teacher of the church school, covering such matters as enrollment, the educational progress of the school, baptisms among the school children, and the results of the children's efforts in denominational endeavors.

　　i.　A report from the Home and School Association leader, covering the activities and needs of that organization.

j.   A report from the Communication secretary covering press, radio, television, and other related activities involving church and community.

10. *Committees of the Board*—(See p. 84.)—In very large churches, a committee for evangelistic planning may be appointed by the board. This will be composed of the heads of the church outreach departments with an elder as chairman. This committee will report to the church board and will also assume the task of department coordination of outreach programs.

CHAPTER 9

Auxiliary Organizations of the Church and Their Officers

The structure of the church, under the guidance of the Holy Spirit, is vital for the spiritual growth of members and for the fulfillment of the mission of the church. It is the skeleton of the body. And "the whole body, joined and knit together by every joint with which it is supplied, when each part is working properly, makes bodily growth and upbuilds itself in love" (Eph. 4:16, RSV). The most important elements of the local church structure and organization are the church officer roles (see chapter 7) and the auxiliary organizations or departments. This chapter is a description of their design, objectives, leadership, functions, and activities. The departments in the local church are expected to cooperate with the corresponding departments of the local field/mission/conference, union, and division.

The work of the departments in the local church is closely tied to the work of the pastor because both are equally engaged in the same program of the church. The pastor serves as a close counselor to the committees of all auxiliary organizations, and the departments assist in correlation with the church in implementing its program. In case of emergency, or where circumstances require such action, the pastor may call a meeting of any committee or organization of the church to conduct necessary business in the interest of the church. Every local church should utilize the services of the departments described in this chapter to nurture its members and accomplish the mission given by Christ to the Christian church, and particularly to the remnant church in the end time (Matt. 28:19; Rev. 10:11; Rev. 14:6).

The Personal Ministries Department

The Personal Ministries Department provides resources and trains church members to unite their efforts with the ministry and church officers in the final proclamation of the gospel of salvation in Christ. The aim of the department is to enlist every member in active soul-winning service for God.

Personal Ministries Council—The Personal Ministries Council guides the outreach (missionary) efforts of the local church and works under the direction of the church board. The council should meet at least once each month. This council shall consist of the following: Personal Ministries leader (chairperson), Personal Ministries secretary, pastor, an elder, church treasurer, Dorcas Society leader, Dorcas Society secretary, Adventist Men's organization leader, Interest coordinator, Health Ministries leader, Communication secretary, Sabbath School superintendent, Youth leader, coordinator for Ministry to People with Disabilities, Children's Ministries coordinator, Women's Ministries leader, director of Community Services center or Community Services leader, and other members as deemed necessary. The Personal Ministries Council may assign subcommittees for specialized tasks as deemed necessary. All subcommittees report to the Personal Ministries Council. (See Notes, #1, p. 123.)

Personal Ministries Leader—The Personal Ministries leader is elected by the church to lead in training and directing the church in active outreach (missionary) service and is chairperson of the Personal Ministries Council. It is the leader's duty to present to the church, in the monthly Sabbath Personal Ministries service and in the church business meetings, a report on the total outreach (missionary) activities of the church.

Personal Ministries Secretary—The Personal Ministries secretary is elected by the church and serves as the representative of the Adventist Book Center for all departments of the church. The secretary works closely with the Personal Ministries leader in developing the outreach (missionary) programs of the church. (See Notes, #2, p. 124.)

Community Services/Dorcas Society—The Community Services/ Dorcas Society is an important feature of the outreach (missionary) activities of the church. The leader of this society, the assistant leader (if needed), and the secretary-treasurer, are elected at the regular church election. This society gathers and prepares clothing, food, and other supplies for the poor, needy, and unfortunate. This organization works in close cooperation with the deacons and deaconesses of the church. Community Services/Dorcas ministry, however, includes more than giving material aid; it encompasses also adult education, visiting, homemaking, home nursing, counseling, and other services. The church Personal Ministries Department has primary responsibility for this work.

Adventist Men—Adventist Men is another subsidiary group within the Personal Ministries Department. (See Notes, #3, p. 124.)

Community Services Center—Where a church operates a Community Services Center, the Personal Ministries Council is the governing committee of the center. The director of the center is appointed by the Personal Ministries Council and is a member of the council. (See Notes, #4, p. 125.)

Ministry to People with Disabilities—Through the Ministry to People with Disabilities, a local church Personal Ministries Council should give special attention to members and others with disabilities. It should develop programs for witnessing to people who have disabilities; make recommendations to the church board regarding possible actions which could make the church facilities more accessible for people with disabilities; assist the church in transportation solutions for people with disabilities; and advise departmental and church leadership regarding possible involvement of members who have disabilities.

The coordinator of Ministry to People with Disabilities serves as a liaison with organizations providing services for people with disabilities such as Christian Record Services and promotes Christian Record Services programs in the local church.

The Sabbath School Department

The Sabbath School is the primary religious education system of the Seventh-day Adventist Church and has four purposes: study of the Scripture, fellowship, community outreach, and world mission emphasis.

In cooperation with world divisions, the specific mission of the General Conference Sabbath School Department is to distribute the *Sabbath School Bible Study Guide* for all age levels, provide designs for Sabbath School programming within the context of the various world division cultures, provide resources and training systems for Sabbath School teachers, and promote world mission Sabbath School offerings.

"The Sabbath school is an important branch of the missionary work, not only because it gives to young and old a knowledge of God's word, but because it awakens in them a love for its sacred truths, and a desire to study them for themselves; above all, it teaches them to regulate their lives by its holy teachings."—*Counsels on Sabbath School Work,* pp. 10, 11.

"The Sabbath school, if rightly conducted, is one of God's great instrumentalities to bring souls to a knowledge of the truth."—*Counsels on Sabbath School Work,* p. 115.

The officers, teachers, and entire Sabbath School membership should cooperate with the other departments of the church in all outreach (missionary) work and soul-saving activities, as well as energetically carrying on Sabbath School evangelism by means of the regular Sabbath

School classes, and such activities as Decision Days, pastors' Bible classes, Community Guest Days, Vacation Bible Schools, and branch Sabbath Schools, including Neighborhood Bible Clubs and Story Hours. In churches which have a Children's Ministries Department, Vacation Bible Schools, children's branch Sabbath Schools, Neighborhood Bible Clubs, and Story Hours will come under the direction of the Children's Ministries Department. (See p. 120.) Likewise, all departments of the church should work together with the Sabbath School to make the work of the entire church as effective as possible.

The officers of the Sabbath School should be members of the local church. They are elected for one or two years as determined by the local church. (See p. 47.) The officers who serve as members of the Sabbath School Council are elected in the same manner and at the same time as the officers of the church. The list of Sabbath School officers and their assistants who are to be elected by the church is as follows: superintendent, with one or more assistants; secretary, with one or more assistants; a leader for each division, including the adult and extension divisions; Children's Ministries coordinator and/or Vacation Bible School director; and Investment secretary.

The Sabbath School Council—The Sabbath School Council is the administrative body of the Sabbath School. It consists of the following: superintendent (to serve as chairperson), assistant superintendent(s), secretary (to serve as secretary of the council), assistant secretaries, division leaders, Investment secretary, Personal Ministries leader, Children's Ministries coordinator and/or Vacation Bible School director, an elder (appointed by the church board or by the board of elders), and the pastor. As soon as possible after the officers are elected, the superintendent should call a Sabbath School Council meeting to appoint, as needed for the various divisions, other officers who do not serve as members of the Sabbath School Council. These may include assistant division leaders, division secretaries, music directors, pianists and/or organists, and greeters.

In addition to the appointed officers listed in the paragraph above, the Sabbath School Council appoints the teachers for all divisions, who are then approved by the church board. Careful study should be given to the needs of all groups. It is advisable to consult with the division leaders, particularly when selecting teachers for the children's divisions.

Because of the importance of maintaining the integrity of the truths being taught and maintaining a high quality of teaching, great care should be exercised in the choice of Sabbath School teachers. The time allotted for teaching should be at least thirty minutes. All teachers shall be members of the church in regular standing.

The Sabbath School Council is responsible for the successful operation of the entire Sabbath School through the leadership of its chairperson, the superintendent. The council should meet regularly as needed to affect proper coordination of the program for all divisions. The council should ensure that program helps and materials, including the *Sabbath School Bible Study Guide* prepared by the General Conference, are supplied in sufficient quantities and in a timely manner.

The Superintendent—The Sabbath School superintendent is the leading officer of the Sabbath School. As soon as the superintendent is elected, he/she should begin planning for the smooth and effective operation of the school. The superintendent should support the plans and emphases of the Sabbath School Department of the conference/mission/field. The superintendent is expected to abide by the decisions of the Sabbath School Council concerning the operation of the Sabbath School. (See Notes, #5, p. 125.)

The Assistant Superintendent—One or more assistant superintendents may be elected to assist the superintendent as needed. The assistant(s) may be assigned specific responsibilities such as: promoting Sabbath School evangelism and world missions; coordinating the weekly mission emphasis, and planning and promoting offering goals; fostering and coordinating evangelistic outreach plans and activities in the community; and caring for membership by checking Sabbath School records with the church membership records, and then making and implementing plans to increase Sabbath School attendance and membership. Such plans should encourage individual and class outreach to contact non-attending and new members.

The Secretary—Faithfulness, accuracy, and Christian courtesy are especially necessary in the work of the secretary. (See Notes, #6, p. 125.)

Assistant Secretary—In the absence of the secretary, an assistant secretary assumes the responsibilities. The assistant secretary should be present at each Sabbath School service, ready to assist by doing whatever the superintendent or the secretary may require.

If desired, the assistant may act as secretary of the teachers' meeting and report to the secretary any business that should be recorded.

Investment Secretary—The Investment secretary gives promotional leadership to the Investment Plan for mission support. He/She encourages investment activity in all divisions of the Sabbath School, keeping all members informed of progress.

Vacation Bible School Director—The Vacation Bible School director leads in organizing, promoting, and launching community evangelism through the annual Vacation Bible School. (In some churches this responsibility may be given to the Children's Ministries coordinator.)

The Music Director—A music director may be appointed by the Sabbath School Council to lead the music of the school and plan with the division leader for the presentation of this phase of worship each Sabbath.

As an expression of worship, care should be taken to provide music which will glorify God. Singers should be as carefully selected as are the workers for other parts of the Sabbath School service and should be measured by the same standards. (See p. 70.)

The Pianist and/or Organist—The Sabbath School pianists and/or organists are appointed by the Sabbath School Council.

Sabbath School Division Leaders—A leader is elected for each division of the Sabbath School by the church board. Assistants, as needed, may be appointed by the Sabbath School Council. More information on the age-related divisions, ranging from beginners through adult, is detailed in the *Sabbath School Handbook* which may be obtained from the Adventist Book Center or the conference/mission/field Sabbath School Department.

Duties of division leaders include arranging for the weekly program of the Sabbath School. Every division should follow the suggested schedule for that division as outlined in the *Sabbath School Handbook* and should always include a time for mission emphasis and for the Bible study discussion appropriate to the age level of those in that Sabbath School division. Division leaders need to be sure that there are adequate physical facilities and supplies of the *Sabbath School Bible Study Guide* and weekly papers for all members and visitors, as well as goal devices, charts, and other teaching aids as needed.

Extension Division—The extension division cares for those who are unable to attend Sabbath School due to age or infirmity. Special information on the work of the extension division leader may be found in the *Sabbath School Handbook*.

Sabbath School Teachers—All teachers are chosen by the Sabbath School Council and approved by the church board to serve for one year. These individuals should have an aptitude for teaching and be willing to study ways to improve their teaching ability. They should be diligent in their preparation, be regular and punctual in attendance, and set an example to the class in the daily study of the *Sabbath School Bible Study Guide.*

Special effort should be made to select teachers for children and youth from among those members who have their special interest at heart and who have the ability to meet their needs.

All teachers should be encouraged to participate in the teacher training courses published by the General Conference and/or division which are available through the conference/mission/field Sabbath School Department.

The Sabbath School Teachers' Meeting—It is recommended that every Sabbath School have a weekly teachers' meeting. The superintendent should have charge, although someone else may be appointed to conduct the survey of the next Sabbath's Bible study. The best results are obtained when the teachers' meeting is held prior to the Sabbath, as this provides opportunity for private study both before and after the meeting; it is also likely to be less hurried than if held on Sabbath morning. Sufficient time should be allowed for the teachers' meeting, and at least three things should be accomplished: a profitable survey of the next Sabbath's Bible study, a brief consideration of one or more Sabbath School goals, and discussion of any general problem requiring attention.

Sabbath School Lessons—Realizing that "None but those who have fortified the mind with the truths of the Bible will stand through the last great conflict" (*The Great Controversy*, pp. 593, 594), the Sabbath School Department leaders should do all that is possible to encourage regular systematic study of the Word. The *Sabbath School Bible Study Guide* is designed to encourage the habit of daily feasting on the Word. This time-honored practice has done much to maintain Christian unity throughout the world church.

The General Conference publishes a *Sabbath School Bible Study Guide* for each division of the Sabbath School. Every member should have access to those materials through the *Sabbath School Bible Study Guide* appropriate to the member's age level. Helps for leaders and teachers are produced by the General Conference and/or division, and the appropriate helps should be made available to every leader and teacher in each Sabbath School division.

Sabbath School Offerings—All Sabbath School offerings are to be carefully recorded by the Sabbath School secretary and handed to the church treasurer at the earliest suitable moment. When the extension division offerings are received, they should be added to the offerings already received from the Sabbath School.

With the exception of the expense fund, all Sabbath School offerings are General Conference offerings and are to be passed on in their entirety by the church treasurer to the conference/mission/field for transfer to the General Conference. These funds include the regular Sabbath School weekly offering, the Thirteenth Sabbath offering, Sabbath School Investment, and Birthday-Thank offering. They are all mission funds, each of which is to be identified as a separate fund in the regular system of records from the local church to the General Conference. This is necessary to enable the General Conference to appropriate the percentages used for special projects according to church policy. No mission funds may be retained by the local church or conference/mission/field.

Expense Money—Many Sabbath Schools take offerings at stated periods for Sabbath School expense. (See Notes, #7, p. 126.)

The Sabbath School expense offering and the mission offering shall not be taken as one offering and divided according to an agreed-upon formula or percentage. Sabbath School expense offerings must be kept entirely separate from the mission offerings.

The Quarterly Report—The Quarterly Report should be completed immediately after the last Sabbath of the quarter and mailed before the stated deadline to the conference/mission/field Sabbath School and Personal Ministries director(s). It should be presented at the quarterly business meeting of the church. The secretary should send the report on the appropriate form to the conference/mission/field Sabbath School and Personal Ministries director(s), place a copy in the secretary's permanent file, and provide copies for the Sabbath School superintendent and the pastor.

Adventist Youth Society

The Adventist Youth Society is a department of the church through which the church works for and through her youth.

"Moses answered, 'We will go with our young and old, with our sons and daughters, and with our flocks and herds, because we are to celebrate a festival to the Lord'" (Ex. 10:9, NIV). "These commandments that I give you today are to be upon your hearts. Impress them on your children. Talk about them when you sit at home and when you get up. Tie them as symbols on your hands and bind them on your foreheads. Write them on the door frames of your houses and on your gates" (Deut. 6:6-8, NIV). "Don't let anyone look down on you because you are young, but set an example for the believers in speech, in life, in love, in faith and purity" (1 Tim. 4:12, NIV).

"We have an army of youth today who can do much if they are properly directed and encouraged. . . . We want them to be blessed of God. We want them to act a part in well-organized plans for helping other youth."— Ellen G. White, in *General Conference Bulletin*, Jan. 29, 30, 1893, p. 24.

The servant of God called for the establishment of a youth organization in each church and told what kind of organization it should be. "Let there be a company formed somewhat after the order of the Christian Endeavor Society. . . ."—*Counsels on Health*, p. 537. "Let there be companies organized in every church to do this work."—Ellen G. White, in *Signs of the Times*, May 29, 1893.

"When the youth give their hearts to God, our responsibility for them does not cease. They must be interested in the Lord's work, and led to see that He expects them to do something to advance His cause. It is not enough to show how much needs to be done, and to urge the youth to act a part. They must be taught how to labor for the Master. They must be trained, disciplined, drilled, in the best methods of winning souls to Christ. Teach them to try in a quiet, unpretending way to help their young companions. Let different branches of missionary effort be systematically laid out, in which they may take part, and let them be given instruction and help. Thus they will learn to work for God."—*Gospel Workers*, p. 210.

"With such an army of workers as our youth, rightly trained, might furnish, how soon the message of a crucified, risen, and soon-coming Saviour might be carried to the whole world!"—*Messages to Young People*, p. 196.

While there is to be an active Adventist Youth Society in every church, it is important that the youth program not be isolated from the rest of the church. In addition to their participation in the youth organization, the young people should be integrated into responsible leadership and involvement in the entire church program. There should be young elders, young deacons and deaconesses, et cetera, working with experienced church officers. In all lines of church work the youth should be active. "In order that the work may go forward in all its branches, God calls for youthful vigor, zeal, and courage. He has chosen the youth to aid in the advancement of His cause. To plan with clear mind and execute with courageous hand demands fresh, uncrippled energies. Young men and women are invited to give God the strength of their youth, that through the exercise of their powers, through keen thought and vigorous action, they may bring glory to Him and salvation to their fellow-men."—*Gospel Workers*, p. 67.

Mission Statement—The primary focus of youth ministry is the salvation of youth through Jesus Christ. We understand youth ministry to be

that work of the church that is conducted for, with, and by young people.*
    Our task is to:
    1.   Lead youth to understand their individual worth and to discover and develop their spiritual gifts and abilities.
    2.   Equip and empower youth for a life of service with God's church and the community.
    3.   Ensure the integration of youth into all aspects of church life and leadership in order that they might be full participants in the mission of the church. (See Notes, #8, p. 126.)

Objectives—In response to these inspired directives, the Youth Department was organized to give leadership training and to provide resource materials and evangelistic plans for the Adventist Youth Society in the local churches. The Spirit of Prophecy sets forth the objectives of the youth organization as follows: (1) to train the youth to work for other youth, (2) to recruit the youth to help their church and "those who profess to be Sabbathkeepers", and (3) to work "for those who are not of our faith."— *Signs of the Times*, May 29, 1893.
    In seeking to reach these objectives the youth are called upon (1) to pray together, (2) to study the Word together, (3) to fellowship together in Christian social interaction, (4) to act together in small groups to carry out well-laid plans for witnessing, (5) to develop tact and skill and talent in the Master's service, and (6) to encourage one another in spiritual growth.
    The *Aim* of the Adventist Youth Society is: "The Advent Message to All the World in My Generation."
    The *Motto* is: "The Love of Christ Constrains Me."

Membership in the Adventist Youth Society—There are three categories of membership in the Adventist Youth Society. (See Notes, #9, p. 127.)

The Adventist Youth Ministries Committee—The Adventist Youth Ministries Committee is the umbrella organization in the local church responsible for the general planning of the youth ministry program. (See p. 78.) It includes the elected officers of the society plus the Personal Ministries leader, youth Sabbath School division leader, Health Ministries leader, Pathfinder Club director, Adventurer Club director, principal of the

---

*Adopted by the General Conference and Division Youth Directors, July 1993.

school, if there is such, the sponsor, and the pastor. The Adventist Youth Society leader, who is a member of the local church board, chairs this committee.

The committee should meet as often as necessary to plan and direct a successful youth ministry in the local church. Committee meetings should include time for prayer, a study of ways to help the youth spiritually, and plans for witnessing activities. The committee will also be responsible for seeing that regular meetings are scheduled for the youth and will work with other departments in coordinating the youth program in the local church. There should be short- and long-range goals if youth ministry is to be effective in reaching its objectives.

The Adventist Youth Society Committee—The Adventist Youth Society Committee is responsible for senior youth activities of the local church and works in coordination with the other youth entities through the Adventist Youth Ministries Committee. Where there is no Pathfinder or Adventurer program, the AYS will include these younger members in a Junior Society.

Officers of the Adventist Youth Society—A chief factor in the success of any Adventist Youth Society is its leadership. When the officers are dedicated, active Christians, with initiative and ability to organize and inspire others, the work will go forward, young people will be saved and trained in God's service, and the whole church will be strengthened.

The officers of the Adventist Youth Society which are elected by the local church are: youth leader, associate youth leader, secretary-treasurer, assistant secretary-treasurer, chorister, pianist or organist, and sponsor, who may be one of the local elders. Since music plays such an important role in the formation of the youth character, musicians should be as carefully selected as the rest of the officers of the Adventist Youth Society. (See p. 70.) This group forms the nucleus for the Adventist Youth Society Committee which in counsel with the young people appoints other officers such as fellowship or social leader, devotional leader, librarian, publicity leader, and the various action group leaders. In smaller churches one person will of necessity carry several responsibilities. As many youth as possible should be involved in the planning and execution of the youth program.

Youth Leader and Associate Youth Leader—The Youth leader as a follower of Jesus must exemplify the graces of a genuine Christian, with a burden for soul-winning and a contagious enthusiasm. In helping motivate the youth to work together and take responsibilities, the leader will be in the background—guiding, counseling, and encouraging the youth, helping them to gain experience and the joys of achievement. It will be necessary to study the youth profile of the church and seek to involve every youth in the society.

The Youth leader will keep in close touch with pastors and sponsors and with the conference/mission/field Youth director, taking advantage of every opportunity for in-service training and leading the society into a cooperative relationship with the church and the conference/mission/field.

The associate Youth leader will assist the Youth leader in this work and in the absence of the Youth leader will chair the Adventist Youth Society Committee and perform the duties of the leader. The associate will also be assigned certain responsibilities as determined by the committee. In smaller churches the committee may assign the assistant to the office of secretary-treasurer.

Secretary-Treasurer and Assistant—As in the case of the other officers, the secretary-treasurer's first qualification is spirituality and dedication. One should know the Lord, be able to speak from personal experience, and have a burden for young people. The secretary-treasurer will keep a record of the activities of the society and send in a monthly report on special forms provided to the local conference/mission/field Youth director who will also encourage the young people to report their witnessing activities during the ten-minute Personal Ministries period at the close of the Sabbath School Bible study. (See Notes, #10, p. 127.)

The assistant secretary-treasurer (when needed) assists with the secretary-treasurer's work as may be mutually arranged and acts in the absence of the secretary-treasurer.

Adventist Youth Society Sponsor—This may be an elder or other qualified person on the church board who understands thoroughly the objectives of the society and who is sympathetic with the youth and their involvement in the church's ministries. This individual serves as a guide or counselor to the Adventist Youth Society officers and meets with them regularly at the time of the Adventist Youth Society Committee meeting. The sponsor will be one whom the young people love and look to for counsel, working with the Youth leader in bringing the needs of the society before the church board.

The sponsor should become acquainted with the local conference/mission/field Youth director, keeping him or her informed of any changes in officer personnel and other matters relating to the Adventist Youth Society. Along with the society officers, the sponsor should attend the youth training institutes of the local conference/mission/field to keep pace with what is developing in youth ministry and thus be more effective in giving counsel. It would be well if the sponsor could serve over a several-year period for continuity.

Adventist Youth Features—As young people grow in their relationship with Jesus Christ, the Youth Department seeks to provide them with age-related, dynamic, active programming that provides an environment for development of spiritual gifts in preparation for this life and the life to come. These include the following:

1. *Devotional and Educational*—Morning Watch, Bible reading plans, Encounter series, Adventist Youth Week of Prayer, Youth Bible Conference, Youth Ministry Training Course, Pathfinder Staff Training Course, Adventist Youth Book Club, Guide, Master Guide and related leadership training classes, Adventist Youth Honors, Outdoor Club, and others.

2. *Witnessing*—Voice of Youth, Friendship Teams, branch Sabbath Schools, Story Hours, Adventist Youth Taskforce, Adventist Youth Service Volunteers, Festival of the Word, Youth Rallies, Sunshine or Singing Band, Community Services, Literature and Correspondence Action Group, Youth Music Witnessing Teams, and AY Honors.

3. *Recreation*—Social to Save, nature exploration, outdoor clubs, Adventist Youth Camping, specialty camps, Adventist Youth Honors, Silver Award, Gold Award.

The Adventist Junior Youth Society

The Adventist Junior Youth Society (AJY) has as its objectives the training of junior youth for Christian leadership and service and the development of each individual to the fullest potential. In those churches where there are church schools, the Adventist Junior Youth Society is a part of the school curriculum, with the teacher as the leader of the society. When the Adventist Junior Youth Society is conducted in the church school, each classroom is considered a society, with pupils in the lower elementary designated as preparatory members. Pupils in the upper elementary are regular members of the Adventist Junior Youth Society.

While the teacher is leader or sponsor of the society, the students should lead out in the meetings, which are usually held weekly during the first class period. The student officers— which would include student leader, associate leader, secretary, treasurer, song leader, pianist, and any other leadership responsibility the class may decide upon—are selected by the class in counsel with the teacher. Usually the officers serve from one month to one quarter in order to give all the students opportunity for leadership training and responsibility. Where there is no church school the junior youth may be integrated into the youth ministry program of the church, or a separate Adventist Junior Youth Society may be conducted at an appropriate time. The Pathfinder Club has taken the place of the Adventist Junior Youth Society in some churches, since its specialized program incorporates the same objectives plus other opportunities. Where there is a Pathfinder Club and an Adventist Junior Youth Society there must be close coordination and cooperation between the two, with the leader of the Adventist Junior Youth Society being on the Pathfinder Club Staff Council (as per the *Pathfinder Staff Manual*) and vice versa. (See Notes, #11, p. 127.)

Members of the Adventist Junior Youth Society will learn and by the grace of God strive to follow the Adventist Junior Youth Pledge and Law and its ideals:

Adventist Junior Youth Pledge

By the grace of God—
    I will be pure and kind and true,
    I will keep the Adventist Junior Youth Law,
    I will be a servant of God and a friend to man.

Adventist Junior Youth Law

The Adventist Junior Youth Law is for me to—
    Keep the Morning Watch,
    Do my honest part,
    Care for my body,
    Keep a level eye,
    Be courteous and obedient,
    Walk softly in the sanctuary,
    Keep a song in my heart,
    Go on God's errands.

The Aim and Motto are the same as for the senior youth.

AY Classes—Six personal development classes are offered the junior youth. These are Friend, Companion, Explorer, Ranger, Voyager, and Guide. An insignia is awarded to those who qualify in each class. Achievement classes are also offered to children ages 6 through 9: Busy Bee, Sunbeam, Builder, and Helping Hand.

Adventist Youth Honors—A wide range of Adventist Youth Honors—in arts and crafts, health and science, household arts, mechanics, outreach (missionary) endeavor, nature, outdoor industries, and recreational pursuits—includes levels of achievement in all of these for both junior youth and senior youth. A Master Award achievement program presents a further challenge to young people.

Pathfinder Club

The Pathfinder Club is a church-centered program which provides an outlet for the spirit of adventure and exploration that is found in every junior youth. This includes carefully tailored activities in outdoor living, nature exploration, crafts, hobbies, or vocations beyond the possibilities in an average Adventist Junior Youth Society. In this setting spiritual emphasis is well received, and the Pathfinder Club has well demonstrated its soul-winning influence. In many local churches Pathfinder Clubs have replaced the traditional Adventist Junior Youth Society, and where there is a church school the Pathfinder Club should supplement the work of the Adventist Junior Youth Society.

A sampling of activities in the Pathfinder Club includes camporees, fairs, craft study, nature exploration, Bible study, witnessing projects, field trips, bikeathons, and many other interesting adventures.

Youth from ages 10 to 15 are eligible to become members of the Pathfinder Club through a special induction ceremony. The triangular emblem has been adopted internationally even though there is sometimes a change in the name "Pathfinder" through translation and local equivalence. Members wear an approved Pathfinder uniform to all club functions, including the weekly club meeting, Pathfinder fairs, and camporees, and on Sabbath morning to church for Pathfinder Day. In some churches the age groups are divided into the Junior Pathfinder Club and the Teen Pathfinder Club and when older Pathfinders reach the age of 15 they may become staff members through a Teen Leadership Training (TLT) program.

The Pathfinder Club director and deputy director(s) are elected for one or two year terms by the church at the time of the general elections. (See p. 47.) If two deputy directors are elected there should be one of each sex. One of the deputy directors may also serve as club scribe and treasurer. The director is a member of the church board and also of the Adventist Youth Ministries Committee. Additional Pathfinder staff include instructors of craft and nature classes and counselors who are responsible for a unit of six to eight Pathfinders.

Many resource materials are available from the conference/mission/field Youth director.

Adventurer Club

The Adventurer Club is a parent/church-centered program which provides parents with a tool useable with their 6- through 9-year-old children and is designed to stimulate the children's budding curiosity towards the world about them. This program includes age-specific activities that involve both parent and child in recreational activities, simple crafts, appreciation of God's creation, and other activities that are of interest to that age. All is carried out with a spiritual focus setting the stage for participation in the church as a Pathfinder. (See Notes, #12, p. 128.)

The Adventurer Club director and that person's immediate associates are elected for one or two year terms by the church at the time of general elections. (See p. 47.) Additional staff are selected by the administrative staff of the club. The director is a member of the church board and of the local church Adventist Youth Ministries Committee. The resource materials are available from the conference/mission/field Youth director.

Christian Education and the Church School

Philosophy—The church operates a school system to ensure that its youth may receive a balanced physical, mental, spiritual, social, and vocational education in harmony with denominational standards and ideals, with God as the source of all moral value and truth. The stated interest of the church is the restoration in man of the image of his Maker, resulting in the optimum development of the whole person for both this life and the life hereafter.

The church conducts its own schools, kindergarten through university, for the purpose of transmitting to its children its own ideals, beliefs, attitudes, values, habits, and customs. Secular schools seek to prepare patriotic and law-abiding citizens, and teach certain values; Adventist schools, in addition, aim at developing loyal, conscientious Seventh-day Adventist Christians. A true knowledge of God, fellowship and companionship with Him in study and service, and likeness to Him in character development are the source, the means, and the aim of Seventh-day Adventist education.

Objectives—Schools operated by the church will endeavor to provide for all of their students an education within the framework of the science of salvation. The fundamentals and common branches of knowledge are to be studied to develop proficiency in their use.

Specifically, these schools will endeavor to operate for each student in the upgrading of health and temperance principles, in the command of fundamental learning processes, and in the teaching of worthy home membership, vocational skills, civic education, worthy use of leisure, and ethical maturity. They will aim to reach objectives of spiritual dedication, self-realization, social adjustment, civic responsibility, world mission and service, and economic sufficiency through high quality, Christ-centered teaching.

Education Secretary—Recognizing that a comprehensive understanding and clear vision of Christian education—whose ultimate aims harmonize with those of redemption—can be developed and fostered only where the church is continually reminded of the preeminent mission of such an education, each church shall elect an Education secretary to promote and generate support for Christian education. The Education secretary shall be a member of the Home and School Association executive committee, and will work in cooperation with the Association. (See Notes, #13, p. 128.)

Home and School Association

Purpose—The purpose of the association is twofold:
1. To provide parent education.
2. To unite the home, the school, and the church in their endeavors to provide Seventh-day Adventist Christian education for the children.

Objectives—1. To educate parents in cooperation with the church and school in their work of fostering the development of the whole child—"the harmonious development of the physical, the mental, and the spiritual powers."—*Education*, p. 13.
2. To promote cooperation between parents and teachers in the educational process.
3. To give guidance for establishing in the home an atmosphere of love and discipline in which Seventh-day Adventist Christian values can be instilled in children through Bible study, prayer, family worship, and the example of the parents.
4. To provide an opportunity for parents and teachers to develop a positive relationship in their work for the children.
5. To support the church school in its effort to more fully harmonize the principles of Christian education in philosophy, content, and methodology.
6. To strengthen the relationship between home and school by promoting such activities as:
   a. Providing suggestions to the administration and school board for curriculum improvement.

b. Encouraging frequent communication between home and school.

c. Encouraging parents to visit the school.

d. Encouraging teachers to visit the homes of students.

e. Providing volunteer services as requested by the school.

f. Assisting in providing the school with additional equipment and facilities not provided by the church or conference/mission/field.

7. To work toward the goal of enrolling every child of the church in the church school. Earnest endeavor should be made to provide ways for disadvantaged children to attend church school so that no Seventh-day Adventist child will miss the opportunity of a Seventh-day Adventist education.

Membership—Members of the church and patrons of the school are members of the association.

Officers—All parents of students are encouraged to be active in the Home and School Association. However, the officers of this association shall be members of the Seventh-day Adventist Church. The officers shall consist of a leader, assistant leader, secretary-treasurer, librarian, and the church educational secretary. (See p. 146.) To give continuity, it is recommended that some of the officers be reelected for a second term.

Leader—The leader of the Home and School Association shall be a church member with experience and success in training children and whose mind is open to new ideas, who is apt to teach, and who believes in the importance of Christian education.

Secretary-Treasurer—The secretary-treasurer is to keep the records of the association and to report to the director of the Department of Education of the conference/mission/field at the beginning and close of the school year.

Association funds are to be channeled through the church/school treasurer, kept as a separate account, and audited in harmony with denominational policy.

Ex Officio—The school principal shall be an ex officio member of the Home and School Association Committee by virtue of position.

The Church School Board

Membership—The administrative body of every elementary school and junior academy operated by a single church shall be a board elected by the church or a school committee appointed by the church board. Hence, this body may be a separate school board, the church board, or a school committee of the church board appointed for this purpose.

Where two or more churches unite to operate a school the administrative body shall be a union school board. (See Notes, #14, p. 128.)

One or more members of the school board may be chosen from among the members of the church board, so that the school board may be closely related to the church board.

The pastor of the church should be a member of the school board. Where the school is operated by more than one church, it is the general practice that the pastors of the churches concerned are members of the school board.

In junior academies and in elementary schools the principal or the head teacher of the school should be a member of the board.

Some members of the board may be parents of children attending the school, so that the board may profit from parental viewpoints and counsel which result from close-up observation and experience.

Officers—The officers shall consist of a chairperson and a secretary. In union school boards serving a school sponsored by two or more churches a treasurer, a vice-chairperson, and an assistant secretary should also be appointed. Where the school is operated by one church, the chairperson should be elected by the church; where the school is operated by two or more churches, the chairperson should be elected by the board from among its own members at the first meeting after its election. In the event that agreement between the churches is not possible, the appointment will be made by the conference/mission/field board of education or the conference/mission/field committee. The principal of the school is generally appointed as secretary of the board.

Relation of Union School Boards to the Local Churches—Where two or more churches operate a union school, any action of the board which involves the churches in financial obligations must be submitted to the respective boards of the churches for approval.

Term of Office—Where a separate school board is elected, one of two plans may be followed with reference to the time when its members are elected and the term of office: (1) All the members may be elected at the close of the calendar or fiscal year and function for one year; (2) the members of the first board may be chosen for terms of one, two, and three years, respectively, the new members being chosen each succeeding year for a period of three years. The purpose of this plan is to have a nucleus of experienced members on the board to ensure a continuity of successful educational policy.

Vacancies are filled in the same way as vacancies in any other church office, the one filling the vacancy to officiate for only the remainder of the unexpired term.

Meetings—The school board or school committee should meet at a regular time and place at least once each month during the school year.

Qualifications —The members of the school board shall be chosen for their consecration, their belief in and loyalty to the principles of Christian education, their good judgment and tact, their experience in school matters, and their financial judgment and ability. They should believe in, and have a willingness to follow, denominational educational policies and recommendations.

Because the elementary school and/or junior academy board is an important organization in the local church, the members of it should be chosen with great care. Persons who do not believe in Christian schools or are unsympathetic with their program should not be chosen as members of the school board. Conviction as to God-given plans, faith, courage, and understanding are as essential for success in this as in other enterprises.

Duties of the Officers—The chairperson calls meetings, presides, and sees that the actions of the board are carried out. He/She also countersigns all financial orders issued by the secretary.

The chairperson is a member ex officio of the elementary school and junior academy Inspection Committee. This committee has the responsibility of surveying and evaluating the elementary school and junior academy and their work.

The secretary keeps a record of each meeting in a permanent record book, issues orders for money in the payment of accounts or obligations, and carries on the necessary correspondence for the board.

Where a single church operates a school the work of the treasurer is usually carried by the church treasurer or an assistant church treasurer, who receives tuition and other money; pays out money on the order of the secretary, countersigned by the chairperson; keeps a careful account of all money passing through his/her hands, making a permanent record of the same in a suitable record book; and at each monthly meeting renders a detailed report to the board. In a union board, where two or more churches are involved, a treasurer is appointed by the board to do this work.

Functions—(For North American Division see the *North American Division Working Policy*, F 30 35, School Operating Board—Functions.)

Communication Department

Importance of Effective Communication—Through the years divine instruction has come to the church concerning the importance of using contemporary communication media in spreading the gospel. We have been counseled:

"We must take every justifiable means of bringing the light before the people. Let the press be utilized, and let every advertising agency be employed that will call attention to the work."—*Testimonies*, vol. 6, p. 36.

"Means will be devised to reach hearts. Some of the methods used in this work will be different from the methods used in the work in the past. . . ."—*Evangelism*, p. 105.

The Organization—The organization of this ministry calls for the enlistment of support from every denominational worker, layperson, and Seventh-day Adventist institution. The Communication Department promotes the use of a sound program of public relations and all contemporary communication techniques, sustainable technologies, and media in the promulgation of the everlasting gospel. It calls for the election of a Communication secretary in every local church and, where needed, a Communication Committee.

The Communication Secretary's Work—The church Communication secretary is responsible for the gathering and dissemination of news. As opportunity presents, the secretary will place on the air persons of interest in interview-type programs, and arrange for news features on such persons. Every effort will be made to maintain a friendly, cooperative relationship with editors and other communications/media personnel. (See Notes, #15, p. 129.)

The Communication secretary will cooperate with the conference/mission/field Communication secretary in carrying out the plans of the conference/mission/field and reporting as requested and will also present periodic reports to the church business meeting.

The Communication Committee—In a large church a Communication Committee may more adequately handle the many facets of the public relations and communication program of the church than can a secretary working alone. This committee, with the Communication secretary as chairperson, will be elected at the time of the general election of church officers. Individual members of the committee may be assigned specific communication responsibilities such as working with the press, with media producers and on-line personnel, and with the internal media of the church. Where there is a church institution in the area a member of its public relations staff should be invited to sit with the committee. (See Notes, #16, p. 129.)

The pastor, who is primarily responsible for the communication program of his church, will work closely in an advisory capacity with the Communication secretary and/or the Communication Committee.

Relation to Other Departments of Church—To serve the church properly the Communication secretary should be alerted regarding plans and scheduled events. Any auxiliary unit of the church organization may appoint an individual to provide the Communication secretary or Communication Committee with news of that particular department's activities.

In Large Adventist Centers—If several churches in a city arrange for a central Communication Committee, each Communication secretary should be a member and should work in harmony with any general plan that will better coordinate the handling of news and other media activities for the several churches. The establishment of this committee would be initiated by the conference/mission/field Communication director. Meetings of such a central committee would be called and presided over by a chairperson selected by the group.

The Communication Departments of the division, union, and local conference/mission/field provide detailed instruction for Communication secretaries and, by their printed materials, correspondence, and other means, give constant help and inspiration.

Qualifications—The Communication secretary should be carefully chosen for (1) the ability rightly to represent the church, (2) sound judgment, (3) organizational ability, (4) ability to put facts down on paper in attractive and persuasive grammatical form, (5) willingness to carry out an assignment, (6) ability to meet people.

Health Ministries Department

The church accepts its responsibility to make Christ known to the world and believes this includes a moral obligation to preserve human dignity by obtaining optimal levels of physical, mental, and spiritual health. In addition to ministering to those who are ill, this responsibility extends to the prevention of disease through effective health education and leadership in promoting optimum health, free of tobacco, alcohol, other drugs, and unclean foods. Where possible, members shall be encouraged to follow a primarily vegetarian diet.

Health Ministries Leader—For an efficient program to be planned and implemented in the church, it is necessary for the church to elect a Health Ministries leader. He/She should be health-oriented and interested in promoting the church's standards in healthful living among the members and in the community through church-operated health ministries programs. The leader should be able to screen programs and information that are representative of the ideals and philosophy of the Seventh-day Adventist Church and to integrate them into an effective spiritual-physical witness. (See Notes, #17, p. 129.)

Associate Health Ministries Leader—The associate leader's duties shall be to assist in the leader's responsibilities.

Health Ministries Council—Where practical, a Health Ministries Council may be appointed. This council is designed to provide dedicated leadership to the church membership and to the community in the field of healthful living, and to assist in cooperative soul-saving activities through a viable program of health and temperance and spiritual emphasis. (See Notes, #18, p. 130.)

The pastor, if not serving as the chairman, should be an ex officio member of the council.

Health Ministries Activities—The Health Ministries Council, in collaboration with the Personal Ministries Council, shall lead out in developing a schedule of health ministries activities that will include programs such as stop-smoking plans, cooking schools, health classes, stress-control programs, and other related endeavors.

Health Ministries Society—In some areas Health Ministries or Temperance societies may be established as separate entities as distinct from church organizations. The conference/mission/field director should be involved in establishing such organizations.

World Health Ministries Sabbath Offering—The entire offering is sent to the local conference/mission/field to be distributed according to policy among the General Conference, division, union, and conference/mission/field. Upon request to the conference/mission/field, up to 25 percent of the offering received in the local church may revert to the church for health ministries programs.

Stewardship Department

The Stewardship Department was organized to help members become effective stewards and to assist in the implementation of God's plan of systematic benevolence throughout the church. Since stewardship responsibility includes the proper management of the entire life, stewardship concepts encourage the proper care and use of the body temple, time, abilities, and material possessions. The department gives assistance in the planning and organization of church resources for a completed work. Its spiritual and financial objectives are summarized in the following statement: "When they shall arouse and lay their prayers, their wealth, and all their energies and resources at the feet of Jesus, the cause of truth will triumph."—*Testimonies*, vol. 4, p. 475.

Stewardship Leader—The Stewardship leader, elected by the church, is chosen for an ability to implement the concepts and objectives outlined by the Stewardship Department and should possess the following qualifications: (1) be a spiritual leader, (2) be one who practices the principles of Christian stewardship, (3) have an understanding of the spiritual and financial program of the church, (4) be willing to dedicate the necessary time to plan, organize, and lead out in designated areas of responsibility in cooperation with the conference/mission/field Stewardship director, the pastor, and the church board.

The Stewardship leader acts in a liaison capacity between the conference/mission/field Stewardship Department and congregation. (See Notes, #19, p. 130.)

Department of Family Ministries

The over-arching objective of Family Ministries is to strengthen the family as a discipling center. The family was established by divine creation as the fundamental human institution. It is the primary setting in which values are learned and the capacity for close relationships with God and with other human beings is developed.

Family Ministries is a ministry of grace which acknowledges as normative the biblical teachings relating to the family and holds high God's ideals for family living. At the same time, it brings an understanding of the brokenness experienced by individuals and families in a fallen world. Thus Family Ministries seeks to enable families to stretch toward divine ideals, while at the same time ever extending the good news of God's saving grace and the promise of growth possible through the indwelling Spirit. Family Ministries focuses on people in relationship. It is concerned with the needs of married couples, parents and children, the family needs of singles and all members of the wider family circle as they pass through life's predictable stages and contend with unexpected changes in their lives.

Family Ministries reinforces and encourages wholesome families. It helps individuals build and maintain strong family relationships because it recognizes that healthy Christian families make strong members for the kingdom of God and present a winsome witness to the community around them. Family Ministries promotes understanding, acceptance, and love within the family and in the larger family of God and fosters the reconciliation and healing between the generations promised in the Elijah message of Malachi 4:5, 6. It extends hope and support to those who have been injured and hurt by abuse, family dysfunction, and broken relationships. Family Ministries fosters competence in a variety of interpersonal skills needed in relationships. It provides growth opportunities through family life education and enrichment. It encourages individuals, married couples, and families to avail themselves of professional counseling when necessary.

An adequate ministry to families will include: premarital guidance available to all couples before marriage; marriage strengthening opportunities; parent education, with attention given to the special needs of single parents and step-families; instruction in family to family evangelism; and support ministries to help families with special needs.

The Family Ministries Committee—To more effectively meet the needs of families in the church, the church board may establish a Family Ministries Committee, chaired by the Family Ministries leader(s). (See Notes, #20, p. 130.)

Family Ministries Leader(s)—An individual or married couple may be elected to serve as the Family Ministries leader(s). The individual(s) should have a positive attitude about God, self, others, and the church. The leader(s) should model strong and growing family relationships and exhibit a sincere interest in fostering the well-being of all families. In order to be effective, it is necessary for the Family Ministries leader(s) to have an understanding of God's redemptive plan for dealing with the brokenness in relationships which sin has brought. It is also important that the leader(s) be able to maintain confidentiality and know when and how to encourage individuals in critical situations to seek professional counseling. (See Notes, #21, p. 131.)

Department of Women's Ministries

The Department of Women's Ministries exists to uphold, encourage, and challenge Seventh-day Adventist women in their daily walk as disciples of Jesus Christ and as members of His world church. The mission of Women's Ministries is, in the larger sense, common to all Christians—that of uplifting Christ in the church and in the world.

Objectives—This ministry seeks to:
1.   Foster spiritual growth and renewal among women.
2.   Affirm that women are of inestimable worth by virtue of their creation and redemption, and equip them for service in the church.
3.   Minister to the broad spectrum of women's needs across the life span, being sensitive to multicultural and multiethnic perspectives.
4.   Liaise and cooperate with other specialized departments of the church to facilitate the ministry to women and of women.
5.   Build goodwill among women in the world church that encourages bonds of friendship, support for church service, and the creative exchange of ideas and information.
6.   Mentor and encourage Seventh-day Adventist women, creating paths for their involvement in the church as they reach for their potential in Christ.
7.   Find ways and means to challenge each Seventh-day Adventist woman to use her gifts to complement the talents of others as they work side by side to further the global mission of the church.

Women's Ministries Leader—The Women's Ministries leader is elected by the church to develop specific ministries to nurture women and equip them for service to God and to the church. She serves as chair of the Women's Ministries Committee, and encourages ideas and plans which maximize women's contributions to the mission of the church. As chair, she is responsible for putting together the agenda, moderating discussion, and developing group cohesion through personal sharing, prayer, and fellowship.

She also serves as a member of the church board, integrating activities and programs for women into the larger church program. It is her responsibility to keep the church informed of the contribution of Women's Ministries to church life. The leader's liaison for training and resource material is the local conference/mission/field Women's Ministries Director.

Qualifications of the Women's Ministries Leader—The Women's Ministries leader should be a woman with a sensitive, caring nature, a burden for women's ministry and concerns, a balance in her perspectives so as to represent a broad spectrum of women, and an ability to encourage other women to cultivate their spiritual gifts. She should be able to work well with women in the church, the pastor, and the church board.

The Women's Ministries Committee—The Women's Ministries leader works with the pastor and church board to establish a Women's Ministries Committee to foster a ministry to women in the church. This committee should be composed of persons interested in the broad spectrum of women's needs and services. To form a balanced team, the members should be persons with varied talents and experience. (See Notes, #22, p. 131.)

Department of Children's Ministries

The Department of Children's Ministries is organized to promote and coordinate ministry to the children of the church, as well as to involve children in service to others. Christ's instruction to feed the lambs provides the impetus for the church to meet the needs of children for nurture, fellowship, worship, stewardship, and outreach.

Children's active minds construct meaning from every experience. "The lessons that the child learns during the first seven years of life have more to do with forming his character than all that it learns in future years."—*Child Guidance*, p. 193. This is the time to begin to educate them "to be thinkers, and not mere reflectors of other men's thought."— *Education*, p. 17.

"When Jesus told the disciples not to forbid the children to come to Him, He was speaking to His followers in all ages,—to officers of the church, to ministers, helpers, and all Christians. Jesus is drawing the children, and He bids us, Suffer them to come; as if He would say, They will come if you do not hinder them."—*The Desire of Ages*, p. 517.

"Every child may gain knowledge as Jesus did."—*The Desire of Ages*, p. 70.

Ministry to Seventh-day Adventist Children—It is the responsibility of each individual in the church community to exert a positive influence on children. Providing children with the opportunity for participation, interaction, and leadership in a variety of religious education settings gives them a sense of inclusion as valued members of the church family, leads them to Jesus, and teaches them to view life through a Seventh-day Adventist perspective. (See Notes, #23, p. 132.)

Ministry to Children Outside the Church—The Bible makes it clear that God has a special burden for children who are not enfolded in the church family. Outreach to children within the influence of the church will have far-reaching results, one of which will be winning parents to the Lord. The Department of Children's Ministries carries responsibility for the traditional outreach programs such as: Vacation Bible Schools, children's branch Sabbath Schools, Neighborhood Bible Clubs, and Story Hours. (See Notes, #24, p. 132).

In churches which do not have a Department of Children's Ministries, Vacation Bible Schools, children's branch Sabbath Schools, Neighborhood Bible Clubs, and Story Hours will come under the direction of the Sabbath School Department. (See p. 96.)

Involving Seventh-day Adventist Children in Service to Others— Participation not only increases capabilities and assures children that they are a necessary part of the church family but, more importantly, involvement in service to others is a major part of their growth in grace. Creative efforts to involve children will help them establish a pattern of outreach to others that may well continue through life. (See Notes, #25, p. 133.)

Safeguarding Children—In Matthew 18:6 Christ spoke strongly about those who would intentionally hurt children: "But whoso shall offend one of these little ones which believe in me, it were better for him that a millstone were hanged about his neck, and that he were drowned in the depth of the sea." The local church should take reasonable steps to safeguard children engaged in church-sponsored activities by choosing individuals with high spiritual and moral backgrounds as leaders and participants in programs for children.

Children's Ministries Committee—The Children's Ministries Committee works under the direction of the church board or Personal Ministries Council. Members will be chosen on the strength of their interest and expertise in working with children. The number of members will vary according to the needs of each church. (See Notes, #26, p. 133.)

Children's Ministries Coordinator—The Children's Ministries coordinator is elected by the church and should be an individual of moral and ethical excellence who demonstrates love and commitment to God, church, and children, and who has ability and experience in working with children. (See Notes, #27, p. 133.)

Department of Public Affairs and Religious Liberty

The Department of Public Affairs and Religious Liberty (PARL) promotes and maintains religious liberty, with particular emphasis upon liberty of conscience. Religious liberty includes the human right to have or adopt the religion of one's choice; to change religious belief according to conscience; to manifest one's religion individually or in community with fellow believers, in worship, observance, practice, witness, and teaching, subject to respect for the equivalent rights of others.

Since religious liberty includes the right to observe days of rest and worship in accordance with the precepts of one's religion, the department actively supports the right of Seventh-day Adventists to keep the Sabbath in accordance with the fourth commandment of God's Word. The department also monitors and interprets current events that may reflect prophetic scenario.

To safeguard religious liberty, the Department of Public Affairs and Religious Liberty encourages, where possible, the separation of church and state, as commended by our Lord when He said, "Render therefore unto Caesar the things which are Caesar's; and unto God the things that are God's" (Matt. 22:21). "The union of the church with the state, be the degree never so slight, while it may appear to bring the world nearer to the church, does in reality but bring the church nearer to the world."—*The Great Controversy Between Christ and Satan,* p. 297.

The state should never invade the distinct realm of the church to affect in any way the complete freedom of conscience or the right to profess, practice, and promulgate religious beliefs; and the church should never invade the distinctive realm of the state except, where appropriate, to bring moral principle to bear on public policy.

The department seeks to guard against intrusions upon religious liberty, especially in view of the persecutions prophesied in Revelation 13. "It is our duty to do all in our power to avert the threatened danger."—*Testimonies,* vol 5, p. 452.

Religious Liberty Associations—The Department of Public Affairs and Religious Liberty carries on many of its functions through the International Religious Liberty Association, and its affiliated associations throughout the world.

Religious Liberty Association in the Local Church—Each church is considered an informal Religious Liberty Association, and every church member is a member of the association. The pastor or the local elder is the chairperson of the association in each local church.

Religious Liberty Leader of the Local Church—The Religious Liberty leader of the local church shall be elected and shall work in close cooperation with the pastor or district leader in all phases of religious liberty and cooperate with the conference/mission/field or union department. Such a person should be of positive spiritual influence, able to meet the general public, interested in public affairs, proficient as a correspondent, and concerned with the preservation of the liberty of the people of God to do the Master's service. (See Notes, #28, p. 134.)

Induction Service

If an induction service (see p. 62) is being held for the newly elected officers of the local church, the officers of the auxiliary organizations should be included.

Notes

These notes contain explanatory material regarding how a local church may proceed in a particular matter. A local church may adopt alternate ways of handling such items. Such alternative methods should be in harmony with generally accepted principles of Seventh-day Adventist Church organization and operation.

1. **Personal Ministries Council**—(See p. 93.)—The duties of this council shall be the following:

    a. To arrange for the outreach (missionary) meetings of the church, to study its field of outreach (missionary) activity, and to enlist every church member in definite lines of service.

    b. To enlist the members' involvement in outreach (missionary) activities sponsored by the Personal Ministries Department, such as:

        1) Literature distribution and circulation of outreach (missionary) periodicals, including subscription magazines.

        2) Bible course enrollments.

        3) Community Services and/or Dorcas Society activities.

        4) Entry events such as stop-smoking clinics, cooking schools, stress management seminars, etc.

        5) Outreach (missionary) activities such as Bible studies and follow up of contacts, public evangelistic meetings, seminar evangelism, and other outreach plans and projects.

    c. To be responsible for the planning and implementation of the annual Ingathering campaign where conducted.

    d. To train and lead members in Christian witnessing, such as:

        1) Conducting or arranging for classes in how to give Bible studies, methods of personal witnessing, the operation of Community Services programs, and provision of disaster relief services.

        2) Giving practical demonstrations in how to do this work.

    e. To encourage reporting through the Personal Ministries secretary.

    f. To supervise the Community Services activities of the church and serve as the governing committee of the church's Community Services center.

g.   To cooperate with the Personal Ministries Department of the local conference/mission/field in carrying out its program.

h.   To authorize disbursement of local church Personal Ministries funds.

i.   To plan for and conduct the weekly and monthly Personal Ministries meetings as called for in the church calendar.

2. *Personal Ministries Secretary*—(See p. 94.)—The duties of the Personal Ministries secretary are:

a.   To serve as secretary of the Personal Ministries Council, recording the minutes of Personal Ministries' meetings and taking an active part in implementing departmental plans. The secretary should record reports of outreach (missionary) work done by church members and complete and send all required reports and other information about such activities to the conference/mission/field Personal Ministries Department promptly each quarter.

b.   To give a report of Personal Ministries activities to the church during the monthly Sabbath Personal Ministries service and during church business meetings.

c.   To be responsible for all local church transactions with the Adventist Book Center or other suppliers. The secretary will maintain careful accounts with the suppliers, using a duplicate order at all times and, in cooperation with the church treasurer, will see that accounts are settled speedily, with clearance of outstanding items on a monthly basis.

d.   To call the attention of the church to resources that are available for use.

e.   To plan periodic offerings to provide Personal Ministries supplies for the members when such are not provided for through the church budget or the conference/mission/field approved offering schedule. A church Personal Ministries offering for this purpose may be received on the first Sabbath of the month. If this offering does not provide sufficient funds, offerings may be taken at the weekly Personal Ministries meeting. The disposition of such Personal Ministries funds shall be made by action of the Personal Ministries Council.

f.   To record details of services and reports of work done by church members, and to be prompt in sending a summary to the Personal Ministries director of the conference/mission/field at the appointed time.

3. *Adventist Men*—(See p. 94.)—The chief outreach (missionary) programs carried on by this group are lay preaching efforts, prison ministry, and Community Services.

4. *Community Services Center*—(See p. 95.)—Where a number of churches within a single district operate a Community Services Center jointly, a governing committee for the center should be appointed by the supporting churches of the district, with representatives from each church, the district pastor serving as the chairman.

Where a center is operated by two or more districts of churches, the center governing committee should be composed of representatives of the supporting churches, with additional representatives appointed by the conference/mission/field committee. The committee elects its own chairperson, but sometimes is chaired by the conference/mission/field Personal Ministries or Community Services director.

5. *The Superintendent*—(See p. 97.)—The superintendent is to:

a. Serve the church as administrator of all divisions of the Sabbath School. He/She is not the leader of the adult division by virtue of being general superintendent, although he/she may also be elected as leader of the adult or another division.

b. Study and follow the counsel and guidelines found in *Counsels on Sabbath School Work* by Ellen G. White, and the *Sabbath School Handbook* published by the General Conference Sabbath School Department. The superintendent should encourage the church to make these books available to leaders and teachers in all divisions of the Sabbath School.

c. Become conversant with the promotion plans of the mission program of the world church and lead the Sabbath School in such sacrificial giving as will enlist their wholehearted support of world missions.

d. Call and chair the Sabbath School Council meetings to care for immediate needs, including recommendations dealing with officer or teacher vacancies.

e. Receive from division leaders all agenda items pertaining to the operation and finances of the Sabbath School and present them to the Sabbath School Council.

f. Implement the decisions of the Sabbath School Council.

g. Be in general charge of the teachers' meeting. While others may have duties in particular lines, such as teaching the Bible study, the superintendent should take the lead and seek to make the teachers' meeting a vital part of the Sabbath School work and through it endeavor to build up a strong, spiritual teaching force.

6. *The Secretary*—(See p. 97.)—The secretary's duties are as follows:

a. To keep all records called for on the official report form supplied by the conference/mission/field, to compile a complete and accurate quarterly Sabbath School report, and to promptly forward the report form to the appropriate individuals. The secretary should also bring before the Sabbath School appropriate reports of Sabbath School work.

b.   To distribute supplies to the teachers and gather class records and offerings from each division.

c.   To ensure that the various Sabbath School divisions are supplied with materials as needed.

d.   To keep a record of the weekly Sabbath School offerings—Thirteenth Sabbath special projects offerings, Birthday-Thank offerings, Investment funds, and Sabbath School expense money, if the latter is not included in the church budget, and to give all offerings to the church treasurer. The financial records kept by the secretary should agree with those of the church treasurer.

e.   To order through the Personal Ministries secretary the Sabbath School supplies, materials, and resources agreed upon by the Sabbath School Council.

f.   To keep the minutes of meetings of the Sabbath School Council.

7. *Expense Money*—(See p. 100.)—All such money should be recorded by the secretary, passed on to the local church treasurer, and used only for paying Sabbath School expense as authorized by the Sabbath School Council. In many churches, Sabbath School expenses are included in the church budget and expended as authorized by the Sabbath School Council.

8. *Mission Statement*—(See p. 101.)—To accomplish our task:

a.   We will achieve a balanced ministry by incorporating the biblical dynamics of fellowship, nurture, worship, and mission.

b.   We will be committed to maintaining relevance and effectiveness in ministry by relating all ministry to the needs of the youth. It is imperative that we listen to and are informed by their perceptions, concerns, and suggestions. Effective ministry becomes possible in an atmosphere of love, acceptance, and forgiveness. We will conduct ongoing research to discover areas that need attention. We are committed to experimentation and innovation in our programs because we recognize the ever changing nature of today's youth.

c.   We will find inspiration in God's Word and our history, and have faith in God for the future. Our philosophy will find expression in a wide variety of God-ordained ministry styles and programs.

d.   We will provide regular evaluation to ensure that our primary focus is achieved.

9. *Membership in the Adventist Youth Society*—(See p. 102.)—
There are three categories of membership in the Adventist Youth Society:

a. *Regular Members*—Young people 16 to 30 years of age who are members of the Seventh-day Adventist Church in regular standing and who, subscribing to the objectives of the society, desire to engage in active service for Christ may enroll as regular members.

b. *Associate Members*—Young people who are not members of the Seventh-day Adventist Church, but who have Christian ideals and desire to be associated with the young people of the church in missionary work should be accepted as associate members. Associate members may not hold office, but they should be cordially received into all the society work and into its bands, and encouraged to become regular members as soon as possible.

c. *Honorary members*—Adult members of the church who support the youth may enroll as honorary members. Many persons who have passed the age of 30 would like to continue attending Adventist Youth Society meetings and to participate in whatever way possible. Whenever it may seem advisable, they should receive an honorary membership card. Their membership is not included in the secretary's report, and they report their outreach (missionary) work in the regular way through the church.

Upon joining the Adventist Youth Society, new members take the following membership pledge:

"Loving the Lord Jesus, I promise to take an active part in the work of the Adventist Youth Society, doing what I can to help others and to finish the work of the gospel in all the world."

10. *Secretary-Treasurer and Assistant*—(See p. 104.)—Another important responsibility of the secretary-treasurer is to keep an accurate record of the receipts and disbursements of all funds of the Adventist Youth Society. Society funds are deposited with the church treasurer and held in trust until such times as their disbursement is ordered by the Adventist Youth Society Committee. This committee shall also review the financial records of the society each quarter and have them audited once each year by the church treasurer. Many churches include the youth organization in their budget.

11. *The Adventist Junior Youth Society*—(See p. 105.)—The activities of the Adventist Junior Youth Society include good reading, Bible study and Bible quizzes, music, and programs developed by the youth from resources available from the teacher and the local conference/mission/field Youth department. Since music is a very important element in the youth program, care should be taken to provide music which will glorify God.

(See p. 84.) Student leaders should be encouraged to develop original program ideas that will involve participation by the class. Witnessing activities should be planned, and a special mission project may be adopted each year toward which a portion of the society offerings can be applied. Social activities may also be encouraged. Some of the Adventist Junior Youth Society meetings should be devoted to the study of the AY classes in preparation for Investiture near the close of the school year.

12. *Adventurer Club*—(See p. 108.)—A sampling of activities as presented in the *Adventurer Manual* includes special day trips, study and application of Bible stories, talent shows, nature activities, crafts, social skills development, and many others. The club has its own flag, uniform, emblems, award patches, and pins and scarves which are different from Pathfinders and must not be mixed or confused with the Pathfinder items. An entire component of the club activities involves parental training in child development, and understanding how to be the model Christian parents all wish to become.

13. *Education Secretary*—(See p. 109.)—The secretary's duties shall be:

a.   To be responsible for the regular promotion of Christian education and to plan, in cooperation with the pastor and Home and School Association leader, periodic programs or services that emphasize the values of Christian education.

b.   To contact all Seventh-day Adventist homes where there are school-age children or young people, to encourage attendance at the local church school or at a Seventh-day Adventist secondary school, college, or university, and to suggest possible solutions to problems.

c.   To make every reasonable effort, where church schools are not available, to encourage the church to provide Seventh-day Adventist education in the area.

d.   To maintain contact with students from the church who are in attendance at Seventh-day Adventist or other schools away from the home church.

e.   To contact members who have no school-age children, encouraging them to provide financial aid for needy Seventh-day Adventist students.

f.   To maintain an up-to-date census of all the children and youth of the church.

14. *Membership*—(See p. 110)—Wherever a separate school board is desired it shall consist of from five to seven members where a single church

operates the school, and seven or more members where two or more churches unite to operate the school.

Where two or more churches unite to operate a school a meeting of these churches should be arranged in counsel with the local conference/mission/field president. At this meeting a plan should be adopted for the appointment of the union school board, including the number of members and the apportionment of the members among the several churches operating the school. The apportionment should be determined on the basis of the memberships of the sponsoring churches, the financial obligations to the school, and the number of pupils attending from each church.

15. *The Communication Secretary's Work*—(See p. 113.)—The Communication secretary will assist in organizing support for the denomination's media programs. This may include the placement of announcements and advertisements for broadcast and Bible correspondence school courses, the promotion of the media ministry offerings, and participation in events for the distribution of radio, television, and Bible correspondence school materials.

16. *The Communication Committee*—(See p. 113.)—Other communication activities that fall within the sphere of interest of this committee include planning for special church events and ceremonies, the preparation of church exhibits and parade floats, placement of church advertising, and providing public libraries and other information centers with information on the Seventh-day Adventist Church. The division of responsibilities will depend largely on the abilities of those comprising the committee. All activities of the committee will be coordinated by the chairperson.

17. *Health Ministries Leader*—(See p. 115.)—The Health Ministries leader's duties should include the following:

a. To outline, plan, and budget, in consultation with the pastor, church Health Ministries Council, and the church board, programs for the year that will emphasize total health and temperance for the church and the community.

b. To promote an ongoing witness in the community concerning the destructive effects of tobacco, alcohol, and other health-destroying drugs and substances.

c. To foster good relationships with community health and temperance organizations.

d. To encourage the study of the biblical principles and the Spirit of Prophecy counsels on health and temperance.

 e.   To encourage the application of the principles of healthful living among church members.

 f.   To arrange for and promote the holding of health and temperance education programs for the church and the community it serves, in close cooperation with the conference/mission/field Health Ministries director.

 h.   To serve as secretary of the Health Ministries Council, except when asked to serve as chairperson.

18. *Health Ministries Council*—(See p. 115.)—Members should be appointed by the church, and might include:
 a.   The pastor or local elder as chairman of the council.
 b.   The Health Ministries leader.
 c.   The Community Services director.
 d.   The Adventist Youth leader or two representatives from the youth group.
 e.   Three representatives from among the following: physician, dentist, dietitian, nurse, health educator, Stewardship leader, or others interested in health and temperance activities.
 f.   The director of the Health Ministries Society when an active society exists.
 g.   A representative of the local Seventh-day Adventist health-care institution.

19. *Stewardship Leader*—(See p. 116.)—The leader will implement the general educational program of the Stewardship Department as it is presented and expanded periodically to meet a continuing need. This responsibility includes assisting the pastor in World Stewardship Day emphasis, conducting stewardship classes, tithe and offering education, and teaching the basic stewardship concepts during Sabbath services or on other occasions.

The leader's organizational responsibilities will include being (1) a member of the church board, involved in and conversant with the spiritual and financial program of the church, (2) a member of the Stewardship and Finance Committees, and (3) an active assistant to the pastor in the annual Stewardship Guidance Program and in the follow-up throughout the year as outlined in the *Stewardship Manual*.

20. *The Family Ministries Committee*—(See p. 117.)—Although this committee should not be too large in order to remain effective, appropriate church leaders should be included as well as persons who understand the varied needs of families within the church. Persons who have faced

traumatic life and family experiences and have grown spiritually through them may make valuable contributions as members of the committee. The committee should include both men and women and, where possible, at least one single person, at least one married couple, one or more parents, and a representative cross-section of the various age groups in the church. The duties of the committee shall be the following:

    a.   To assist church leadership in compiling family demographic data both within the church and in the surrounding community to clarify target groups for a ministry to families.

    b.   To assist church leadership in assessing the needs of church members for family life education, enrichment, and counseling; and in developing a plan for utilizing community and church resources to address these needs.

    c.   To encourage sensitivity to the impact of church programs on family life in terms of the expenditure of time, energy, money, and other family resources required.

    d.   To participate with the conference/mission/field Family Ministries Department in implementing family emphasis programs promoted by the department.

    e.   To cooperate with church leadership to design, plan, and implement additional family life features and programs as needed, both for family nurture within the membership and evangelistic outreach to the community.

    f.   To foster a climate of warmth and fellowship, engendering a sense of "familiness" in the congregation and a redemptive spirit toward families in need of support and encouragement.

   21. *Family Ministries Leaders(s)*—(See p. 117.)—The duties of the Family Ministries leader(s) are:

    a.   To chair the Family Ministries Committee.

    b.   To represent the needs and interests of families through membership on the church board, and to coordinate Family Ministries plans with the overall church program.

    c.   To inform the pastor and church board of Family Ministries concerns and achievements, and to encourage funding and support for ministry to families.

    d.   To identify church and community resources which foster relational growth and provide help to meet critical needs, and to heighten awareness of these resources among church leadership and families.

   22. *The Women's Ministries Committee*—(See p. 119.)—The major responsibilities of the Women's Ministries Committee shall be as follows:

a.   To assess the needs of women in the local church and community, by utilizing surveys and interviews, and in counsel with the pastor and church leaders;

b.   To brainstorm, develop strategies, and cooperate with other specialized departments of the church to foster programs and activities which minister to women;

c.   To plan and implement these and other initiatives which relate to women's specific and varied needs, in cooperation with the pastor, departmental specialists, and other church leaders;

d.   To facilitate local church participation in annual programs and activities initiated by the field/mission/conference/union/division/General Conference such as the International Women's Day of Prayer, Women's Ministries Day, and small group ministries to support women and encourage them in service. Information regarding these programs is available through the conference/mission/field Department of Women's Ministries.

23. *Ministry to Seventh-day Adventist Children*—(See p. 119.)— Ways to strengthen the spiritual life of Seventh-day Adventist children could include:

a.   Sabbath School (under the responsibility of the Sabbath School Department).

b.   Pathfinder and Adventurer Clubs (under the responsibility of the Youth Department).

c.   Children's prayer meeting at the same time and place as the adult midweek prayer meeting.

d.   An on-going baptismal class for children who express a desire to be baptized, but are considered too young.

e.   Children's Bible club on Sabbath afternoon that would involve them in meaningful and appropriate Sabbath observance.

f.   Weekly religious instruction for Seventh-day Adventist children not attending church school.

g.   Children's small groups ministry bringing children each week for discussion, Bible study, and fellowship.

h.   Children's choir.

i.   Children's congress (city or district or field/mission/conference wide) to provide opportunities for children and their parents to experience leadership training, inspiration, and fellowship.

24. *Ministry to Children Outside the Church*—(See p. 119)—In addition, the church can extend ministry to children by the following kinds of programs:

a.   Seventh-day Adventist day care.

b. Radio and television programs.
c. Children's choirs.
d. Evangelistic meetings for children.
e. Correspondence Bible courses.
f. Other creative outreach, e.g. children's gymnastics clubs.

25. *Involving Seventh-day Adventist Children in Service to Others*— (See p. 120.)—Here are some suggestions for tapping the unlimited potential of children:

a. Participation in divine services.
b. Participation in church outreach.
c. Visitation to shut-ins.
d. Musical performances.
e. Community service.
f. Leadership opportunities in evangelism, Bible study, and prophecy seminars.

26. *Children's Ministries Committee*—(See p. 120.)—The committee's responsibilities could include:

a. Providing cooperation and balance among the religious education activities planned for children.

b. Working together to coordinate all activities in order to avoid overlaps or gaps in the plans for children, and preparing a yearly activities calendar that incorporates all children's programs.

c. Keeping up-to-date records of church members' children and community children who have participated in church activities.

d. Conducting a needs assessment of children in the congregation and/or community.

27. *Children's Ministries Coordinator*—(See p. 120.)—The role of the Children's Ministries coordinator may include responsibilities such as:

a. Scheduling and chairing the Children's Ministries Committee, encouraging a spirit of teamwork among those working for and with children, and being the team leader in creating a ministry for children that draws them to Christ and provides for their participation in all church activities.

b. Serving as an advocate of the interests of children to:

1) The Church Board—by keeping the board members informed of concerns and successes, by reporting the results of the children's needs assessment, and by encouraging funding for children's programs.

2) The pastor—by working together to make the various aspects of church life meaningful to children.

3) The Personal Ministries Council—by participating in the council's planning for the church, suggesting ways to involve children.

4) The leaders of children's activities—by supporting and encouraging them.

c. Taking reasonable steps to maintain a high moral and ethical quality of leadership for the children.

d. Maintaining communication with parents and leaders of children's activities, informing them about workshops, conventions, camp meetings, and other resources, and encouraging their growth in understanding children.

e. Seeking opportunities to spend time with children in order to stay in touch with their thinking and their needs.

28. *Religious Liberty Leader of the Local Church*—(See p. 121.)— The Religious Liberty leader's duties are:

a. To interact with the Public Affairs and Religious Liberty director of the conference/mission/field, or union where appropriate, and deal with the suggestions that come through proper channels.

b. To advise concerning matters affecting religious liberty.

c. To promote the circulation of religious liberty magazines and other materials approved by the division or the General Conference.

d. To organize or facilitate religious liberty meetings, seminars, programs, and activities as circumstances indicate.

CHAPTER 10

Ministers and Workers in Relation to the Church

A Divinely Appointed Ministry

"God has a church, and she has a divinely appointed ministry. 'And He gave some, apostles; and some, prophets; and some, evangelists; and some, pastors and teachers; for the perfecting of the saints, for the work of the ministry, for the edifying of the body of Christ: till we all come in the unity of the faith, and of the knowledge of the Son of God, unto a perfect man, unto the measure of the stature of the fullness of Christ . . . .'

"The Lord has His appointed agencies, and a church that has lived through persecution, conflict, and darkness. Jesus loved the church, and gave Himself for it, and He will replenish, refine, ennoble, and elevate it, so that it shall stand fast amid the corrupting influences of this world. Men appointed of God have been chosen to watch with jealous care, with vigilant perseverance, that the church may not be overthrown by the evil devices of Satan, but that she shall stand in the world to promote the glory of God among men."—*Testimonies to Ministers*, pp. 52, 53.

The Conference/Mission/Field President

The president of the conference/mission/field should be an ordained minister of experience and good report. He stands at the head of the gospel ministry in his conference/mission/field and is the chief elder, or overseer, of all the churches. He works for the spiritual welfare and upbuilding of the churches. He counsels them regarding their activities and plans. He has access to all the churches, church services, business meetings, and church boards, without vote unless granted by the church, and may, by virtue of his office, preside over the sessions of any of the churches when such a course is necessary. He has access to all church records, report books, et cetera.

He will not set aside the duly elected officers of the church but work in cooperation with them. They in turn are bound, in recognition of the ties of conference/mission/field fellowship, to counsel with him over all that pertains to the welfare of the church. They should not attempt to exclude him from a proper discharge of his duties.

Pastors and District Leaders Not Executives

Ordained ministers appointed by the conference/mission/field committee to act as pastors or district leaders do not take the place of the president in their respective fields; they are not charged with administrative powers as is the president, but they cooperate with him in carrying out the plans and policies of the conference/mission/field.

President and Committee Direct Departmental Directors

Departmental directors are employed by the conference/mission/field to foster important lines of denominational work. In order to successfully carry on the work assigned to them, these workers must have access to the churches. They should be given opportunity to present and develop their plans in the churches. It is expected that these workers will have sympathetic consideration for all church plans, even outside their respective departments. These directors work under the general direction of the conference/mission/ field committee in counsel with the conference/mission/ field president, who is the responsible head of all lines of the work.

Work of Departmental Directors Not Administrative

Departmental directors are not vested with administrative or executive authority in conference/mission/field or church work, but their relation to the field is an advisory one. Their work does not bear the same relationship to the churches as that of the conference/mission/field committee or president. Their work, however, is primarily of a specific kind, and in the promotion of their lines of work they labor throughout the entire conference/mission/ field. It is not expected that they will counsel the churches regarding church elections and other administrative duties or any other line of service, unless especially requested by the conference/mission/field president to do so.

Relation of Ordained Minister to Church Work

On assignment to a local church as pastor, the ordained minister ranks above the local elder or elders; these serve as his assistants. By virtue of his ordination to the ministry he is qualified to function in all church rites and ceremonies. He should be the spiritual leader and adviser of the church. He should instruct the church officers in their duties and plan with them for all lines of church work and activity. When a minister is appointed by the conference/mission/field committee as pastor of the church, it is understood that he is a member of the church board and serves as its chairman. In a case where the pastor desires to be relieved of the responsibility of acting as chairman of a church board, a church elder serves as chairman. Between the pastor and the church elder there needs to be the closest cooperation. (See pp. 49, 83.) The minister, with the assistance of the elders, is expected to plan for and lead out in all spiritual services of the church, such as Sabbath morning worship and prayer meeting, and should officiate at the communion service and baptism. He should not surround himself with any special body of counselors of his own choosing, but always work in cooperation with the duly elected officers of the church.

When an ordained minister of the conference/mission/field, or one sent by the conference/mission/field, visits a church, it is expected that the local elder will show him proper deference by inviting him to occupy the pulpit. This also applies to unordained workers sent by the conference/mission/ field. (See pp. 69, 140.)

Churches Do Not Elect Pastor

Pastors or assistant pastors are not nominated or elected to such positions by the church. Their connection with the church is by the appointment of the conference/mission/field committee, and such appointments may be changed at any time. (See pp. 49, 50.)

Licensed Ministers

To give young men an opportunity to demonstrate their call to the ministry, especially in the area of soul-winning, prospective candidates are granted ministerial licenses by the conference/mission/field. The granting of such licenses confers the opportunity and the right to develop the ministerial gift. The licensed minister is authorized to preach, to engage in evangelism, to lead out in outreach (missionary) work, and to assist in any church activities.

There are circumstances in many fields, however, where it is necessary for the conference/mission/field to appoint a licensed minister to carry responsibility as a pastor or assistant pastor of a church or group of churches. In order to open the way for him to perform certain ministerial functions, the church or group of churches he is to serve may elect him as a local elder. However, since he is employed by the conference/mission/field and appointed by it he represents it, and it may consider, in varying degrees as circumstances require, that his authority and responsibilities should be extended in order to enable him to discharge his duties satisfactorily. The right to permit this extension of authority and responsibility rests, in the first instance, with the division executive committee. Its action is necessary before any conference/mission/field may extend the authority and responsibility of the licensed minister. Such action shall define specifically and clearly what additional ministerial functions a licensed minister may perform but always on the understanding that his functions as a church elder and his extended functions be always and only within the church or group of churches which he serves. (See p. 50.)

In its actions the conference/mission/field committee shall not go beyond that which the division committee authorizes. It shall not authorize a licensed minister to go from church to church outside the church or group of churches of which he is a local elder, performing church rites which pertain to the functions of an ordained minister. A conference/mission/field committee action cannot be substituted for church election or ministerial ordination.

Bible Instructors

A very important line of service is that of the Bible instructor. This is recognized by conferences/missions/fields in employing suitable persons to engage in this line of work. They may be transferred from place to place as the work requires. They may be assigned to work in connection with an evangelistic effort, in which case they are under the immediate direction of the evangelist in charge of the effort, or they may be stationed in a city to labor in connection with a local church. In such a case they come under the immediate direction of the pastor of the church but, as already seen, are under the general direction of the conference/mission/field. A conference/mission/field Bible instructor should not, except by special arrangement with the conference/mission/field, be asked to carry any church office, but should be left free to carry on personal soul-winning work.

Adventist Book Center Managers

These are conference/mission/field workers, and as such are under the direction of the conference/mission/field committee and the president. While they are in a special way in close touch with church publishing houses, they are not chosen, elected, or directed by publishing house boards, but by the conference/mission/field. In selecting such workers it is well to consider available personnel who have received a training in connection with church publishing houses.

The Pastor Should Assist the Evangelist

When an evangelist is asked to conduct an evangelistic effort in a locality or city in which there is a church with a pastor in charge, the pastor should be invited by the conference/mission/field to assist the evangelist, thus giving the pastor an opportunity of becoming acquainted with the prospective members.

President and Committee Direct
Conference/Mission/Field Workers

The conference/mission/field president in counsel with the conference/mission/field committee directs the workers of the conference/mission/field in their varied activities. It is his duty to acquaint the workers with the plans and policies of the committee and to secure the cooperation of the workers in carrying them out. The president should take a special interest in fostering the evangelistic work of the conference/mission/field, doing all he can to encourage a constant soul-winning endeavor on the part of all the workers. He should actively recruit and assist in training young men for the ministry. Departmental secretaries are employed by the conference/mission/field to foster important lines of denominational work.

All conference/mission/field workers—ministers, Bible instructors, departmental directors, et cetera—are under the direction of the conference/mission/field committee. They receive their credentials from and are responsible to the conference/mission/field, and not to any local church in the conference/mission/field. Churches may request the services or help of conference/mission/field workers, lodging such requests with the conference/mission/field president, but the appointment in all cases rests with the conference/mission/field committee. Workers may be appointed to labor with certain churches, and when in the judgment of the conference/mission/field committee the appointment should be changed, the committee is at liberty to do so. The worker or the church may appeal to the conference/mission/field committee for a hearing on the decision to move the worker from his field of labor. This will be carefully considered in the light of the needs of the entire conference/mission/field, and the decision will be made accordingly. Should such a situation develop in which the worker refuses to cooperate with the committee and declines to work in harmony with its decisions, his conduct may be regarded as insubordination and be dealt with as such. In no case should he appeal to the church regarding such decisions. Any church supporting a worker in his stand under such circumstances becomes subject to the discipline of the conference/mission/field.

Credentials and Licenses

God's work is to be jealously safeguarded by the responsible leaders in every step of organization, from the local church to the General Conference. In order that enemies of the work may not gain access to our pulpits, it is most strongly urged that no one be allowed to speak to any congregation unless he/she presents valid and up-to-date denominational credentials. It is recognized, however, that there are times when it is proper for our congregations to be addressed by government officials or by civic leaders; but all unauthorized persons should be excluded from the pulpit. (See pp. 69, 137, 205-207.)

The churches in their collective capacity through the conferences/ missions/fields confer upon certain individuals the authority to represent and speak for the church as ministers and gospel workers. This authority is represented by the granting of credentials, which are written commissions, properly dated and signed by the officers of the conference/mission/field. The authority thus conveyed is not personal or inherent in the individual holding the credentials, but is inherent in the body granting the credentials, and may be recalled at any time if sufficient cause exists. The credentials granted workers are never to be regarded as the personal property of the workers, but as belonging to the organization granting the same. The worker is honor bound to return them upon the request of the organization.

Official credentials are issued to all authorized Seventh-day Adventist workers, and are granted by controlling committees for limited periods.

Expired Credentials

Credentials are granted for the duration of the conference/mission/field term, either annually, triennially, or quinquennially. The credentials are renewed by a vote of the conference/mission in session. If for any reason it is deemed inadvisable to renew credentials to any minister, he ceases to function as a worker in the conference/mission/field. The possession of out-of-date or expired credentials does not authorize him to function in any of the offices of a minister. In such a case he has no more authority or standing than any other laymember in the church.

Removing a Minister From Office

A minister may be removed from office by conference/mission/field committee action, without the individual's church membership being affected. When a minister is removed from membership in the church and subsequently restored to church membership, that person is not thereby restored to the ministry. The individual is readmitted to the church as a laymember.

Retired Workers

Throughout the various conferences/missions/fields are workers who, on account of age or condition of health, have retired from active service. As a class these workers are deserving of honor and consideration. In many cases they have spent long years in helping to build up the cause of God. Their presence is a blessing and help to our churches.

Retired workers usually hold their church membership in the church nearest their place of residence. They may be elected to any office in the church, in which case they function freely in all that pertains to the office in which they serve. They also may exercise their ministerial functions under the direction of the conference/mission/field committee.

Ministers Without Credentials Serving in Our Churches

There may be instances of men who years ago were ordained as ministers but who, for some valid reason, are not carrying credentials from the organization. They may be elected as elders of churches and, should their ordination not have been invalidated, such men need not be ordained as elders, but in their service they are limited to the work and prerogatives of a local elder.

CHAPTER 11

The Church Election

In view of the responsibilities of church officers and the character of the work required of them, the electing of church officers is an important work. This duty should be entered upon in a prayerful, well-ordered, and serious manner. Only such persons should be chosen who fully expect to fulfill the specific duties of the office for which they have been elected.

Nominating Committee

In the Seventh-day Adventist Church, officers are elected every one or two years (see p. 47) through an appointed nominating committee. This committee brings its report to the church, which then acts on the names presented. This procedure enables the church to give careful study to each name prior to election, and avoids the public competitive element that may arise when nominations are made from the floor.

The nominating committee shall study the needs of the church and make careful inquiry into the fitness of members to serve in the different offices. For this reason officers shall not be nominated from the floor or by general ballot.

The *Church Manual* does not determine the size of the nominating committee. It will range from five members in a small church to a larger number in a large church. The exact number to be chosen is left to the discretion of each church. This matter should be studied by the church board prior to presentation to the church. A suitable recommendation may then be brought to the church, using a minimum of time in the Sabbath worship hour.

When the Nominating Committee Is Appointed—The nominating committee should be appointed early in the closing quarter of the church year and report at least three weeks before the final Sabbath of the church year.

How the Nominating Committee Is Appointed—The minister or, in the absence of a minister, the church elder should bring the matter to the attention of the church. The church shall then appoint a special committee that will be responsible to nominate the nominating committee. This special committee may be chosen in one of two ways:

1. By nominations, verbal or written, from the floor. If verbal nominations are made from the floor, it must be understood that no member may nominate more than one person. The effort of one individual or a small group to dictate to the entire membership of the church is disapproved. Everything of a political nature should be avoided.

2. By the church's authorizing the church board, together with five to seven additional persons chosen by the church, in accordance with paragraph 1. above, to function as the special committee.

The sequential steps are as follows:

a. The church appoints by vote a special committee by either of the two methods listed above.

b. The special committee recommends to the church names for the nominating committee, with suggestions for chairperson and secretary.

c. The church appoints by vote the nominating committee, naming the chairperson and secretary.

d. The nominating committee meets to prepare the list of church officers, which will be presented to the church for approval.

e. The church appoints by vote the various church officers for the ensuing year.

Who Should be Members of the Nominating Committee—Only members who are in regular standing should be chosen to serve on the nominating committee. They should be persons of good judgment and, above all, have the welfare and prosperity of the church at heart. There are no ex officio members of the nominating committee, except the pastor or district leader who serves as the chair of the committee. Should the pastor or district leader choose not to chair the committee, or in case the conference/mission/field has not yet appointed a pastor or district leader to the church, the special committee appointed by the church to nominate the nominating committee should recommend to the church the name of a local member to serve as chair of the nominating committee.

Work of the Nominating Committee—As soon as possible after its election, the nominating committee should be called together by the one chosen to act as chairperson. With earnest prayer for guidance the committee should begin its work of preparing a list of names to submit to the church for officers and assistants comprised of members in regular standing on the roll of the church making the appointments. These will be placed in nomination for office and presented to the church at a Sabbath service or at a specially called business meeting of the church. In making their selections, the committee may counsel with others who are well informed. This committee does not nominate either the pastor or the assistant pastor(s). These appointments are made by the executive committee of the conference/mission/field.

The church nominating committee deals with the following:

Elder(s)
Deacon(s)
Deaconess(es)
Clerk
Treasurer
Assistant treasurer(s)
Children's Ministries coordinator
Church chorister or song leader
Church organist or pianist
Education secretary
Family Ministries leader(s)
Women's Ministries leader
Ministry to People with Disabilities coordinator
Personal Ministries leader
Personal Ministries secretary
Interest coordinator
Community Services director
Sabbath School superintendent(s)
Sabbath School assistant superintendent(s)
Sabbath School secretary
Sabbath School assistant secretary
Sabbath School division leaders, including leaders for the adult and
    extension divisions
Sabbath School Investment secretary
Vacation Bible School director
Home and School Association leader
Home and School Association secretary-treasurer
Dorcas Society leader
Dorcas Society secretary-treasurer
Adventist Junior Youth Society leader
Adventist Junior Youth assistant leader(s)
Adventist Youth Society leader
Adventist Youth Society associate leader
Adventist Youth Society sponsor
Adventist Youth Society secretary-treasurer
Adventist Youth Society assistant secretary-treasurer

Adventist Youth Society music director
Adventist Youth Society pianist or organist
Pathfinder Club director
Pathfinder Club deputy director
Adventurer Club director   ,
Religious Liberty leader
Communication secretary or Communication Committee
Health Ministries leader
Stewardship leader
Church board
Church school board
Such other leadership personnel as the church may deem advisable,
   except Sabbath School teachers who shall be appointed by the
   Sabbath School Council and approved by the church board.

Home and School Association officers are nominated where the local church is the only church that supports the school. Such nominations are provided to the school board which makes the appointment. Where more than one church supports a school, this whole process is fulfilled by the school board. (See pp. 109-110.)

The size of the church will naturally determine the number of church officers to be nominated. If the church is small, many of the assistant leaders may be omitted. In a large church all the officers and leaders named in the preceding list may be necessary.

Nominating Committee to Consult Prospective Officers—Having nominated for the various offices persons who are faithful, loyal members of the local church,* the appropriate members of the nominating committee should inform them of their nomination to office and secure their consent to serve.

Member May Appear Before the Nominating Committee—If any member of the church desires to appear before the committee during its sessions to make suggestions or objections, he/she should be given opportunity to do so. After the one appearing before the committee has retired from the committee room, the suggestions or objections should be considered on their merits. When this has been done and everything is clear

---

*Any exception to this shall be by approval of the conference/mission/field. (See p. 49, Work of the Church Elder is Local.)

to the satisfaction of the committee, the committee is ready to report to the church.

Nominating Committee Discussions Are Confidential—It is a violation of Christian ethics and the spirit of the golden rule for a member of a nominating committee to repeat outside of a committee session any report, discussion, or conversation regarding any member whose name may be under consideration for any office. To offend in this regard is ample reason for excluding such a member from participating in the work of a nominating committee. All inquiries and discussions regarding the fitness of members to hold church office should be confidential. Should the necessity arise for inquiries to be made outside the committee, the chairperson of the committee should make them.

These principles apply to the work of all nominating committees, in both church and conference/mission/field work.

Reporting to the Church—This report is rendered to the church as a whole and not to the church board. The board has no jurisdiction in these matters. The report of this committee may be presented at the Sabbath service or at a specially called business meeting of the church.

When the nominating committee is ready to render its report, the minister or elder should give the chairperson of the nominating committee opportunity to make appropriate remarks to the church. A copy of the report should be placed in the hands of members, or it should be read aloud by the secretary of the nominating committee. The chairperson should announce that the report will be voted on the following week or two weeks later.

Objecting to the Report of the Nominating Committee—It is the right of any member to raise an objection to the nominating committee's report. Any such objection should be presented in person to the nominating committee for consideration before the second reading of the report by making an appointment through the chairperson or church pastor. Or, at the time of the second reading of the report, it is in order for the objector to request that the whole report be referred, without discussion, to the nominating committee for further consideration. It is the usual procedure for the chairperson to accept the referral. However, if the request becomes a motion it is nondebatable and is decided by majority vote. The chairperson of the committee should then announce when and where the committee will be in session to hear the objections to any name. At that time the member making the objection, or any other member who desires to do so, should appear before the committee. If the election is deferred on the objection of any member, it would be a serious matter for that member to fail to appear before the committee. Trivial or groundless objections to any name should never be made, but if there are serious reasons why any nomination should be changed, these reasons should be stated. The committee should give due consideration to the objections presented. If they are found to be justified, the committee will need to substitute another name for the one to which objection was made. When the report is again presented to the church, the church proceeds to vote on the report of the committee. Every church member should vote in the election of church officers. The election is by the majority vote of those present and voting.

Vacancies—If an office of the church becomes vacant during the year because of death, removal, resignation, or for any other reason, the church board nominates a successor to fill the vacancy for the remainder of the term of office and submits the nomination to the church for election.

Election of
Delegates to Local Conference/Mission Session

In local and union conference/mission organizations all administrative authority springs from the constituency. The local churches in conference/mission organizations elect delegates to the local conference/ mission session. These are duly authorized to represent the churches in the councils of the conference/mission. The conference/mission session elects officers, grants credentials and licenses, adopts or changes the constitution if such actions be necessary, and transacts other business. One of its most important acts is the election of the executive committee, whose duty is to function for the constituency between sessions. In this committee is vested the delegated power and authority of all the churches within the conference/mission.

Choosing Delegates—"He [God] has so arranged matters that chosen men shall go as delegates to our conferences. These men are to be tried and proved. They are to be trustworthy men. The choosing of delegates to attend our conferences is an important matter. These men are to lay the plans that shall be followed in the advancement of the work; and therefore they are to be men of understanding, able to reason from cause to effect."— *Testimonies*, vol. 9, p. 262.

The number of delegates from each church to a local conference/ mission session is determined by the provisions of the conference/mission constitution. When the time comes to select delegates the pastor, or the head elder in cooperation with the pastor, should bring the matter before the church. A committee may be appointed to nominate delegates or the church board may be asked to nominate them. Nothing of a political nature should be allowed to come into this work. Men and women of known piety and loyalty and who are able to attend the session should be nominated as delegates. (See pp. 52, 57.)

When the committee or church board has completed its work, it should report to the church, nominating as delegates the members it has agreed upon. The church then votes on these nominations. No church officer by virtue of office is a delegate ex officio. After the election, the clerk of the church will fill out the delegates' credential blanks, furnished for the purpose, and return them to the secretary of the conference/mission. The chosen delegates become the representatives of the church, to unite with the delegates of other churches in the conference/mission in the election of officers for the conference/mission and for the transaction of all other conference/mission business. The delegates to a union conference/mission session are chosen by the local conferences/missions, not by the churches. The delegates to a General Conference session are chosen by the divisions and the union conferences/missions. The respective terms of office for these organizations are determined by the terms of their respective constitutions.

Duty of Delegates—A delegate to a conference/mission session or constituency meeting is not chosen to represent merely the church or conference/mission. A seated delegate should view the work as a whole, remembering that he/she is responsible for the welfare of the work in every part of the field. It is not permissible for church or conference/mission delegations to organize or attempt to direct their votes as a unit. Nor is it permissible for the delegates from a large church or conference/mission to claim pre-eminence in directing affairs in a conference/mission session. Each delegate should be susceptible to the direction of the Holy Spirit and vote according to personal convictions. Any church or conference/mission officer or leader attempting to control the votes of a group of delegates would be considered disqualified for holding office.

Responsibility of Conference/Mission Officers

The local church has no authority outside its own local body. It unites with other churches in the conference/mission in delegating authority and responsibility to the conference/mission officers and executive committee to carry on the work of the conference/mission between sessions. These officers are answerable to the conference/mission as a whole and not to any one local church.

Conference/Mission/Field Committee Members to
Represent the Entire Conference/Mission/Field

Conference/Mission/Field committee members are elected to represent the work in the entire territory of the conference/mission/field; they do not represent merely a local church, or district, or any particular institution in the conference/mission/field. Each member should feel a definite responsibility to foster all interests of the work in all parts of the field. The decisions and votes of the committee are not to be controlled or influenced by any church, group, or individual. Decisions are reached after prayerful and careful study of all aspects of the matters that come before them pertaining to the administration of the work.

CHAPTER 12

Gospel Finance

The gospel plan for the support of the work of God in preaching the everlasting gospel is by the tithes and offerings of His people. The Seventh-day Adventist Church has followed this plan from its earliest days.

The biblical basis for the returning of tithes and giving of offerings will be found in the following references: Lev. 27:30; Mal. 3:8-12; Matt. 23:23; 1 Cor. 9:9-14; 2 Cor. 9:6-15. Observe also the following from the Spirit of Prophecy:

"The system of tithes and offerings was intended to impress the minds of men with a great truth—that God is the source of every blessing to His creatures, and that to Him man's gratitude is due for the good gifts of His providence."—*Patriarchs and Prophets*, p. 525.

"Tithes and offerings for God are an acknowledgment of His claim on us by creation, and they are also an acknowledgment of His claim by redemption. Because all our power is derived from Christ, these offerings are to flow from us to God. They are to keep ever before us the claim of redemption, the greatest of all claims, and the one that involves every other. The realization of the sacrifice made in our behalf is ever to be fresh in our minds and is ever to exert an influence on our thoughts and plans. Christ is to be indeed as one crucified among us."—*Testimonies*, vol. 6, p. 479.

"The tithe is sacred, reserved by God for Himself. It is to be brought into His treasury to be used to sustain the gospel laborers in their work."—*Testimonies*, vol. 9, p. 249.

"He has given His people a plan for raising sums sufficient to make the enterprise self-sustaining. God's plan in the tithing system is beautiful in its simplicity and equality. All may take hold of it in faith and courage, for it is divine in its origin. In it are combined simplicity and utility, and it does not require depth of learning to understand and execute it. All may feel that they can act a part in carrying forward the precious work of salvation. Every man, woman, and youth may become a treasurer for the Lord and may be an agent to meet the demands upon the treasury. Says the apostle: 'Let every one of you lay by him in store, as God hath prospered him.'"—*Testimonies*, vol. 3, pp. 388, 389.

"That which has been set apart according to the Scriptures as belonging to the Lord constitutes the revenue of the gospel and is no longer ours. It is no better than sacrilege for a man to take from God's treasury in order to serve himself or to serve others in their secular business."—*Testimonies,* vol. 9, pp. 246, 247.

"Every church member should be taught to be faithful in paying an honest tithe."—*Testimonies,* vol. 9, p. 251.

"This is not a request of man; it is one of God's ordinances, whereby His work may be sustained and carried on in the world. . . . No one can excuse himself from paying his tithes and offerings to the Lord."—*Testimonies to Ministers,* p. 307.

"God has made the proclamation of the gospel dependent upon the labors and the gifts of His people. Voluntary offerings and the tithe constitute the revenue of the Lord's work. Of the means entrusted to man, God claims a certain portion,—the tenth. He leaves all free to say whether or not they will give more than this."—*The Acts of the Apostles,* p. 74.

"God has given special direction as to the use of the tithe. He does not design that His work shall be crippled for want of means. That there may be no haphazard work and no error, He has made our duty on these points very plain. The portion that God has reserved for Himself is not to be diverted to any other purpose than that which He has specified. Let none feel at liberty to retain their tithe, to use according to their own judgment. They are not to use it for themselves in an emergency, nor to apply it as they see fit, even in what they may regard as the Lord's work."—*Testimonies,* vol. 9, p. 247.

Stewardship

Christians are God's stewards, entrusted with His goods and, as His partners, responsible to manage them in harmony with His guidelines and principles as outlined in Scripture and the Spirit of Prophecy. The divine counsel is that "it is required in stewards, that a man be found faithful" (1 Cor. 4:2). The question of stewardship in its fullest form covers many aspects of Christian life and experience, such as our time, our influence, and our service, but there is no doubt that the stewardship of our means is a vitally important phase of this question. It is one which concerns the entire church family. It involves our recognition of the sovereignty of God, of His ownership of all things, and of the bestowal of His grace upon our hearts. As we grow in the understanding of these principles we shall be led into a fuller appreciation of the way God's love operates in our lives.

While this aspect of Christian stewardship concerns our material possessions, it is, nevertheless, something which reacts very definitely upon our Christian experience. The Lord requires certain things of us, in order that He may do certain things for us. Our yielding obedience to what our heavenly Father requires places this phase of stewardship upon a high spiritual plane. Our God is not exacting. He does not arbitrarily demand either that we serve Him or that we recognize Him with our gifts. But He has so arranged that when we work in harmony with Him in these things there will flow to our own hearts great spiritual blessings. If, on the other hand, we fail to cooperate with Him in carrying out His plans, we deprive ourselves of His richest blessings when we need them most.

"God desires all His stewards to be exact in following divine arrangements. They are not to offset the Lord's plans by performing some deed of charity or giving some gift or some offering when or how they, the human agents, shall see fit. It is a very poor policy for men to seek to improve on God's plan, and invent a makeshift, averaging up their good impulses on this and that occasion, and offsetting them against God's requirements. God calls upon all to give their influence to His own arrangement. He has made His plan known, and all who would co-operate with Him must carry out this plan instead of daring to attempt an improvement on it."—*Testimonies*, vol. 9, p. 248.

The Tithe

In recognition of the Bible plan and the solemn privilege and responsibility that rest upon church members as children of God and members of His body, the church, all are encouraged to return a faithful tithe (one tenth of their increase or personal income) into the denomination's treasury.

The tithe is not used or disbursed by the local church but is remitted to the conference/mission/field treasurer. Thus the tithe from all the churches flows into the local conference/mission/field treasury, which in turn remits one tenth of its total tithe income to the union. The union in turn forwards to the General Conference, or its divisions, one tenth of its total tithe income. Thus the local conference/mission/field, the union, and the General Conference are provided with funds with which to support the workers employed and to meet the expense of conducting the work of God in their respective spheres of responsibility and activity.

In addition to remitting to the union ten percent of their tithe income, local conferences/missions/fields also remit through the union to the General Conference, or its divisions, an additional percentage of their tithe as determined by the General Conference Executive Committee or division committee for the financing of the church's program.

These policies have been developed for the gathering and disbursing of funds in all the world and for the conducting of the business affairs of the cause. The financial and business aspect of the work are of great importance.

They cannot be separated from the proclamation of the message of salvation; they are indeed an integral part of it.

Systematic Benevolence and Unity—The financial plan of the denomination serves a larger purpose than appears in its financial and statistical reports. The arrangement is more than a means of gathering and distributing funds. It is, under God, one of the great unifying factors of the Advent Movement. God's people are a united people. The church's system of dividing the tithe between the conference/mission/field and the union and between the union and the General Conference and of sharing the funds with the world fields has served a wonderful purpose in unifying the work throughout the world.

How the Tithe Is to be Used—The tithe is to be held sacred for the work of the ministry, for Bible teaching, and for the support of conference/mission/field administration in the care of the churches and of field outreach (missionary) endeavors. The tithe is not to be spent on other work, on paying church or institutional debts, or on building programs.

"A very plain, definite message has been given to me for our people. I am bidden to tell them that they are making a mistake in applying the tithe to various objects which, though good in themselves, are not the object to which the Lord has said that the tithe should be applied. Those who make this use of the tithe are departing from the Lord's arrangement. God will judge for these things."—*Testimonies*, vol. 9, p. 248.

How the Tithe Is Handled—The tithe is the Lord's and is to be brought, as an act of worship, to the conference/mission/field treasury through the church in which the person's membership is held. Where unusual circumstances exist, church members should consult with the officers of their conference/mission/field.

Conference/Mission/Field Workers and Church Officers to Set Example in Returning Tithe—Conference/Mission/Field workers and church elders, other officers, and institutional leaders are to recognize that as a principle of leadership in God's work, a good example is to be set in the matter of returning tithe. No one shall be continued as either a church officer or conference/mission/field worker who does not conform to this standard of leadership.

Tithing—a Scriptural Obligation—Although the returning of tithe is not held as a test of fellowship, it is recognized as a scriptural obligation that every believer owes to God and as one of the spiritual exercises in which the giver should have part in claiming by faith the fullness of blessing in Christian life and experience.

"Bring ye all the tithes into the storehouse, that there may be meat in mine house, and prove me now herewith, saith the Lord of hosts, if I will not open you the windows of heaven, and pour you out a blessing, that there shall not be room enough to receive it" (Mal. 3:10).

Offerings

In addition to the tithe, the Scriptures emphasize our obligation to bring offerings to the Lord. The withholding of offerings is classed with the withholding of tithe and is called robbery (Mal. 3:8). The Seventh-day Adventist Church has from its early days followed the practice of giving liberal offerings to the cause of God. Great prosperity and blessing have attended the work as a result. People of wealth, professional people with larger incomes, farmers, laborers, ministers and workers, including the converts in other lands where wages are small, have all united in generously supporting the cause by giving offerings in proportion to their incomes.

Sabbath School Offerings—Our most widely used method of regular systematic giving is through our Sabbath Schools. The Sabbath School offerings are devoted to our world mission work. Sabbath by Sabbath large sums come in through this channel.

Other Offerings—Other offerings are taken from time to time for world mission work and for general and local enterprises. When any offering is taken for world mission work or for general or local enterprise, all money placed in the offering plate, unless otherwise indicated by the donor, shall be counted as part of that particular offering.

Special Gifts to Fields—The financial support of the worldwide work of the church is based on the budget system. Appropriations are made to the various fields on the basis of budgeted needs. This is a fair and equitable method of distributing the funds. It ensures every field's receiving a just share. Where special gifts outside the regular budget plan are made to a particular field, a disparity is created to the disadvantage of all the other fields. If such gifts are given for the purpose of starting new work, the work thus started would languish when the special gift was used up, or it would have to be included in the budget for its future support. Thus other fields, with perhaps greater needs, but without the opportunity of making them known, would be deprived of their equitable part of general funds, which would be diverted to care for work started by special gifts. The entire history of this cause has proved over and over again the wisdom of having our members generously and loyally give their offerings and gifts through the accepted channels, with the satisfaction of knowing that every field shares in the benefits of such giving.

Assisting the Poor and Needy—Offerings for the poor and needy are taken to assist the members of the church who may require help. As far as possible a reserve should be kept in this fund for emergency cases. However, the church should take a benevolent attitude toward *all* in need, and the church board may make appropriations from the church fund for the needy to assist the health and welfare work carried on by the church for families in the community.

Church Budget for Local Expenses—The most satisfactory method of providing for local church expenses is the budget plan. Before the beginning of the new year, the church board should prepare a carefully drawn-up budget of expenses for the maintenance of church activities through the next annual period. This budget should make provision for all repairs, heat, light, janitor service (if paid for), church school expense and teacher's salary, fund for the poor and needy, et cetera. The budget should be presented to the church for its study and adoption, and for plans to assure that funds shall be provided to balance the budget during the coming year. Funds to meet the church expense budget may be raised by offerings and subscriptions. Every member in proportion to his/her financial circumstances should have a part in supporting the local church as well as the cause in general.

Sample Budget—The following budget will serve as an example. It can be adapted to meet the needs of a church of any size.

Church Budget

Estimated Receipts—

Sabbath School Expense Collections	$ 1,500.00
Church Fund for the Needy	375.00
Combined (Church) Budget Giving	27,055.00
Welfare Fund	300.00
	$29,230.00

Estimated Expenses—

Repairs and Painting Church Building	$ 2,250.00
Fuel	2,350.00
Janitor and Supplies	1,475.00
Insurance on Building and Furnishings	750.00
Church Fund for the Needy	1,450.00
Sabbath School Supplies	1,250.00
Emergency Expense	2,000.00
Light	3,220.00
Water	360.00
Gas	550.00
Stationery and Supplies	500.00
Laundry	75.00
Church School Subsidy	8,000.00
Welfare Expense	1,000.00
Church Planting	4,000.00
	$29,230.00

Provision should be made in each church's budget for all receipts and expenses, including those relating to the various departments.

General Counsel

On Solicitation of Funds—The matter of soliciting funds is covered in the following regulations:

1. No conference/mission/field, church, or institution, without special counsel and arrangement, shall plan work requiring solicitation of funds from outside its own territory. Any solicitation within its own territory shall be in harmony with local, union, and General Conference policies.

2. For the protection of churches from unauthorized and fraudulent and undenominational solicitation, the following principles and methods are recognized:

    a. Ministers and church officers shall not grant the privilege of the pulpit to persons for the raising of funds who have not recognition or recommendation from the conference/mission/field authorities. (See pp. 69, 137.)

    b. No permission shall be granted to solicit funds either publicly or privately without such recognition.

    c. Literature approved for solicitation purposes shall be provided only to responsible persons.

    d. All funds contributed for any cause in response to appeals shall be passed through the regular channels of the church.

    e. No authority is granted denominational workers representing special interests in one part of the field to solicit help for that work in any other part of the field or in any other conference/mission/field, without arrangement with and written authorization from the conference/mission/field officers.

    f. Conference/mission/field and church officers shall take such steps as may be necessary to prevent unauthorized or illegal public solicitation.

    3. No campaign other than the Ingathering, which involves using Ingathering literature and containers with Ingathering labels, shall be conducted for the solicitation of money for either home or overseas mission work. Union and local conferences/missions/fields should take such steps as may be necessary to prevent any violations of this regulation.

    4. Interdivision employees visiting the home churches or in touch with the home base by correspondence are asked to solicit funds only for enterprises included in the budget of appropriations, working in cooperation with churches and conferences/missions/fields to raise the funds required to meet the appropriations on which our world mission work depends. All such funds shall be passed through the regular channels.

    On Questionable Methods for Raising Church Funds—Seventh-day Adventists have always taken a strong stand against any and all methods of a questionable nature for raising money for local or general work.

    "When money is raised for religious purposes, to what means do many churches resort? To bazaars, suppers, fancy fairs, even to lotteries and like devices. Often the place set apart for God's worship is desecrated by feasting and drinking, buying, selling, and merrymaking. Respect for the house of God and reverence for His worship are lessened in the minds of the youth. The barriers of self-restraint are weakened. Selfishness, appetite, the love of display, are appealed to, and they strengthen as they are indulged."—*Testimonies*, vol. 9, p. 91.

    "As God's work extends, calls for help will come more and more frequently. That these calls may be answered, Christians should heed the command, 'Bring ye all the tithes into the storehouse, that there may be meat in Mine house.' Malachi 3:10. If professing Christians would faithfully bring to God their tithes and offerings, His treasury would be full. There would then be no occasion to resort to fairs, lotteries, or parties of pleasure to secure funds for the support of the gospel."—*The Acts of the Apostles*, p. 338.

On Tithes and Offerings Not a Personal Trust Fund—Tithes and offerings received by the church do not create a trust fund for the future benefit of the givers. These funds shall be used for the current purposes for which they are given.

On Avoiding Debt—A church board should always counsel with its conference/mission/field officers before incurring debt of any kind. Financial embarrassment has come to many churches through premature or improperly laid plans for the erection or purchase of church or school buildings. This may be avoided if a church seeks counsel before launching such an enterprise, and adheres to the denominational policy for the financing of such undertakings.

On Financing Church Buildings—Churches contemplating either the purchase or erection of church buildings are cautioned against undertaking financial obligations which would be likely to embarrass the membership; and concerning such undertaking, local and union committees shall give careful counsel in each case, taking into consideration the size of the congregation, its financial strength, and the location of the building.

In the purchase or building of church properties, in no case shall commitments be made or building operations be begun until approval has been given by the local conference/mission/field and union conference/mission committees, after these have assured themselves that the financial arrangements are in line with established policies.

On Handling and Accounting for Funds—The gathering and handling of funds for the Lord's work is a sacred responsibility. The proper channel through which these funds flow is first from the individual member to the local church. The church treasurer receives these funds. (See p. 58-62.) The funds intended for local church purposes are disbursed accordingly. Those intended for conference/mission/field use or general purposes the church treasurer passes on to the conference/mission/field treasurer. The conference/mission/field treasurer in turn disburses the funds of the conference/mission/field, but passes on to the union conference/mission treasurer the funds intended for union conference/mission use or for general purposes. The union conference/mission treasurer disburses the funds intended for union conference/mission use, but passes on to either the division or the General Conference treasurer all funds given for general purposes. All these treasurers, from the local church to the General Conference, work under the direction of either the church board or conference/mission/field committees. They do not disburse funds independently of specific action by responsible committees.

On Auditing—Every set of books, from those of the local church treasurer and the Personal Ministries secretary to those of the General Conference treasurer, are subject to audit by auditors appointed for the purpose. This rule of auditing is also applied to the books of every denominationally operated institution. It provides the maximum of safety in the handling of funds. (p. 61.)

CHAPTER 13

Standards of Christian Living

The High Calling of God in Christ Jesus

The Christian's life is not a slight modification or improvement, but a complete transformation of nature. This means a death to self and sin and a resurrection to a new life as a new person in Christ Jesus.

The heart of the Christian becomes the dwelling place of Christ by faith. This is brought about by "the contemplation of Christ, beholding Christ, ever cherishing the dear Saviour as our very best and honored Friend, so that we would not in any action grieve and offend Him." Thus it is that Christians "have the companionship of the divine presence," and it is only as we realize that presence that "our thoughts are brought into captivity to Jesus Christ" (*Testimonies to Ministers*, pp. 387, 388) and our habits of life made to conform to the divine standard.

We should bear in mind that "as a shield from temptation and an inspiration to purity and truth, no other influence can equal the sense of God's presence."— *Education*, p. 255.

A similar thought is expressed in *Patriarchs and Prophets*, pages 217, 218: "If we were to cherish an habitual impression that God sees and hears all that we do and say and keeps a faithful record of our words and actions, and that we must meet it all, we would fear to sin. Let the young ever remember that wherever they are, and whatever they do, they are in the presence of God. No part of our conduct escapes observation. We cannot hide our ways from the Most High. . . . Every act, every word, every thought, is as distinctly marked as though there were only one person in the whole world, and the attention of heaven were centered upon him."

God's love extends to everyone, and to His children in particular. His ear is ever open to the appeals of His people, those who have turned from the world and given themselves to Him. Out of this sacred relationship grows a respect and a reverence which is manifested every day and everywhere. As Christians we are members of the royal family, children of the heavenly King. Therefore, we should say no word, perform no act, that would bring dishonor upon "that worthy name by the which ye are called." In every phase of life we should "study carefully the divine-human character, and constantly inquire, 'What would Jesus do were He in my

161

place?' This should be the measurement of our duty."—*The Ministry of Healing*, p. 491.

It is through the remnant church that God will make final demonstration to the entire universe of the adequacy of the gospel completely to save men and women from the power of sin. There is need today that as members of that church we should emphasize again the great standards of Christian conduct, and that we renew our allegiance to these God-given principles. All should come up to the high standards of the Christian life and be separated from the world. To this end we would emphasize the Lord's admonition: "Love not the world, neither the things that are in the world. If any man love the world, the love of the Father is not in him" (1 John 2:15).

Bible Study and Prayer

Spiritual life is maintained by spiritual food. The habit of devotional Bible study and prayer must be maintained if we are to perfect holiness. In a time when a great flood of reading matter pours forth from printing presses everywhere, when the very ether is filled with thousands of voices, pleading for a hearing, it is incumbent upon us to close our eyes and our ears to much of that which is seeking entrance to our minds, and devote ourselves to God's book—the Book of all books, the Book of Life. If we cease to be the people of the Book, we are lost, and our mission has failed. Only as we daily talk to God in prayer and listen to His voice speaking to us from the Bible, can we hope to live the life that is "hid with Christ in God" (Col. 3:3), or finish His work.

Prayer is a two-way conversation in which believers listen to God and talk to Him. "Prayer is the opening of the heart to God as to a friend."— *Steps to Christ*, p. 93. "Through sincere prayer we are brought into connection with the mind of the Infinite," but "without unceasing prayer and diligent watching we are in danger of growing careless and of deviating from the right path."—*Steps to Christ*, pp. 97, 95.

The home is the cornerstone of the church, and a Christian home is a house of prayer. "Fathers and mothers" says the Spirit of Prophecy, "however pressing your business, do not fail to gather your family around God's altar. . . . Those who would live patient, loving, cheerful lives must pray."—*The Ministry of Healing*, p. 393.

Community Relationships

While our "citizenship is in heaven; from whence also we wait for a Saviour" (Phil. 3:20, RV), we are yet in the world as an integral part of human society, and must share with our fellows certain responsibilities in the common problems of life. In every community where they live Seventh-day Adventists, as children of God, should be recognized as outstanding citizens in their Christian integrity and in working for the common good of all. While our highest responsibility is to the church and its commission to preach the gospel of the kingdom to all the world, we should support by our service and our means, as far as possible and consistent, all proper efforts for social order and betterment. Even though we must stand apart from all political and social strife, we should always, quietly and firmly, maintain an uncompromising stand for justice and right in civic affairs, along with strict adherence to our religious convictions. It is our sacred responsibility to be loyal citizens of the governments to which we belong, rendering "unto Caesar the things which are Caesar's; and unto God the things that are God's" (Matt. 22:21).

Sabbathkeeping

The sacred institution of the Sabbath is a token of God's love to humanity. It is a memorial of God's power in the original creation and also a sign of His power to recreate and sanctify the life (Eze. 20:12), and its observance is an evidence of our loyalty to Him. The proper observance of the Sabbath is an evidence of our fidelity to our Creator and of fellowship with our Redeemer. In a special sense the observance of the Sabbath is a test of obedience. Unless we can pass that test as individuals, how can we adequately present the Sabbath message to the world?

The Sabbath holds a very special place in the lives of Seventh-day Adventists. The seventh day of the week, from sunset Friday to sunset Saturday (Lev. 23:32), is a gift from God, a sign of His grace in time. It is a privilege, a special appointment with the One who loves us and whom we love, a sacred time set aside by God's eternal law, a day of delight for worshiping God and sharing with others (Isa. 58:13). The believer welcomes the Sabbath with joy and gratitude. "God's love has set a limit to the demands of toil. Over the Sabbath He places His merciful hand. In His own day He preserves for the family opportunity for communion with Him, with nature, and with one another."—*Education*, p. 251.

The Sabbath hours belong to God, and are to be used for Him alone. Our own pleasure, our own words, our own business, our own thoughts, should find no place in the observance of the Lord's day (Isa. 58:13). Let us gather round the family circle at sunset and welcome the holy Sabbath with prayer and song, and let us close the day with prayer and expressions of gratitude for His wondrous love. The Sabbath is a special day for worship in the home and in the church, a day of joy to ourselves and our children, a day in which to learn more of God through the Bible and the great lesson book of nature. It is a time to visit the sick and to work for the salvation of souls. The ordinary affairs of the six working days should be laid aside. No unnecessary work should be performed. Secular reading or secular broadcasts should not occupy our time on God's holy day. "The Sabbath is not intended to be a period of useless inactivity. The law forbids secular labor on the rest day of the Lord; the toil that gains a livelihood must cease; no labor for worldly pleasure or profit is lawful upon that day; but as God ceased His labor of creating, and rested upon the Sabbath and blessed it, so man is to leave the occupations of his daily life, and devote those sacred hours to healthful rest, to worship, and to holy deeds."—*The Desire of Ages*, p. 207.

A rightly directed program of activities in harmony with the spirit of true Sabbathkeeping will make this blessed day the happiest and best of all the week, for ourselves and for our children—a veritable foretaste of our heavenly rest.

Reverence for the Place of Worship

Christians who appreciate God's omnipotence, His holiness, and His love will always and under all circumstances manifest a spirit of deep reverence for God, His word, and His worship. "Humanity and reverence should characterize the deportment of all who come into the presence of God."—*Patriarchs and Prophets*, p. 252. They will recognize that "the hour and place of prayer are sacred, because God is there."—*Gospel Workers*, p. 178. They will come to the house of worship, not carelessly, but in the spirit of meditation and prayer, and will avoid unnecessary conversation.

Parents should reverently instruct their children as to how they should behave in "the house of God" (1 Tim. 3:15). Faithful instruction and discipline in the home, Sabbath School, and church during the days of childhood and youth in regard to reverence for God and His worship will go far in holding their loyalty in after years.

The minister who senses the sacredness of God's service will, by his example, instruction, and conduct in the pulpit, foster reverence, simplicity, good order, and decorum in the church. "But the Lord is in his holy temple: let all the earth keep silence before him" (Hab. 2:20).

Health and Temperance

The body is the temple of the Holy Spirit (1 Cor. 6:9). "Both mental and spiritual vigor are in great degree dependent upon physical strength and activity; whatever promotes physical health, promotes the development of a strong mind and a well-balanced character."—*Education*, p. 195. For this reason, Seventh-day Adventists take care to live intelligently in accordance with health principles of physical exercise, respiration, sunshine, pure air, use of water, sleep, and rest. By conviction, they choose to eat healthfully, freely choosing to follow the principles of health, of self-control, and of wholesome diet. Therefore, they abstain from all forms of alcohol, tobacco, and addictive drugs. They strive to preserve their physical and psychological balance by avoiding any excess.

Health reform and the teaching of health and temperance are inseparable parts of the Advent message. Instruction came to us through the Lord's chosen messenger "that those who are keeping His commandments must be brought into sacred relationship to Himself, and that by temperance in eating and drinking they must keep mind and body in the most favorable condition for service."—*Counsels on Health*, pp. 132, 133. Also, "it is the Lord's design that the restoring influence of health reform shall be a part of the last great effort to proclaim the gospel message."—*Medical Ministry*, p. 259.

We belong to God, body, soul, and spirit. It is therefore our religious duty to observe the laws of health, both for our own well-being and happiness and for more efficient service to God and our fellow men. The appetite must be kept under control. Health is promoted by an intelligent observance of the hygienic principles having to do with pure air, ventilation, suitable clothing, cleanliness, proper exercise and recreation, adequate sleep and rest, and an adequate, wholesome diet. God has furnished man with a liberal variety of foods sufficient to satisfy every dietary need. Fruits, grains, nuts, and vegetables prepared in simple ways "make, with milk or cream, the most healthful diet."—*Christian Temperance and Bible Hygiene*, p. 47.

When the principles of healthful living are practiced the need for stimulants will not be felt. The use of intoxicants and narcotics of any kind is forbidden by nature's law. From the early days of this movement abstinence from the use of liquor and tobacco has been a condition of membership in the Seventh-day Adventist Church. (See pp. 16, 33, 34, 185, 211.)

God has given us great light on the principles of health, and modern scientific research has abundantly verified these principles. These cannot be safely ignored, for we are told that those "who choose to follow their own preferences in this matter, eating and drinking as they please, will gradually grow careless of the instruction the Lord has given regarding other phases of the present truth and will lose their perception of what is truth; . . ."—*Testimonies*, vol. 9, pp. 156, 157.

Dress

As Seventh-day Adventists we have been called out from the world. We are reformers. True religion which enters into every phase of life must have a molding influence on all our activities. Our habits of life must stem from principle and not from the example of the world about us. Customs and fashions may change with the years, but principles of right conduct are always the same. Dress is an important factor in Christian character. Early in our history instruction was given as to the way Christians should dress, the purpose of which was "to protect the people of God from the corrupting influence of the world, as well as to promote physical and moral health, . . ."—*Testimonies*, vol. 4, p. 634. Truly a comprehensive purpose! There is no virtue in dressing differently from those about us just to be different, but where the principles of refinement or morality are involved the conscientious Christian will be true to his/her convictions rather than follow the prevailing customs.

Christians should avoid gaudy display and "profuse ornamentation." Clothing should be, when possible, "of good quality, of becoming colors, and suited for service. It should be chosen for durability rather than display." Our attire should be characterized by "modesty," "beauty," "grace," and "appropriateness of natural simplicity." —*Messages to Young People*, pp. 351, 352. That it may not be conspicuous, it should follow the conservative and most sensible styles of the time.

The adoption of fads and extreme fashions in men's or women's dress indicates a lack of attention to serious matters. Regardless of how sensibly people generally may dress, there are always extremes in style that transgress the laws of modesty and thus have a direct bearing on the prevalence of immoral conditions. Many who blindly follow the styles are at least partly unconscious of these effects, but the results are no less disastrous. The people of God should always be found among the conservatives in dress, and will not let "the dress question fill the mind."—*Evangelism*, p. 273. They will not be the first to adopt the new styles of dress or the last to lay the old aside.

"To dress plainly, abstaining from display of jewelry and ornaments of every kind, is in keeping with our faith."—*Testimonies*, vol. 3, p. 366. It is clearly taught in the Scriptures that the wearing of jewelry is contrary to the will of God. ". . . not with broided hair, or gold, or pearls, or costly array" is the admonition of the apostle Paul (1 Tim. 2:9). The wearing of ornaments of jewelry is a bid for attention which is not in keeping with Christian self-forgetfulness.

In some countries the custom of wearing the wedding ring is considered imperative, having become, in the minds of the people, a criterion of virtue, and hence it is not regarded as an ornament. Under such circumstances we have no disposition to condemn the practice.

Let us remember that it is not the "outward adorning" which expresses true Christian character, but "the hidden man of the heart . . . a meek and quiet spirit, which is in the sight of God of great price" (1 Peter 3:3, 4). The use of cosmetics not in keeping with good taste and the principles of Christian modesty should be avoided. Cleanliness and Christlike deportment should be observed in the care and grooming of the individual who is seeking at all times to please and rightly represent Christ our Lord.

Christian parents should bring to bear the weight of their example, instruction, and authority to lead their sons and daughters to attire themselves modestly, and thus win the respect and confidence of those who know them. Let our people consider themselves well dressed only when the demands of modesty are met in the wearing of tasteful, conservative clothing.

Simplicity

Simplicity has been a fundamental feature of the Seventh-day Adventist Church from its foundation. We must continue to be a plain people. Increase of pomp in religion always parallels a decline in spiritual power. As "the life of Jesus presented a marked contrast" to the display and ostentation of His time (*Education*, p. 77), so the simplicity and power of the Advent message must be in marked contrast to the worldly display of our day. The Lord condemns "needless, extravagant expenditure of money to gratify pride and love of display."—*Testimonies to Ministers*, p. 179. In harmony with these principles, simplicity and economy should characterize our graduating exercises, the weddings in our churches, and all other church services.

Reading

Like the body, the inner being also needs wholesome nourishment for renewal and strengthening (2 Cor. 4:6). The mind is the measure of the person. Food for the mind is therefore of the utmost importance in developing character and in carrying out our life's purposes. For this reason our mental habits should be carefully checked. There is no better index to character than what we choose to read and hear. Books and other literature are among the most valuable means of education and culture, but these must be well chosen and rightly used. There is a wealth of good literature, both books and periodicals; but equally there is a flood of evil literature, often in most attractive guise but damaging to mind and morals. The tales of wild adventure and of moral laxness, whether fact or fiction, which are presented in print or other communication media are unfit for the youth or adult.

"Those who indulge the habit of racing through an exciting story are simply crippling their mental strength, and disqualifying their minds for vigorous thought and research."—*Counsels to Parents, Teachers, and Students*, p. 135. Along with other evil results from the habit of reading fiction, we are told that "it unfits the soul to contemplate the great problems of duty and destiny," and "creates a distaste for life's practical duties."—*Counsels to Parents, Teachers, and Students*, p. 383.

Radio and Television

Radio and television have changed the whole atmosphere of our modern world and have brought us within easy contact with the life, thought, and activities of the entire globe. Radio and television are great educational agencies. By these means we can greatly enlarge our knowledge of world events and enjoy important discussions and the best in music.

Unfortunately, however, radio and television also bring to their audiences almost continuous theatrical performances and many influences that are neither wholesome nor uplifting. If we are not discriminating and decisive, radio and television will turn our homes into theaters and minstrel shows of a cheap and sordid kind.

Safety for ourselves and our children is found in a determination, by God's help, to follow the admonition of the apostle Paul: "Finally, brethren, whatsoever things are true, whatsoever things are honest, whatsoever things are just, whatsoever things are pure, whatsoever things are lovely, whatsoever things are of good report; if there be any virtue, and if there be any praise, think on these things" (Phil. 4:8).

Recreation and Entertainment

Recreation is a purposeful refreshing of the powers of body and mind. A vigorous, wholesome mind will not require worldly amusement, but will find a renewal of strength in good recreation.

"Many of the amusements popular in the world today, even with those who claim to be Christians, tend to the same end as did those of the heathen. There are indeed few among them that Satan does not turn to account in destroying souls. Through the drama he has worked for ages to excite passion and glorify vice. The opera, with its fascinating display and bewildering music, the masquerade, the dance, the card table, Satan employs to break down the barriers of principle and open the door to sensual indulgence. In every gathering for pleasure where pride is fostered or appetite indulged, where one is led to forget God and lose sight of eternal interests, there Satan is binding his chains about the soul."—*Patriarchs and Prophets*, pp. 459, 460. (See p. 212.)

We earnestly warn against the subtle and sinister influence of the moving-picture theater, which is no place for the Christian. Dramatized films that graphically present by portrayal and by suggestion the sins and crimes of humanity—murder, adultery, robbery, and kindred evils—are in no small degree responsible for the present breakdown of morality. We appeal to parents, children, and youth to shun those places of amusement and those theatrical films that glorify professional acting and actors. If we will find delight in God's great world of nature and in the romance of human agencies and divine workings, we shall not be attracted by the puerile portrayals of the theater.

Another form of amusement that has an evil influence is social dancing. "The amusement of dancing, as conducted at the present day, is a school of depravity, a fearful curse to society."—*Messages to Young People*, p. 399. (See 2 Cor. 6:15-18; 1 John 2:15-17; James 4:4; 2 Tim. 2:19-22; Eph. 5:8-11; Col. 3:5-10.)

Let us not patronize the commercialized amusements, joining with the worldly, careless, pleasure-loving multitudes who are "lovers of pleasures more than lovers of God."

Recreation is essential. We should endeavor to make the friendships and recreations of our people church centered. We recommend that in every home where there are children, materials be provided which will afford an outlet for the creative energies of youth. Wholesome association and recreation may be provided through music organizations, AJY class projects, and outreach (missionary) service bands.

Music

"Music was made to serve a holy purpose, to lift the thoughts to that which is pure, noble, and elevating, and to awaken in the soul devotion and gratitude to God."—*Patriarchs and Prophets*, p. 594. Jesus "held communion with heaven in song."—*The Desire of Ages*, p. 73.

Music is one of the highest arts. Good music not only gives pleasure but elevates the mind and cultivates the finest qualities. Spiritual songs have often been used of God to touch the hearts of sinners and lead to repentance. Debased music, on the contrary, destroys the rhythm of the soul and breaks down morality.

Great care should be exercised in the choice of music. Any melody partaking of the nature of jazz, rock, or related hybrid forms, or any language expressing foolish or trivial sentiments, will be shunned by persons of true culture. Let us use only good music in the home, in the social gathering, in the school, and in the church. (See p. 70.)

Social Relationships

The social instinct is given us of God, for our pleasure and benefit. ". . . by mutual contact minds receive polish and refinement; by social intercourse, acquaintances are formed and friendships contracted which result in a unity of heart and an atmosphere of love which is pleasing in the sight of heaven."—*Testimonies*, vol. 6, p. 172. Proper association of the sexes is beneficial to both. Such associations should be conducted upon a high plane and with due regard to the conventions and restrictions which, for the protection of society and the individual, have been prescribed. It is the purpose of Satan, of course, to pervert every good thing; and the perversion of the best often leads to that which is worst. So it is highly important that Christians should adhere to very definite standards of social life.

Today the ideals that make these social relationships safe and happy are breaking down to an alarming degree. Under the influence of passion unrestrained by moral and religious principle, the association of the sexes has to an alarming extent degenerated into freedom and license. Sexual perversions, incest, and sexual abuse of children prevail to an alarming degree. Millions have abandoned Christian standards of conduct and are bartering the sweet and sacred experiences of marriage and parenthood for the bitter, remorseful fruits of lust. Not only are these evils damaging the familial structure of society, but the breakdown of the family in turn fosters and breeds these and other evils. The results in distorted lives of children and youth are distressing and evoke our pity, while the effects on society are not only disastrous but cumulative.

These evils have become more open and threatening to the ideals and purposes of the Christian home. Adultery, sexual abuse of spouses, incest, sexual abuse of children, homosexual practices, and lesbian practices are among the obvious perversions of God's original plan. As the intent of clear passages of Scripture (see Ex. 20:14; Lev. 18:22, 29 and 20:13; 1 Cor. 6:9; 1 Tim. 1:10; Rom. 1:20-32) is denied and as their warnings are rejected in exchange for human opinions, much uncertainty and confusion prevail. This is what Satan desires. It has always been his plan to cause people to forget that God is their Creator and that when He "created man in His own image" He created them "male and female" (Gen. 1:27). The world is witnessing today a resurgence of the perversions of ancient civilizations.

The degrading results of the world's obsession with sex and the love and pursuit of sensual pleasure are clearly delineated in the Word of God. But Christ came to destroy the works of the devil and reestablish the relationship of human beings with their Creator. Thus, though fallen in Adam and captive to sin, those who are in Christ receive full pardon and the right to choose anew the better way, the way to complete renewal. By means of the cross and the power of the Holy Spirit, all may be freed from the grip of sinful practices as they are restored to the image of their Creator.

It is incumbent upon the parents and the spiritual guides of the youth to face with no false modesty the facts of social conditions, to gain more fully a sympathetic understanding of the problems of this generation of young people, to seek most earnestly to provide for them the best environment, and to draw so near to them in spirit as to be able to impart the ideals of life and the inspiration and power of Christian religion, that they may be saved from the evil that is in the world through lust.

But to our young men and young women we say, The responsibility is yours. Whatever may be the mistakes of parents, it is your privilege to know and to hold the highest ideals of Christian manhood and womanhood. Reverent Bible study, a deep acquaintance with the works of nature, stern guarding of the sacred powers of the body, earnest purpose, constancy in prayer, and sincere, unselfish ministry to others' needs will build a character that is proof against evil and that will make you an uplifting influence in society.

Social gatherings for old and young should be made occasions, not for light and trifling amusement, but for happy fellowship and improvement of the powers of mind and soul. Good music, elevating conversation, good recitations, suitable still or motion pictures, games carefully selected for their educational value, and, above all, the making and using of plans for outreach (missionary) effort can provide programs for social gatherings that will bless and strengthen the lives of all. The Youth Department of the General Conference has published helpful information and practical suggestions for the conduct of social gatherings and for guidance in other social relations.

The homes of the church are by far the best places for social gatherings. In large centers where it is impossible to hold them there, and where there is no social center of our own, a proper place free from influences destructive to Christian standards should be secured rather than a place that is ordinarily used for commercial amusements and sports, such as social halls and skating rinks, which suggest an atmosphere contrary to Christian standards.

Chaperonage

The happy and cordial association of those older in years with the young people is one of the most wholesome influences in the lives of children and youth. "There is danger that both parents and teachers . . . fail to come sufficiently into social relation with their children or scholars."—*Counsels to Parents, Teachers, and Students*, p. 76. It is the duty of our schools and other institutions to care for the morals and reputation of those placed in their charge. Chaperonage is an obligatory duty with them. It is equally the duty of the home. Parents should strongly sustain the regulations of the institutions in which their youth and children are placed, and should institute in their homes equal safeguards. To make this possible, it is their duty to learn how to be welcome companions of their children; but it rests chiefly upon the young people themselves to make of chaperonage not an irksome and repugnant association but an honored and happy relationship.

Courtship and Marriage

Courtship is recognized as a preparatory period during which a man and a woman, already mutually attracted, become more thoroughly acquainted with each other in preparation for intended marriage. Christian marriage is a divinely sanctioned union between a believing man and a believing woman for the fulfillment of their mutual love, for mutual support, for shared happiness, and for the procreation and rearing of children who will in turn become Christians. According to God's design, this union lasts until dissolved by the death of one of the partners.

Marriage is the foundation of human society, and true affection between man and woman is ordained of God. "Let those who are contemplating marriage weigh every sentiment and watch every development of character in the one with whom they think to unite their life destiny. Let every step toward a marriage alliance be characterized by modesty, simplicity, sincerity, and an earnest purpose to please and honor God. Marriage affects the afterlife both in this world and in the world to come. A sincere Christian will make no plans that God cannot approve."—*The Ministry of Healing*, p. 359.

The failure to follow these principles in Christian courtship may lead to tragedy. Unity of husband and wife in ideals and purposes is a requisite to a happy and successful home. The Scriptures counsel, "Be ye not unequally yoked together with unbelievers" (2 Cor. 6:14). Differences regarding religion are likely to mar the happiness of a home where partners hold different beliefs and lead to confusion, perplexity, and failure in the rearing of children.

"The family tie is the closest, the most tender and sacred, of any on earth. It was designed to be a blessing to mankind. And it is a blessing wherever the marriage covenant is entered into intelligently, in the fear of

God, and with due consideration for its responsibilities."—*The Adventist Home*, p. 18.

Worship of God, Sabbathkeeping, recreation, association, use of financial resources, and training of children are responsible components of happy family relationships. Because differences in these areas can often lead to a deterioration of these relationships, to discouragement, and even to a complete loss of Christian experience, an adequate preparation for marriage should include premarital pastoral counseling in these areas.

"'Can two walk together, except they be agreed?' (Amos 3:3). The happiness and prosperity of the marriage relation depends upon the unity of the parties; but between the believer and the unbeliever there is a radical difference of tastes, inclinations, and purposes. They are serving two masters, between whom there can be no concord. However pure and correct one's principles may be, the influence of an unbelieving companion will have a tendency to lead away from God."—*Patriarchs and Prophets*, p. 174.

The Spirit of Prophecy consistently counsels against marriage between "the believer and the unbeliever" and further cautions against uniting with fellow Christians who have "not accepted the truth for this time."—*Testimonies*, vol. 5, p. 364. Marriages are more likely to endure and family life to fulfill the divine plan, if husband and wife are united and are bound together by common spiritual values and lifestyles. For these reasons, the Seventh-day Adventist Church strongly discourages marriage between a Seventh-day Adventist and a non-Seventh-day Adventist, and strongly urges Seventh-day Adventist ministers not to perform such weddings.

The church recognizes that it is the prerogative of the individual to make the final decision relative to the choice of a marriage partner. However, it is the hope of the church that, if the member chooses a marriage partner who is not a member of the church, the couple will realize and appreciate that the Seventh-day Adventist pastor, who has covenanted to uphold the principles outlined above, should not be expected to perform such a marriage. If an individual does enter into such a marriage, the church is to demonstrate love and concern with the purpose of encouraging the couple toward complete unity in Christ. (For further information on the subject of marriage, see Chapter 15, *Marriage, Divorce, and Remarriage*.)

Conclusion

Standing amid the perils of the last days, bearing the responsibility of speedily carrying the last offer of salvation to the world, and facing a judgment that will culminate in the establishment of universal righteousness, let us with true heart consecrate ourselves to God, body, soul, and spirit, determining to maintain the high standards of living that must characterize those who wait for the return of their Lord.

CHAPTER 14

Church Discipline

General Principles

The attention of all ministers, church officers, and members is called to the important quotations in this chapter from the Spirit of Prophecy. These statements are worthy of careful and prayerful study; they set forth in clear, unmistakable language the solemn responsibility that rests upon the people of God in maintaining the purity, the integrity, and the spiritual fervor of the church. If members grow cold and indifferent, the church must seek to arouse them from their lethargy. Should some be drifting away from the truth, efforts must be made to bring them back into the narrow way.

Dealing With Erring Members—"In dealing with erring church members, God's people are carefully to follow the instruction given by the Saviour in the eighteenth chapter of Matthew."—*Testimonies*, vol. 7, p. 260.

"Moreover if thy brother shall trespass against thee, go and tell him his fault between thee and him alone: if he shall hear thee, thou hast gained thy brother. But if he will not hear thee, then take with thee one or two more, that in the mouth of two or three witnesses every word may be established. And if he shall neglect to hear them, tell it unto the church: but if he neglect to hear the church, let him be unto thee as an heathen man and a publican. Verily I say unto you, Whatsoever ye shall bind on earth shall be bound in heaven: and whatsoever ye shall loose on earth shall be loosed in heaven" (Matt. 18:15-18).

"Human beings are Christ's property, purchased by Him at an infinite price, bound to Him by the love that He and His Father have manifested for them. How careful, then, we should be in our dealing with one another! Men have no right to surmise evil in regard to their fellow men. Church members have no right to follow their own impulses and inclinations in dealing with fellow members who have erred. They should not even express their prejudices regarding the erring, for thus they place in other minds the leaven of evil. Reports unfavorable to a brother or sister in the church are communicated from one to another of the church members. Mistakes are made and injustice is done because of an unwillingness on the part of some one to follow the directions given by the Lord Jesus.

"'If thy brother shall trespass against thee,' Christ declared, 'go and tell him his fault between thee and him alone.' Matthew 18:15. Do not tell others of the wrong. One person is told, then another, and still another; and continually the report grows, and the evil increases, till the whole church is made to suffer. Settle the matter 'between thee and him alone.' This is God's plan. 'Go not forth hastily to strive, lest thou know not what to do in the end thereof, when thy neighbor hath put thee to shame. Debate thy cause with thy neighbor himself; and discover not a secret to another.' Proverbs 25:8, 9. Do not suffer sin upon your brother; but do not expose him, and thus increase the difficulty, making the reproof seem like a revenge. Correct him in the way outlined in the word of God."— *Testimonies*, vol. 7, pp. 260, 261.

To Seek Reconciliation—"Do not suffer resentment to ripen into malice. Do not allow the wound to fester and break out in poisoned words, which taint the minds of those who hear. Do not allow bitter thoughts to continue to fill your mind and his. Go to your brother, and in humility and sincerity talk with him about the matter.

"Whatever the character of the offense, this does not change the plan that God has made for the settlement of misunderstandings and personal injuries. Speaking alone and in the spirit of Christ to the one who is in fault will often remove the difficulty. Go to the erring one, with a heart filled with Christ's love and sympathy, and seek to adjust the matter. Reason with him calmly and quietly. Let no angry words escape your lips. Speak in a way that will appeal to his better judgment. Remember the words: 'He which converteth the sinner from the error of his way shall save a soul from death, and shall hide a multitude of sins.' James 5:20.

"Take to your brother the remedy that will cure the disease of disaffection. Do your part to help him. For the sake of the peace and unity of the church, feel it a privilege as well as a duty to do this. If he will hear you, you have gained him as a friend.

"All heaven is interested in the interview between the one who has been injured and the one who is in error. As the erring one accepts the reproof offered in the love of Christ, and acknowledges his wrong, asking forgiveness from God and from his brother, the sunshine of heaven fills his heart. The controversy is ended; friendship and confidence are restored. The oil of love removes the soreness caused by the wrong. The Spirit of God binds heart to heart, and there is music in heaven over the union brought about."—*Testimonies*, vol. 7, pp. 261, 262.

"As those thus united in Christian fellowship offer prayer to God and pledge themselves to deal justly, to love mercy, and to walk humbly with God, great blessing comes to them. If they have wronged others they continue the work of repentance, confession, and restitution, fully set to do good to one another. This is the fulfilling of the law of Christ.

"'But if he will not hear thee, then take with thee one or two more, that in the mouth of two or three witnesses every word may be established.' Matthew 18:16. Take with you those who are spiritually minded, and talk with the one in error in regard to the wrong. He may yield to the united appeals of his brethren. As he sees their agreement in the matter his mind may be enlightened.

"'And if he shall neglect to hear them,' what then shall be done? Shall a few persons in a board meeting take upon themselves the responsibility of disfellowshiping the erring one? 'If he shall neglect to hear them, tell it unto *the church*.' Verse 17. Let the church take action in regard to its members."—*Testimonies,* vol. 7, p. 262.

"'But if he neglect to hear the church, let him be unto thee as an heathen man and a publican.' Verse 17. If he will not heed the voice of the church, if he refuses all the efforts made to reclaim him, upon the church rests the responsibility of separating him from fellowship. His name should then be stricken from the books.

"*No church officer should advise, no committee should recommend, nor should any church vote, that the name of a wrong doer shall be removed from the church books, until the instruction given by Christ has been faithfully followed.* When this instruction has been followed, the church has cleared herself before God. The evil must then be made to appear as it is, and must be removed, that it may not become more and more widespread. The health and purity of the church must be preserved, that she may stand before God unsullied, clad in the robes of Christ's righteousness. . . .

"'Verily I say unto you,' Christ continued, 'whatsoever ye shall bind on earth shall be bound in heaven: and whatsoever ye shall loose on earth shall be loosed in heaven.' Verse 18.

"This statement holds its force in all ages. On the church has been conferred the power to act in Christ's stead. It is God's instrumentality for the preservation of order and discipline among His people. To it the Lord has delegated the power to settle all questions respecting its prosperity, purity, and order. Upon it rests the responsibility of excluding from its fellowship those who are unworthy, who by their un-Christlike conduct would bring dishonor on the truth. Whatever the church does that is in accordance with the directions given in God's word will be ratified in heaven."—*Testimonies* , vol. 7, pp. 262, 263. (Italics supplied.)

"Matters of grave import come up for settlement by the church. God's ministers, ordained by Him as guides of His people, after doing their part are to submit the whole matter to the church, that there may be unity in the decision made.

"The Lord desires His followers to exercise great care in dealing with one another. They are to lift up, to restore, to heal. But there is to be in the church no neglect of proper discipline. The members are to regard themselves as pupils in a school, learning how to form characters worthy of their high calling. In the church here below, God's children are to be prepared for the great reunion in the church above. Those who here live in harmony with Christ may look forward to an endless life in the family of the redeemed."—*Testimonies*, vol. 7, pp. 263, 264.

The Authority of the Church—"The world's Redeemer has invested great power with His church. He states the rules to be applied in cases of trial with its members. After He has given explicit directions as to the course to be pursued, He says: 'Verily I say unto you, Whatsoever ye shall bind on earth shall be bound in heaven: and whatsoever [in church discipline] ye shall loose on earth shall be loosed in heaven.' Thus even the heavenly authority ratifies the discipline of the church in regard to its members when the Bible rule has been followed.

"The word of God does not give license for one man to set up his judgment in opposition to the judgment of the church, neither is he allowed to urge his opinions against the opinions of the church. If there were no church discipline and government, the church would go to fragments; it could not hold together as a body."—*Testimonies*, vol. 3, p. 428.

Church Responsible for Dealing With Sin—"God holds His people, as a body, responsible for the sins existing in individuals among them. If the leaders of the church neglect to diligently search out the sins which bring the displeasure of God upon the body, they become responsible for these sins."—*Testimonies*, vol. 3, p. 269.

"He would teach His people that disobedience and sin are exceedingly offensive to Him, and are not to be lightly regarded. He shows us that when His people are found in sin they should at once take decided measures to put that sin from them, that His frown may not rest upon them all. But if the sins of the people are passed over by those in responsible positions, His frown will be upon them, and the people of God, as a body, will be held responsible for those sins. In His dealings with His people in the past the Lord shows the necessity of purifying the church from wrongs. One sinner may diffuse darkness that will exclude the light of God from the entire congregation. When the people realize that darkness is settling upon them, and they do not know the cause, they should seek God earnestly, in great humility and self-abasement, until the wrongs which grieve His Spirit are searched out and put away. . . .

"If wrongs are apparent among His people, and if the servants of God pass on indifferent to them, they virtually sustain and justify the sinner, and are alike guilty and will just as surely receive the displeasure of God; for they will be made responsible for the sins of the guilty. In vision I have been pointed to many instances where the displeasure of God has been incurred by a neglect on the part of His servants to deal with the wrongs and sins existing among them. Those who have excused these wrongs have been thought by the people to be very amiable and lovely in disposition, simply because they shunned to discharge a plain Scriptural duty. The task was not agreeable to their feelings; therefore they avoided it."—*Testimonies*, vol. 3, pp. 265, 266.

Unconsecrated Resist Church Discipline—"There are many who do not have the discretion of Joshua and who have no special duty to search out wrongs and to deal promptly with the sins existing among them. Let not such hinder those who have the burden of this work upon them; let them not stand in the way of those who have this duty to do. Some make it a point to question and doubt and find fault because others do the work that God has not laid upon them. These stand directly in the way to hinder those upon whom God has laid the burden of reproving and correcting prevailing sins in order that His frown may be turned away from His people. Should a case like Achan's be among us, there are many who would accuse those who might act the part of Joshua in searching out the wrong, of having a wicked, faultfinding spirit. God is not to be trifled with and His warnings disregarded with impunity by a perverse people.

"I was shown that the manner of Achan's confession was similar to the confessions that some among us have made and will make. They hide their wrongs and refuse to make a voluntary confession until God searches them out, and then they acknowledge their sins. A few persons pass on in a course of wrong until they become hardened. They may even know that the church is burdened, as Achan knew that Israel were made weak before their enemies because of his guilt. Yet their consciences do not condemn them. They will not relieve the church by humbling their proud, rebellious hearts before God and putting away their wrongs. God's displeasure is upon His people, and He will not manifest His power in the midst of them while sins exist among them and are fostered by those in responsible positions.

"Those who work in the fear of God to rid the church of hindrances and to correct grievous wrongs, that the people of God may see the necessity of abhorring sin and may prosper in purity, and that the name of God may be glorified, will ever meet with resisting influences from the unconsecrated."—*Testimonies*, vol. 3, pp. 270, 271.

Rules and Regulations Necessary—"Brethren, never allow anyone's ideas to unsettle your faith in regard to the order and harmony which should exist in the church. . . . The God of heaven is a God of order, and He requires all His followers to have rules and regulations, and to preserve order."—*Testimonies*, vol. 5, p. 274.

Self-appointed Organizations—The church in its organized capacity is God's instrumentality for preserving order and discipline among His people. Its God-given message is borne to the world not only by the personal testimony of the individual member but in the corporate witness of the church as the body of Christ. Such corporate witness requires the recognized administrative structure that has been established with all duly elected officers and all properly organized channels of work such as the Sabbath School, Personal Ministries, Youth organizations, et cetera. It also acknowledges such self-supporting institutions whose activities contribute to the attainment of the church's objectives. Therefore, although all members have equal rights within the church, no individual member or group of members should start a movement or form an organization or seek to encourage a following for the attainment of any objective or for the teaching of any doctrine or message not in harmony with the fundamental religious objectives and teachings of the Seventh-day Adventist Church. Such a course would result in the fostering of a factional and divisive spirit, in the fragmenting of the effort and witness of the church, and thus in hindering it in the discharge of its obligations to its Head and to the world.

Safeguarding the Unity of the Church

Christians should make every effort to avoid tendencies that would divide them and bring dishonor to their cause. "It is the purpose of God that His children shall blend in unity. Do they not expect to live together in the same heaven? . . . Those who refuse to work in harmony greatly dishonor God."—*Testimonies*, vol. 8, p. 240. The church should discourage every action that would threaten harmony among its members and should consistently encourage unity.

Reconciliation of differences within the church and its membership should, in most cases, be possible without recourse either to a conciliation process provided by the church or to civil litigation. "If matters of difficulty between brethren were not laid open before others, but frankly spoken of between themselves in the spirit of Christian love, how much evil might be prevented! How many roots of bitterness whereby many are defiled would be destroyed, and how closely and tenderly might the followers of Christ be united in His love!"—*Thoughts From the Mount of Blessing*, p. 59. (See Matt. 18:15-18 and pp. 160-162.)

Settlement of Differences Among Members—Every effort should be made to settle differences among church members and contain the controversy within the smallest possible sphere. "Contentions, strife, and lawsuits between brethren are a disgrace to the cause of truth. Those who take such a course expose the church to the ridicule of her enemies and cause the powers of darkness to triumph. They are piercing the wounds of Christ afresh and putting Him to an open shame. By ignoring the authority of the church they show contempt for God, who gave to the church its authority."—*Testimonies*, vol. 5, pp. 242, 243.

Civil litigation is often carried on in a spirit of contention that results from and reveals human selfishness. It is this kind of adversary proceedings that must be discouraged by a church that seeks to exhibit the spirit of Christ. Christian unselfishness will lead followers of Christ to suffer themselves to be defrauded (1 Cor. 6:7) rather than to "go to law before the unjust, and not before the saints" (1 Cor. 6:1).

While there are, in the modern world, occasions for seeking decrees of civil courts, Christians should prefer settlement within the authority of the church, and should limit the seeking of such decrees to cases that are clearly within the jurisdiction of the civil courts and not within the authority of the church or for which the church agrees it has no adequate process for orderly settlement. Such suits before civil courts should never become revengeful adversary proceedings but should develop out of a desire to seek arbitration and to settle differences amicably. Examples of such cases may include, but are not limited to, the settlement of insurance claims, the issuance of decrees affecting the boundaries and ownership of real property, the deciding of some matters involving the administration of estates, and the awarding of custody of minor children. While the church should set up procedures within the constraints of legal practice to avoid the type of litigation referred to in 1 Corinthians 6, it should constantly be on guard against turning from its gospel mission and taking up the duties of a civil magistrate. (See Luke 12:13, 14 and *Testimonies*, vol. 9, pp. 216-218.)

God's ideal for members of His church is that they should, as far as possible, "live peaceably with all men" (Rom. 12:18). The church should use its readily accessible and reasonably prompt process by which many differences among members can be settled. Should the church fail to respond to a member's request for help in reconciling a difference, or if the church acknowledges that the nature of the case is such that it is not within its authority, it should be recognized that the member has exhausted the possibilities of the biblically outlined procedure for the settlement of differences and that what he/she should do beyond that point is a matter for his/her conscience. (See *The SDA Bible Commentary*, vol. 6, p. 698.)

However, when the church, endeavoring to assist in timely and amicable settlement of differences among its members, recommends a solution, they should not summarily reject the recommendation the church has offered. It is no light matter for a church member, outside the orderly processes of the church, to litigate a grievance against another church member. "Now therefore there is utterly a fault among you, because ye go to law one with another" (1 Cor. 6:7).

Church members who demonstrate impatience and selfishness by their unwillingness to wait for and accept recommendations of the church in the settlement of grievances against other church members may properly be subject to the discipline of the church (see p. 179) because of the disruptive effect on the church and their refusal to recognize properly constituted church authority.

Settlement of Grievances of Members Against the Church—The same principles that influence resolution of differences among members apply to the settlement of grievances of members against church organizations and institutions.

A church member should not instigate litigation against any entity of the church except under circumstances where the church has not provided adequate process for orderly settlement of the grievance within the church, or where the nature of the case is such that it is clearly not within the authority of the church to settle.

Settlement of Grievances of the Church Against Members—There may be times when church organizations or institutions will have grievances against church members. At such times, church administrators must, in Christian forbearance, keep in mind the biblical counsel for settling disputes among Christians and apply that counsel to the settlement of grievances of the church against its members. The church should, in preference to litigating matters in a secular court, make every reasonable effort in cooperation with the member to provide a process by which orderly settlement of the problem can be accomplished.

Administering Discipline

If a member falls into sin, sincere efforts must be made for reclamation. "If the erring one repents and submits to Christ's discipline, he is to be given another trial. And even if he does not repent, even if he stands outside the church, God's servants still have a work to do for him. They are to seek earnestly to win him to repentance. And, however aggravated may have been his offense, if he yields to the striving of the Holy Spirit and, by confessing and forsaking his sin, gives evidence of repentance, he is to be forgiven and welcomed to the fold again. His brethren are to encourage him in the right way, treating him as they would wish to be treated were they in his place, considering themselves lest they also be tempted."—*Testimonies, vol. 7*, p. 263.

"We are nearing the judgment, and those who bear the message of warning to the world must have clean hands and pure hearts. They must have a living connection with God. The thoughts must be pure and holy, the soul untainted, the body, soul, and spirit be a pure, clean offering to God, or He will not accept it."—*Testimonies to Ministers*, p. 426.

"Sin and sinners in the church must be promptly dealt with, that others may not be contaminated. Truth and purity require that we make more thorough work to cleanse the camp from Achans. Let those in responsible positions not suffer sin in a brother. Show him that he must either put away his sins or be separated from the church."—*Testimonies*, vol. 5, p. 147.

When grievous sins are involved disciplinary measures must be taken. There are two ways by which this may be done:

1. By a vote of censure.
2. By a vote to remove from church membership.

There may be cases where the offense is not considered by the church to be so serious as to warrant the extreme course of removing the offending member from church membership, yet it may be sufficiently serious to call for an expression of disapproval. Such disapproval may be expressed by a vote of censure.

Censure has a twofold purpose:

1. To enable the church to express its disapproval of a grievous offense that has brought disgrace upon the cause of God.
2. To impress the offending member with the need for amendment of life and reformation in conduct; also to extend to the individual a period of grace and probation during which these steps might be taken.

Discipline by Censure

An erring member may be placed under censure by a vote of the church at any duly called business meeting of the church, provided the member concerned has been notified. The individual may be present if he/she so desires. A vote of censure is for a stated period of time, from a minimum of one month to a maximum of twelve months; it terminates the erring one's election or appointment to any and all offices he/she may hold in the church and removes the privilege of election to office while under censure. A member under censure has no right to participate by voice or by vote in the affairs of the church and can have no public part in the exercises thereof, such as teaching a Sabbath School class, et cetera. Neither may the individual's membership be transferred to another church during the period of censure. He/She is not deprived, however, of the privilege of sharing the blessings of Sabbath School, church worship, or the ordinances of the Lord's house. A vote of censure must not carry any provision involving severance of church membership in case of failure to comply with any conditions imposed. Proper inquiry should be made at the expiration of the period of censure to ascertain whether the member under discipline has changed course. If observed conduct is satisfactory, the individual may then be considered in regular standing without further action. If observed conduct is not satisfactory, the case should again be considered and such discipline administered as is required. Any return to church office must be by election.

Discipline By Removal From Church Membership

Removing an individual from membership in the church, the body of Christ, is always a serious matter; it is the ultimate in the discipline that the church can administer; it is the extreme measure that can be meted out by the church. *Only after the instruction given in this chapter has been followed, and after all possible efforts have been made to win and restore him/her to right paths,* should this kind of discipline be used. It would be advisable to secure counsel from the pastor of the church or, if he is not available, from the conference/mission/field president before any action is taken by the church, when such a step is contemplated.

Reasons for Which Members Shall be Disciplined

Among the grievous sins for which members shall be subject to church discipline are the following:

1. Denial of faith in the fundamentals of the gospel and in the cardinal doctrines of the church or teaching doctrines contrary to the same.

2. Violation of the law of God, such as worship of idols, murder, stealing, profanity, gambling, Sabbathbreaking, and willful and habitual falsehood.

3. Violation of the seventh commandment of the law of God as it relates to the marriage institution, the Christian home, and biblical standards of moral conduct.

4. Such violations as fornication, promiscuity, incest, homosexual practice, sexual abuse of children and vulnerable adults, and other sexual perversions, and the remarriage of a divorced person, except of the spouse

who has remained faithful to the marriage vow in a divorce for adultery or for sexual perversions.

5. Physical violence, including violence within the family.

6. Fraud or willful misrepresentation in business.

7. Disorderly conduct which brings reproach upon the cause.

8. Adhering to or taking part in a divisive or disloyal movement or organization. (See p. 180.)

9. Persistent refusal to recognize properly constituted church authority or to submit to the order and discipline of the church.

10. The use, manufacture, or sale of alcoholic beverages.

11. The use, manufacture, or sale of tobacco in any of its forms for human consumption.

12. The misuse of, or trafficking in, narcotics or other drugs.

The Seventh-day Adventist Church recognizes the need of exercising great care to protect the highest spiritual interests of its members, to ensure fair treatment, and to safeguard the name of the church.

In a case of transgression of the commandments of God where there is deep repentance and full and free confession, giving evidence that genuine conversion has taken place, the church may administer discipline by placing the transgressor under censure for a stated period of time.

However, in a case of flagrant violations of the law of God which have brought public reproach upon the cause, the church may deem it necessary, even though a sincere confession has been made, to remove an individual from church membership to protect its name and its Christian standards. Later, when it is evident that the individual's life is consistent with church standards, the offender may be received back into the fold after rebaptism. The church cannot afford to deal lightly with such sins nor permit personal considerations to affect its actions. It must register its decisive and emphatic disapproval of the sins of fornication, adultery, all acts of moral indiscretion, and other grievous sins; at the same time it must do everything to restore and reclaim the erring ones. As the world continually grows more lax in moral matters, the church must not lower the standards set by God.

Timeliness in the Disciplinary Process

It is the duty of the church to care for the disciplinary process within a reasonable time and then communicate its decisions with kindness and promptness. The application of discipline is a painful process in itself. One thing that increases the frustration and the suffering of the individual member and the local church itself is the delay in administering the discipline.

Caution in Disciplining Members

"Christ has plainly taught that those who persist in open sin must be separated from the church, but He has not committed to us the work of judging character and motive. He knows our nature too well to entrust this work to us. Should we try to uproot from the church those whom we suppose to be spurious Christians, we should be sure to make mistakes. Often we regard as hopeless subjects the very ones whom Christ is drawing to Himself. Were we to deal with these souls according to our imperfect judgment, it would perhaps extinguish their last hope. Many who think themselves Christians will at last be found wanting. Many will be in heaven who their neighbors supposed would never enter there. Man judges from appearance, but God judges the heart. The tares and the wheat are to grow together until the harvest; and the harvest is the end of probationary time.

"There is in the Saviour's words another lesson, a lesson of wonderful forbearance and tender love. As the tares have their roots closely intertwined with those of the good grain, so false brethren in the church may be closely linked with true disciples. The real character of these pretended believers is not fully manifested. Were they to be separated from the church, others might be caused to stumble, who but for this would have remained steadfast."—*Christ's Object Lessons*, pp. 71, 72.

Ministers or Churches Not to Establish Tests of Fellowship—A minister, an individual church, or a conference/mission/field does not have the authority to set up or establish tests of fellowship for the denomination. This authority rests with the entire church body and is exercised through the regularly constituted organization of the church in the General Conference. Anyone seeking to apply tests other than those herein set forth does not, therefore, properly represent the church.

"God is leading out a people, not a few separate individuals here and there, one believing this thing, another that. Angels of God are doing the work committed to their trust. The third angel is leading out and purifying a people, and they should move with him unitedly. Some run ahead of the angels that are leading this people; but they have to retrace every step, and meekly follow no faster than the angels lead."—*Testimonies*, vol. 1, p. 207.

At a Duly Called Meeting—Members may be disciplined by the church for sufficient cause, but only at a duly called business meeting of the church after the church board has reviewed the case. The meeting must be presided over by an ordained minister or a licensed minister who is ordained as a local elder of the church concerned or, in his absence and in counsel with him or with the conference/mission/field president, a local ordained elder of the church concerned.

Majority Vote—Members may be removed from church membership or otherwise disciplined only by a majority vote of the members present and voting at a duly called meeting. ". . . the majority of the church is a power which should control its individual members."—*Testimonies*, vol. 5, p. 107.

Church Board Cannot Remove From Church Membership—The church board may recommend to the church in a business meeting the removal of a member from church membership, but under no circumstances does a church board have the right to take final action. Except in the case of the death of a member, the clerk of the church can remove a name from the church records only on a vote of the church in a business meeting.

Right of the Member to be Heard in Defense—It is a fundamental principle of justice that every member has the right to be heard in his/her own defense and to introduce evidence and produce witnesses. No church should vote to remove a member from church membership under circumstances that deprive an individual of this right, if one chooses to exercise it. Due notice should be given by the church to the member of its intention to consider the problem, thus giving the opportunity for the individual to appear.

Lawyers Not to Represent Members—The work of the church in its administration of order and discipline, is an ecclesiastical function and, in no sense, has to do with civil or legal procedure; therefore, the church does not recognize the right of any member to bring a lawyer to represent him/her in any church meeting or council called to administer order or discipline or for the transaction of any business relating to the church. Therefore, our members should be informed that they will not be given a hearing if they endeavor to bring a lawyer into the meeting for such a purpose. The church should also exclude all nonmembers from any church meeting or council called for the administration of church order or discipline, except as they may be called as witnesses.

Members Not to be Removed from Church Membership for Nonattendance—Absentees should be faithfully visited by the church leadership, and each should be encouraged to revive church attendance, explaining the seriousness of neglecting the obligation of church membership in deliberately absenting oneself for indefinite periods of time and making no report of one's faith and hope to the church. When because of age, infirmity, or other unavoidable cause, a member finds it impossible regularly to attend divine worship, it should be considered an obligation to keep in contact with the church leaders by letter or by other means. However, as long as a person is loyal to the doctrines of the church, nonattendance at church services shall not be considered sufficient cause for removal from church membership.

Members Moving Away and Not Reporting—When members move away from the vicinity, it is their duty to inform the church elder or clerk as to their new location and address. While they remain members of that church they should recognize their responsibility of reporting regularly to the church and sending in their tithes and offerings. It is desirable for such a report to be sent at least once each quarter. If, however, such a member leaves no address behind and makes no effort to reach the home church or send a report and it is found impossible to locate the missing member, then, after an absence of two years, an individual may be removed from the membership of the church by a vote of the church, provided the church officers can certify that they have faithfully endeavored to locate the person but without success. The clerk should record in the proper column, "Whereabouts unknown. Voted to designate as missing."

Members Not to be Removed for Pecuniary Reasons—A member should never be removed from the church records on account of one's inability or failure to render financial help to any of the causes of the church. Church membership rests primarily on a spiritual basis. It is the duty of every member to support the work of the church in a financial way to the extent of one's ability, but an individual should never be deprived of membership simply through inability or failure to render financial help to any of the causes of the church.

Removing a Member From Membership on Personal Request—Great care should be exercised in dealing with a member who requests to be removed from membership. Although we recognize the right of an individual to decide whether or not to belong to the church, ample time should be given such a member for sober thought and reflection, and every effort made to restore these individuals to a satisfactory experience. Letters of resignation should be presented to the church board which will forward them to the church at a duly called business meeting. Out of Christian consideration for the individuals involved, action shall be taken without public discussion.

Notification to Persons Removed from Membership—It is incumbent upon the church that removes a member from church membership to notify the individual in writing of the action that was reluctantly taken with the assurance of enduring spiritual interest and personal concern. This communication should, where possible, be delivered in person by the church pastor or by a church board designee. The erring member should be assured that the church will always hope that reaffiliation will take place and that one day there will be eternal fellowship together in the kingdom of God.

Reinstating a Person Previously Removed From Church Membership—When a person has been removed from church membership, the church should, where possible, maintain contact and manifest the spirit of friendship and love, endeavoring to win him/her back to the fold. A person previously removed from church membership may be received again into membership when confession of wrongs committed is made, evidence is given of real repentance and amendment of life, and it is clear that the member will fully submit to church order and discipline. Such reinstatement should preferably be in the church from which the member was dismissed. This, however, is not always possible. In this case, the church where the person is requesting reinstatement must seek information from the former church as to the reasons for which the person was removed from church membership.

Because removal from church membership is the most serious form of discipline, the period of time before such an individual may be reinstated should be sufficient to demonstrate that the issues which led to removal from membership have been resolved beyond reasonable doubt. Readmission to church membership is normally preceded by rebaptism.

Right of Appeal for Reinstatement—In a case where the church officers refuse to consider the application for reinstatement from a dismissed member, such an individual has a right to appeal to the church for a hearing. The church should not neglect or refuse to grant such a hearing. If it does, the individual has the right to appeal for a hearing to the executive committee of the conference/mission/field in which the church is located. If, after a full and impartial hearing, the conference/mission/field committee is satisfied that an injustice is being inflicted by the church, the committee may recommend the reinstatement of the dismissed member. But if membership is still refused by that church, then the committee may recommend the individual to membership in some other church. On the other hand, if it finds good grounds for sustaining the church in refusing to reinstate the member, it will so record its decision.

Transfer of Members Under Censure—No church shall receive into membership a person who is under the censure of another church. Such a course condones the offense for which another church has applied discipline.

The acceptance into membership of an individual who is under discipline is such a serious violation of church policy that the offending church may be subject to discipline applied by the conference/mission/field constituency.

CHAPTER 15

Marriage, Divorce, and Remarriage

Biblical Teachings on Marriage

The Origin of Marriage—Marriage is a divine institution established by God Himself before the fall when everything, including marriage, was "very good." (Gen. 1:31). "Therefore shall a man leave his father and his mother, and shall cleave unto his wife: and they shall be one flesh" (Gen. 2:24). "God celebrated the first marriage. Thus the institution has for its originator the Creator of the universe. 'Marriage is honourable'; it was one of the first gifts of God to man, and it is one of the two institutions that, after the fall, Adam brought with him beyond the gates of Paradise."—*The Adventist Home*, pp. 25, 26.

The Oneness of Marriage—God intended the marriage of Adam and Eve to be the pattern for all future marriages, and Christ endorsed this original concept saying: "Have ye not read that he which made them at the beginning made them male and female, and said, For this cause shall a man leave father and mother, and shall cleave to his wife: and they twain shall be one flesh? Wherefore they are no more twain, but one flesh. What therefore God hath joined together, let not man put asunder" (Matt. 19:4-6).

The Permanence of Marriage—Marriage is a lifelong commitment of husband and wife to each other and between the couple and God (Mark 10:2-9; Rom. 7:2). Paul indicates that the commitment which Christ has for the church is a model of the relationship between husband and wife (Eph. 5:31, 32). God intended the marriage relationship to be as permanent as Christ's relationship with the church.

Sexual Intimacy in Marriage—Sexual intimacy within marriage is a sacred gift from God to the human family. It is an integral part of marriage, reserved for marriage only (Gen. 2:24; Prov. 5:5-20). Such intimacy, designed to be shared exclusively between husband and wife, promotes ever-increasing closeness, happiness, and security, and provides for the perpetuation of the human race. In addition to being monogamous, marriage, as instituted by God, is a heterosexual relationship (Matt. 19:4, 5).

191

Partnership in Marriage—Unity in marriage is achieved by mutual respect and love. No one is superior (Eph. 5:21-28). "Marriage, a union for life, is a symbol of the union between Christ and His church. The spirit that Christ manifests toward the church is the spirit that husband and wife are to manifest toward each other."—*Testimonies,* vol. 7, p. 46. God's Word condemns violence in personal relationships (Gen. 6:11, 13; Ps. 11:5; Isa. 58:4, 5; Rom. 13:10; Gal. 5:19-21). It is the spirit of Christ to love and accept, to seek to affirm and build others up, rather than to abuse or demean them (Rom. 12:10; 14:19; Eph. 4:26; 5:28, 29; Col. 3:8-14; 1 Thess. 5:11). There is no room among Christ's followers for tyrannical control and the abuse of power (Matt. 20:25-28; Eph. 6:4). Violence in the setting of marriage and family is abhorrent (see *Adventist Home,* p. 343).

"Neither husband nor wife is to make a plea for rulership. The Lord has laid down the principle that is to guide in this matter. The husband is to cherish his wife as Christ cherishes the church. And the wife is to respect and love her husband. Both are to cultivate the spirit of kindness, being determined never to grieve or injure the other."—*Testimonies,* vol. 7, p. 47.

The Effects of the Fall on Marriage—The entrance of sin adversely affected marriage. When Adam and Eve sinned, they lost the oneness which they had known with God and with one another (Gen. 3:6-24). Their relationship became marked with guilt, shame, blame, and pain. Wherever sin reigns, its sad effects on marriage include alienation, desertion, unfaithfulness, neglect, abuse, violence, separation, divorce, domination of one partner by the other, and sexual perversion. Marriages involving more than one spouse are also an expression of the effects of sin on the institution of marriage. Such marriages, although practiced in Old Testament times, are not in harmony with the divine design. God's plan for marriage requires His people to transcend the mores of popular culture which are in conflict with the biblical view.

Restoration and Healing—1. *Divine Ideal to be Restored in Christ* — In redeeming the world from sin and its consequences, God also seeks to restore marriage to its original ideal. This is envisioned for the lives of those who have been born again into the kingdom of Christ, those whose hearts are being sanctified by the Holy Spirit and who have as their primary purpose in life the exaltation of the Lord Jesus Christ. (See also 1 Peter 3:7; *Thoughts From the Mount of Blessing,* p. 64.)

2. *Oneness and Equality to be Restored in Christ*—The gospel emphasizes the love and submission of husband and wife to one another (1 Cor. 7:3, 4; Eph. 5:21). The model for the husband's leadership is the

self-sacrificial love and service that Christ gives to the church (Eph. 5:24, 25). Both Peter and Paul speak about the need for respect in the marriage relationship (1 Peter 3:7; Eph. 5:22, 23).

3. *Grace Available for All*—God seeks to restore to wholeness and reconcile to Himself all who have failed to attain the divine standard (2 Cor. 5:19). This includes those who have experienced broken marriage relationships.

4. *The Role of the Church*—Moses in the Old Testament and Paul in the New Testament dealt with the problems caused by broken marriages (Deut. 24:1-5; 1 Cor. 7:11). Both, while upholding and affirming the ideal, worked constructively and redemptively with those who had fallen short of the divine standard. Similarly, the church today is called to uphold and affirm God's ideal for marriage and, at the same time, to be a reconciling, forgiving, healing community, showing understanding and compassion when brokenness occurs.

Biblical Teachings on Divorce

God's Original Purpose—Divorce is contrary to God's original purpose in creating marriage (Matt. 19:3-8; Mark 10:2-9), but the Bible is not silent about it. Because divorce occurred as part of the fallen human experience, biblical legislation was given to limit the damage it caused (Deut. 24:1-4). The Bible consistently seeks to elevate marriage and to discourage divorce by describing the joys of married love and faithfulness (Prov. 5:18-20; Song of Sol. 2:16; 4:9-5:1), by referring to the marriage-like relationship of God with His people (Isa. 54:5; Jer. 3:1), by focusing on the possibilities of forgiveness and marital renewal (Hosea 3:1-3), and by indicating God's abhorrence of divorce and the misery it causes (Mal. 2:15, 16). Jesus restored the creation view of marriage as a lifelong commitment between a man and a woman and between the couple and God (Matt. 19:4-6; Mark 10:6-9). Much biblical instruction affirms marriage and seeks to correct problems which tend to weaken or destroy the foundation of marriage (Eph. 5:21-33; Heb. 13:4; 1 Peter 3:7).

Marriages can be Destroyed—Marriage rests on principles of love, loyalty, exclusiveness, trust, and support upheld by both partners in obedience to God (Gen. 2:24; Matt. 19:6; 1 Cor. 13; Eph. 5:21-29; 1 Thess. 4:1-7). When these principles are violated, the marriage is endangered. Scripture acknowledges that tragic circumstances can destroy marriage.

Divine Grace—Divine grace is the only remedy for the brokenness of divorce. When marriage fails, former partners should be encouraged to examine their experience and to seek God's will for their lives. God provides comfort to those who have been wounded. God also accepts the repentance of individuals who commit the most destructive sins, even those that carry with them irreparable consequences (2 Sam. 11; 12; Ps. 34:18; 86:5; Joel 2:12, 13; John 8:2-11; 1 John 1:9).

Grounds for Divorce—Scripture recognizes adultery and/or fornication (Matt. 5:32) as well as abandonment by an unbelieving partner (1 Cor. 7:10-15) as grounds for divorce.

Biblical Teachings on Remarriage

There is no direct teaching in Scripture regarding remarriage after divorce. However, there is a strong implication in Jesus' words in Matthew 19:9 that would allow the remarriage of one who has remained faithful, but whose spouse has been unfaithful to the marriage vow.

The Church's Position on Divorce and Remarriage

Acknowledging the teachings of the Bible on marriage, the church is aware that marriage relationships are less than ideal in many cases. The problem of divorce and remarriage can be seen in its true light only as it is viewed from Heaven's viewpoint and against the background of the Garden of Eden. Central to God's holy plan for our world was the creation of beings made in His image who would multiply and replenish the earth and live together in purity, harmony, and happiness. He brought forth Eve from the side of Adam and gave her to Adam as his wife. Thus was marriage instituted—God the author of the institution, God the officiator at the first marriage. After the Lord had revealed to Adam that Eve was verily bone of his bone and flesh of his flesh, there could never arise a doubt in his mind that they twain were one flesh. Nor could ever a doubt arise in the mind of either of the holy pair that God intended that their home should endure forever.

The church adheres to this view of marriage and home without reservation, believing that any lowering of this high view is to that extent a lowering of the heavenly ideal. The belief that marriage is a divine institution rests upon the Holy Scriptures. Accordingly, all thinking and reasoning in the perplexing field of divorce and remarriage must constantly be harmonized with that holy ideal revealed in Eden.

The church believes in the law of God; it also believes in the forgiving mercy of God. It believes that victory and salvation can as surely be found by those who have transgressed in the matter of divorce and remarriage as by those who have failed in any other of God's holy standards. Nothing presented here is intended to minimize the mercy of God or the forgiveness of God. In the fear of the Lord, the church here sets forth the principles and practices that should apply in this matter of marriage, divorce, and remarriage.

Though marriage was first performed by God alone, it is recognized that people now live under civil governments on this earth; therefore, marriage has both a divine and a civil aspect. The divine aspect is governed by the laws of God, the civil by the laws of the state.

In harmony with these teachings, the following statements set forth the position of the Seventh-day Adventist Church:

1. When Jesus said, "Let not man put asunder," He established a rule of conduct for the church under the dispensation of grace which must transcend all civil enactments which would go beyond His interpretation of the divine law governing the marriage relation. Here He gives a rule to His followers who should adhere to it whether or not the state or prevailing custom allows larger liberty. "In the Sermon on the Mount Jesus declared plainly that there could be no dissolution of the marriage tie, except for unfaithfulness to the marriage vow."—*Thoughts From the Mount of Blessing*, p. 63. (Matt. 5:32; 19:9.)

2. Unfaithfulness to the marriage vow has generally been seen to mean adultery and/or fornication. However, the New Testament word for fornication includes certain other sexual irregularities. (1 Cor. 6:9; 1 Tim. 1:9, 10; Rom. 1:24-27.) Therefore, sexual perversions, including incest, child sexual abuse, and homosexual practices, are also recognized as a misuse of sexual powers and a violation of the divine intention in marriage. As such they are just cause for separation or divorce.

Even though the Scriptures allow divorce for the reasons mentioned above, as well as for abandonment by an unbelieving spouse (1 Cor. 7:10-15), earnest endeavors should be made by the church and those concerned to effect a reconciliation, urging the spouses to manifest toward each other a Christ-like spirit of forgiveness and restoration. The church is urged to relate lovingly and redemptively toward the couple in order to assist in the reconciliation process.

3. In the event that reconciliation is not effected, the spouse who has remained faithful to the spouse who violated the marriage vow has the biblical right to secure a divorce and also to remarry.

4. A spouse who has violated the marriage vow (see sections 1. and 2. above) shall be subject to discipline by the local church. (See Chapter 14, *Church Discipline*, pp. 182-190.) If genuinely repentant, the spouse may be

placed under censure for a stated period of time rather than removed from church membership. A spouse who gives no evidence of full and sincere repentance shall be removed from church membership. In case the violation has brought public reproach on the cause of God, the church, in order to maintain its high standards and good name, may remove the individual from church membership even though there is evidence of repentance.

Any of these forms of discipline shall be applied by the local church in a manner that would seek to attain the two objectives of church discipline—to correct and redeem. In the gospel of Christ, the redemptive side of discipline is always tied to an authentic transformation of the sinner into a new creature in Jesus Christ.

5.   A spouse who has violated the marriage vow and who is divorced does not have the moral right to marry another while the spouse who has been faithful to the marriage vow still lives and remains unmarried and chaste. The person who does so shall be removed from church membership. The person whom he/she marries, if a member, shall also be removed from church membership.

6.   It is recognized that sometimes marriage relations deteriorate to the point where it is better for a husband and wife to separate. "To the married I give charge, not I but the Lord, that the wife should not separate from her husband (but if she does, let her remain single or else be reconciled to her husband)—and that the husband should not divorce his wife" (1 Cor. 7:10, 11, RSV). In many such cases the custody of the children, the adjustment of property rights, or even personal protection may make necessary a change in marital status. In such cases it may be permissible to secure what is known in some countries as a legal separation. However, in some civil jurisdictions such a separation can be secured only by divorce.

A separation or divorce which results from factors such as physical violence or in which "unfaithfulness to the marriage vow" (see sections 1. and 2. above) is not involved, does not give either one the scriptural right to remarry, unless in the meantime the other party has remarried, committed adultery or fornication, or died. Should a member who has been thus divorced remarry without these biblical grounds, he/she shall be removed from church membership; and the one whom he/she marries, if a member, shall also be removed from church membership. (See pp. 184, 185.)

7.   A spouse who has violated the marriage vow and has been divorced and removed from church membership and who has remarried, or a person who has been divorced on other than the grounds set forth in sections 1. and 2. above and has remarried, and who has been removed from church membership, shall be considered ineligible for membership except as hereinafter provided.

8.   The marriage contract is not only sacred but also infinitely more

complex than ordinary contracts in its possible involvements; for example, with children. Hence, in a request for readmittance to church membership, the options available to the repentant may be severely limited. Before final action is taken by the local church, the request for readmittance shall be brought by the church through the pastor or district leader to the conference/mission/field committee for counsel and recommendation as to any possible steps that the repentant one, or ones, may take to secure such readmittance.

9. Readmittance to membership of those who have been removed from church membership for reasons given in the foregoing sections shall normally be on the basis of rebaptism. (See p. 189.)

10. When a person who has been removed from membership is readmitted to church membership, as provided in section 8., every care should be exercised to safeguard the unity and harmony of the church by not giving such a person responsibility as a leader; especially in an office which requires the rite of ordination, unless by very careful counsel with the conference/mission/field administration.

11. No Seventh-day Adventist minister has the right to officiate at the remarriage of any person who, under the stipulation of the preceding paragraphs, has no scriptural right to remarry.

Local Church Ministry for Families

The church as a redemptive agency of Christ is to minister to its members in all of their needs and to nurture every one so that all may grow into a mature Christian experience. This is particularly true when members face lifelong decisions such as marriage and distressful experiences such as divorce. When a couple's marriage is in danger of breaking down, every effort should be made by the partners and those in the church or family who minister to them to bring about their reconciliation in harmony with divine principles for restoring wounded relationships (Hosea 3:1-3; 1 Cor. 7:10, 11; 13:4-7; Gal. 6:1).

Resources are available through the local church or other church organizations which can be of assistance to members in the development of a strong Christian home. These resources include: (1) programs of orientation for couples engaged to be married, (2) programs of instruction for married couples with their families, and (3) programs of support for broken families and divorced individuals.

Pastoral support is vital in the area of instruction and orientation in the case of marriage, and healing and restoration in the case of divorce. The pastoral function in the latter case is both disciplinary and supportive. That function includes the sharing of information relevant to the case; however, the disclosure of sensitive information should be done with great discretion.

This ethical concern alone should not be the grounds for avoiding disciplinary actions established in sections 1. to 11. above.

Church members are called to forgive and accept those who have failed as God has forgiven them (Isa. 54:5-8; Matt. 6:14, 15; Eph. 4:32). The Bible urges patience, compassion, and forgiveness in the Christian care of those who have erred (Matt. 18:10-20; Gal. 6:1, 2). During the time when individuals are under discipline, either by censure or by being removed from membership, the church, as an instrument of God's mission, shall make every effort to maintain caring and spiritually nurturing contact with them.

CHAPTER 16

Organizing, Uniting, and Dissolving Churches

Organization of a Church

Churches are organized by an ordained minister on the recommendation of a conference/mission/field committee. Since so much is involved in the organization of a church, the local conference/mission/field president should, whenever possible, be invited to be present.

When a company of baptized believers, fully instructed in the message, is prepared to assume the responsibilities of an organized church, the conference/mission/field president should be taken into counsel and a date should be agreed upon for the organization to take place.

The baptized believers being assembled, it is well to present a brief review of the leading principles of our faith, such as belief in the Godhead with the personhood of God the Father, God the Son, and God the Holy Spirit, salvation by grace through faith, the new birth, the priesthood of Christ, the Second Advent, the law of God, the Sabbath, the nature of man, the state of the dead, the judgment, the church, baptism, the communion service, spiritual gifts, Christian stewardship, health and temperance, the oneness of the human family in Christ Jesus, and Christian social standards. Two or three representative texts should be cited in support of each teaching.

When this has been done a call should be made, asking all who are in agreement with these principles and who desire to unite in church fellowship to come forward. The name of each person should be recorded. If one or more are already members of the conference/mission/field church or any other church, the one officiating will already have ascertained this and will have had letters granted to them to join this new church. These will thus form a nucleus.

If, however, there are none present who have such membership elsewhere, then three members (preferably established Sabbathkeepers among those present) should be selected as a nucleus. The following questions might then be asked: Do you accept Christ as your personal Saviour? Are you in full harmony with the principles of faith that have just been presented? Have you been baptized by immersion? Are you in good fellowship and enjoying one another's confidence?

If these questions are answered in the affirmative, the three are declared to constitute the nucleus of the new church. Then one after another the names on that list are called, and the person is asked the foregoing questions, then a vote is taken among the nucleus to receive the individual into church fellowship. Each person thus received becomes a member of the church and is qualified to vote on the next name. Care should be taken to see that full fellowship and brotherly love exist among those received into membership. Should any difficulty arise in any case over a question either of doctrine or of fellowship, action in such cases should be deferred unless the matter can be adjusted at the time kindly and tactfully.

When all have been received the church is a complete entity and ready for the election of officers. A nominating committee should be chosen, with the officiating minister as chairman. This committee shall bring in nominations to fill the various church offices. When these have been elected, the elders should be ordained. After a brief outline of an elder's duties and the mutual responsibilities of members, the elders should be called to the platform and invited to kneel while the officiating ministers pray and lay hands upon them to signify that the church sets them apart for this service. A similar but shorter dedication should take place for the ordination of the deacons. When this has been done the church is fully organized and ready for service.

Before such a meeting closes, an action should be taken requesting the local conference to receive the newly organized church into the sisterhood of churches at the time of the next local conference/mission session.

Care should be taken to see that all officers are fully instructed concerning their duties. The church should have a communion set provided, also the materials needed for the ordinance of foot-washing. The treasurer, the clerk, and the other officers should be furnished with the necessary record and receipt books. All such details should be given careful attention, for the future prosperity of the church depends in a large degree upon the care that is exercised in its organization and instruction. When it can be arranged the communion service should be celebrated at the time the church is organized.

Uniting Churches

When it is advisable to unite two churches the conference/mission/field committee should take action recommending such a course. In a duly called meeting, presided over by the conference/mission/field president or the pastor or other ordained minister, each church should vote on the question of union. When favorable action has been taken by both churches a joint meeting of the two churches should be arranged with the conference/mission/field president presiding, or in his absence an ordained minister appointed by the conference/mission/field.

A carefully written statement of agreement should be prepared, setting forth the reasons for uniting and stating any special matters that may be involved, such as the disposal of property, the responsibility for financial obligations, et cetera. This statement should set forth the conditions of the agreement on which the union is made. It should provide for the new name of the united church and for the release from service of all officers of the two churches. The adoption of this agreement by the united body consummates the union of the two churches. Then a nominating committee should be chosen to nominate officers for the united church to serve for the remainder of the current year. A copy of the agreement should then be filed with the conference/mission/field.

When such a step has been taken the entire membership of both churches unites in the new organization. It is not permissible under such circumstances to remove any members by failing to include them in the membership list at the time of uniting. The united body becomes responsible for the order and discipline of all the members. Members under discipline should be dealt with as provided elsewhere in this manual.

The books and records of both churches become a part of the records of the united body. The local conference/mission/field should be notified and suitable actions taken at its next session.

Dissolving or Expelling Churches

". . . Christ also loved the church, and gave himself for it; that he might sanctify and cleanse it with the washing of water by the word, that he might present it to himself a glorious church, not having spot, or wrinkle, or any such thing; but that it should be holy and without blemish. . . . For no man ever yet hated his own flesh; but nourisheth and cherisheth it, even as the Lord the church: for we are members of his body, of his flesh, and of his bones" (Eph. 5:25-30).

This should ever be the attitude toward churches in the administering of discipline, either to the individual or to the church as a body—always to help and save for the cause of God. Conditions may make it necessary for a church to be dissolved. So many of the members may move away that the number remaining is not sufficient to support the organization. Occasionally difficulties arise that threaten the life of a church. Where the solution of these problems seems to require disciplinary action, it is advisable that a series of revival meetings be conducted. These meetings can be held with the idea to recover the church from its unfortunate state and to help the members to renew their covenant with the Lord. This is better than taking measures that would lead to a rupture in the church which could make dissolution necessary.

Churches may be dissolved or expelled from the sisterhood of churches for the following reasons:

1. Loss of Members—There are occasions when, in spite of endeavors to preserve a church, so many members are lost by removal from its neighborhood or by death or by apostasy that the existence of the church is threatened. Under such circumstances the conference/mission/field committee should take action recommending to the church concerned its dissolution.

Before a church takes final action to dissolve, the remaining members shall be invited to transfer their membership to other churches.

If enough members remain, this may be done by the calling of a meeting to be presided over by the conference/mission/field president or by a minister designated by him. At such a meeting letters of transfer may be voted to all remaining members who are in regular standing to unite with other churches. In this way the church dissolves itself upon recommendation of the conference/mission/field committee. The way will thus be opened for the conference/mission/field committee to take action recording the dissolution of the church.

If, in the judgment of the conference/mission/field committee, there are too few members available for the calling of such a meeting, the conference/mission/field committee shall have the authority to recommend such members as are in regular standing to other churches or to the conference/mission/field church. In this way the church is dissolved.

If at the time of dissolution there are members who are under discipline, and therefore cannot be granted letters saying they are in regular standing, their membership shall be provisionally held in the conference/mission/field church while conference/mission/field administration ensures that every effort is made as soon as possible to help such members to a satisfactory Christian experience. If the effort is successful, their membership may then be confirmed in the conference/mission/field church or letters may be granted to them for transfer to other churches. If they cannot be helped and reclaimed, they should be removed from membership by vote of the conference/mission/field committee.

2. Discipline—Occasions for expelling churches for disciplinary reasons are fortunately rare, for the mission of the church is to seek and to save. Where serious problems such as apostasy, refusal to operate in harmony with the *Church Manual*, or rebellion against the conference/ mission/field persist, earnest efforts should be made to avert the need for expulsion. The pastor should seek to deepen the spiritual life of the church through his preaching and personal visitation ministry. With conference/ mission/field cooperation, a series of revival meetings should be held to lead the members to renew their covenant with their Lord. If these efforts are not successful, the pastor, in cooperation with the conference/mission/field committee, should counsel with the church and its leadership, seeking to bring healing and reconciliation and to preserve the church as a witness for God and His saving truth.

The spirit of Christ should permeate all efforts to help an erring church and all aspects of any discipline that may be applied. That spirit is beautifully and persuasively portrayed in Ephesians 5:25-30 where Paul tells us that Christ loves the church and gave His life for it that He might have the joy of presenting it as a glorious church to His heavenly Father.

Such remedial measures are preferable to permitting the deterioration of relationships which could lead to expulsion of the church.

However, if all efforts to preserve the church fail, the conference/ mission/field committee should give careful study to the question of expulsion of the church. If such action is decided upon, there should then be recorded in its minutes a recommendation for expulsion with a statement of supporting reasons, and the following procedure shall be followed:

a. The decision to recommend the expulsion, with supporting reasons, shall be presented to the church itself in a business meeting for its information and consideration.

b. In the event that the church does not accept the recommendation, it may respond in one of the following ways:

1) Take an action to eliminate the causes for discipline, accepting the conference/mission/field specifications, and request the conference/mission/field to rescind the recommendation to dissolve or expel.

2) Appeal to the union executive committee to arbitrate on behalf of the church.

c. In the event that the church remains in rebellion, or the union executive committee upholds the conference/mission/field recommendation to expel the church, the conference/mission/field shall call an executive committee meeting and recommend to a conference/mission/field constituency meeting the expulsion of the church, presenting the reasons for the recommendation.

d. If the constituency takes action to expel, the conference/ mission/field shall enforce the decision.

Care of Members—In the membership of a church which has been dissolved or expelled, there may be loyal members who desire to remain with the Seventh-day Adventist communion. To ensure their welfare, their memberships shall be provisionally held for up to ninety days in the conference/mission/field church to allow opportunity for those who desire to do so to have their memberships in the conference/mission/field church confirmed or transferred to another church of their choice. Their standing shall be evaluated by the conference/mission/field committee, and, if satisfactory, they may be recommended for membership in the conference/mission/field church or a church of their choice.

The names of members of a dissolved or an expelled church, who are under discipline, shall be referred to the conference/mission/field secretary for early attention by the conference/mission/field committee as set out in section 1. above regarding dissolution of churches because of loss of members.

Conference/Mission Session to Act in All Cases—In any case of dissolution or expulsion of a church, for whatever reason, a statement of the facts shall be presented at the next session of the conference/mission and a recommendation made to remove the church from the list of constituent churches.

Church Assets, Funds, and Records—On dissolution or expulsion of a church for loss of members or for disciplinary reasons, all offerings, financial accounts, and all property real or personal, whether held in the name of the local church or the conference/mission/field or other denominational legal association, are held in trust for the conference/mission/field. The conference/mission/field therefore has the right, the authority, and the duty to administer, protect, or dispose of said property and funds. All books and records of such a church are to be held in the custody of the conference/mission/field secretary and/or treasurer.

CHAPTER 17

The Pulpit Not a Forum

No minister, church elder, or other person has the right to make the pulpit a forum for advocating disputed points of doctrine or procedure. The church does not confer upon any individual the right to exploit one's personal views and opinions in such a manner.

Those members who think they have new light contrary to the established views of the church should seek counsel from responsible leaders.

"There are a thousand temptations in disguise prepared for those who have the light of truth; and the only safety for any of us is in receiving no new doctrine, no new interpretation of the Scriptures, without first submitting it to brethren of experience. Lay it before them in a humble, teachable spirit, with earnest prayer; and if they see no light in it, yield to their judgment; for 'in the multitude of counselors there is safety.'"— *Testimonies*, vol. 5, p. 293.

This plan was followed in the early church. When a difference of opinion arose at Antioch over an important question, the believers sent representatives to Jerusalem, where the question was submitted to the apostles and elders for consideration. The decision of this council was joyfully accepted by the believers in Antioch, and thus unity and brotherly love were preserved in the church.

The foregoing counsel from the Lord must not be regarded as in any way deterring one from pursuing a diligent study of the Scriptures, but rather as a protection against the infiltration of false theories and erroneous doctrines into the church. God wants His children faithfully to search His Word for light and truth, but He does not want them to be led astray by false teachings.

The Bible is a mine of truth. "The earth itself is not so interlaced with golden veins and filled with precious things as is the word of God."— *Christ's Object Lessons*, p. 104. For this treasure we must seek diligently.

"Let none think that there is no more knowledge for them to gain. The depth of human intellect may be measured; the works of human authors may be mastered; but the highest, deepest, broadest flight of the imagination cannot find out God. There is infinity beyond all that we can comprehend. We have seen only the glimmering of divine glory and of the infinitude of

knowledge and wisdom; we have, as it were, been working on the surface of
the mine, when rich golden ore is beneath the surface, to reward the one who
will dig for it. The shaft must be sunk deeper and yet deeper in the mine, and
the result will be glorious treasure. Through a correct faith, divine
knowledge will become human knowledge."—*Christ's Object Lessons*,
p. 113.

"New light will ever be revealed on the word of God to him who is in
living connection with the Sun of Righteousness. Let no one come to the
conclusion that there is no more truth to be revealed. The diligent, prayerful
seeker for truth will find precious rays of light yet to shine forth from the
word of God. Many gems are yet scattered that are to be gathered together
to become the property of the remnant people of God."—*Counsels on
Sabbath School Work*, p. 34.

When new light shines forth from the sacred page to reward the earnest
seeker after truth, it does not make void the old. Instead it merges with the
old, causing it to grow brighter with added luster. Therefore, "the path of the
just is as the shining light, that shineth more and more unto the perfect day"
(Prov. 4:18).

Although the child of God must stand ready to accept advancing light,
one must never give heed to any voice, however pious and plausible, that
would lead away from the fundamental doctrines of the Bible.

"We are not to receive the words of those who come with a message that
contradicts the special points of our faith. They gather together a mass of
Scripture, and pile it as proof around their asserted theories. This has been
done over and over again during the past fifty years. And while the
Scriptures are God's word, and are to be respected, the application of them,
if such application moves one pillar from the foundation that God has
sustained these fifty years, is a great mistake. He who makes such an
application knows not the wonderful demonstration of the Holy Spirit that
gave power and force to the past messages that have come to the people of
God."—*Counsels to Writers and Editors*, p. 32.

It is important that we keep "the unity of the faith" (Eph. 4:13); it is just
as important that we seek at all times to "keep the unity of the Spirit in the
bond of peace" (verse 3). Hence the need for caution and thorough
investigation, also for counsel with the brethren.

"God is leading a people out from the world upon the exalted platform
of eternal truth, the commandments of God and the faith of Jesus. He will
discipline and fit up His people. They will not be at variance, one believing
one thing and another having faith and views entirely opposite, each moving
independently of the body. Through the diversity of the gifts and
governments that He has placed in the church, they will all come to the unity
of the faith. If one man takes his views of Bible truth without regard to the

opinion of his brethren, and justifies his course, alleging that he has a right to his own peculiar views, and then presses them upon others, how can he be fulfilling the prayer of Christ? And if another and still another arises, each asserting his right to believe and talk what he pleases without reference to the faith of the body, where will be that harmony which existed between Christ and His Father, and which Christ prayed might exist among His brethren?

"Though we have an individual work and an individual responsibility before God, we are not to follow our own independent judgment, regardless of the opinions and feelings of our brethren; for this course would lead to disorder in the church. It is the duty of ministers to respect the judgment of their brethren; but their relations to one another, as well as the doctrines they teach, should be brought to the test of the law and the testimony; then, if hearts are teachable, there will be no divisions among us. Some are inclined to be disorderly, and are drifting away from the great landmarks of the faith; but God is moving upon His ministers to be one in doctrine and in spirit. . . .

"In reviewing our past history, having traveled over every step of advance to our present standing, I can say, Praise God! As I see what God has wrought, I am filled with astonishment, and with confidence in Christ as leader. We have nothing to fear for the future except as we shall forget the way the Lord has led us."—*Testimonies to Ministers*, pp. 29-31.

In view of these considerations, it must be evident that the church cannot confer upon any individual the right to exploit personal views and opinions from the pulpit. The sacred desk must be reserved for the preaching of the sacred truths of the Divine Word and the presentation of denominational plans and policies for the advancement of the work of God. (See pp. 69, 137, 140, 157, 158.)

We should keep consecrated to the Lord day by day and seek Him for divine wisdom in the study of His Sacred Word. According to His own promise, the Holy Spirit will guide into all truth. The heart and mind should ever be kept open to the illumination of the Divine Spirit, that rays of heavenly light may shine across our pathway. Though we should take counsel with our brethren on matters that present problems to us, we should refrain from presenting publicly any questions that are not in full harmony with the views of the established body.

Summary of Doctrinal Beliefs

This summary of doctrinal beliefs is especially prepared for the instruction of candidates for baptism. (See pp. 31-34.)

1. The true and living God, the first person of the Godhead, is our heavenly Father, and He, by His Son, Christ Jesus, created all things. (Matt. 28:18, 19; 1 Cor. 8:5, 6; Eph. 3:9; Jer. 10:10-12; Heb. 1:1-3; Acts 17:22-29; Col. 1:16-18.)

2. Jesus Christ, the second person of the Godhead, and the eternal Son of God, is the only Saviour from sin; and man's salvation is by grace through faith in Him. (Matt. 28:18, 19; John 3:16; Micah 5:2; Matt. 1:21; 2:5, 6; Acts 4:12; 1 John 5:11, 12; Eph. 1:9-15; 2:4-8; Rom. 3:23-26.)

3. The Holy Spirit, the third person of the Godhead, is Christ's representative on earth, and leads sinners to repentance and to obedience of all God's requirements. (Matt. 28:18, 19; John 14:26; 15:26; 16:7-15; Rom. 8:1-10; Eph. 4:30.)

4. Through Christ, believers receive forgiveness of sins which are forsaken and confessed, and for which, as far as lies in their power, restitution is made. (Eph. 1:7; Col. 1:14, 15; 1 John 1:7-9; Isa. 55:6, 7; Eze. 33.15; Matt. 5:23, 24; 6:14, 15.)

5. The Bible is God's inspired word, and is the full, the sufficient, and the only basic rule of faith and practice. (2 Tim. 3:15-17; 2 Peter 1:19-21; Ps. 119:9, 11, 105, 130; 1 Thess. 2:13; Isa. 8:20; Jer. 15:16; Heb. 4:12.)

6. All who enter the kingdom of heaven must have experienced conversion, or the new birth, through which man receives a new heart and becomes a new creature. Thus, regardless of ethnic or social background, he becomes a member of "the whole family in heaven and earth." (Matt. 18:3; John 3:3; 2 Cor. 5:17; Eze. 36:26, 27; Heb. 8:10-12; 1 Peter 1:23; 2:2; Acts 17:26; Eph. 3:15.)

7. Christ dwells in the regenerate heart, writing upon it the principles of God's law, leading the believer to delight to obey its precepts, and imparting power for such obedience. (2 Cor. 6:16; Ps. 40:8; Heb. 8:10-12; John 14:15; Col. 1:27; 3:16; Gal. 2:20; Eph. 3:14-21.)

8. Upon His ascension Christ began His ministry as high priest in the holy place of the heavenly sanctuary, which sanctuary is the antitype of the earthly tabernacle of the former dispensation. As in the type, a work of

investigative judgment began as Christ entered the second phase of His ministry, in the Most Holy Place, foreshadowed in the earthly service by the Day of Atonement. This work of the investigative judgment in the heavenly sanctuary began in 1844, at the close of the 2300 years, and will end with the close of probation. (Heb. 4:14; 8:1, 2; Lev. 16:2, 29; Heb. 9:23, 24; Dan. 8:14; 9:24-27; Rev. 14:6, 7; 22:11.)

9. The second coming of Christ is the hope of the church, the climax of the gospel, and the goal of the plan of redemption, when Jesus will come literally, personally, and visibly, with all His holy angels. Many signs of the times testify that His coming is at hand. And the almost complete fulfillment of all the various lines of prophecy indicates that "he is near, even at the doors." (John 14:1-3; Titus 2:11-14; Heb. 9:28; Acts 1:9-11; Rev. 1:7; Matt. 25:31; Luke 9:26; 21:25-33; Matt. 24:14, 36-39, 33, margin.)

10. The righteous dead will be raised to life at Christ's second advent. Together with the righteous living, they will be caught up to meet the Lord in the air, and will go with Him to heaven, there to spend the one thousand years known as the millennium. (Rev. 1:7; John 5:25, 28, 29; Hosea 13:14; 1 Cor. 15:51-55; 1 Thess. 4:13-18; John 11:24, 25; 14:1-3; Rev. 20:6, 4, 5; Isa. 25:8, 9.)

11. The wicked who are living at the time of Christ's second advent will be slain by the brightness of His coming. These, with the wicked dead of all ages, will await the second resurrection, at the close of the one thousand years. (2 Thess. 1:7-10; 2:8; Jude 14, 15; Rev. 20:5, 12, 15; John 5:28, 29; Acts 24:15; Isa. 24:21, 22.)

12. At the end of the one thousand years, the following events will take place: *(a)* Christ and the righteous will descend from heaven, with the Holy City, the New Jerusalem (Rev. 21:2, 10); *(b)* the wicked dead will be resurrected for final judgment (Rev. 20:11, 12); *(c)* the wicked will receive the final wages of sin when fire comes down from God out of heaven to consume them (Rev. 20:7-10, 14, 15); and *(d)* this fire, which destroys the works of sin, will purify the earth. (2 Peter 3:10-14; Mal. 4:1, 3; Rev. 20:8, 4.)

13. The earth, cleansed by fire and renewed by the power of God, will become the eternal home of the redeemed. (2 Peter 3:9-13; Isa. 65:17-25; 35:1-10; 45:18; Matt. 5:5; Mal. 4:1-3; Prov. 11:31.)

14. The seventh day of the week is the eternal sign of Christ's power as Creator and Redeemer, and is therefore the Lord's day, or the Christian Sabbath, constituting the seal of the living God. It should be observed from sunset Friday to sunset Saturday. (Gen. 2:1-3; Ex. 16:23-31; 20:8-11; John 1:1-3, 14; Eze. 20:12, 20; Mark 1:21-32; 2:27, 28; Isa. 58:13; Luke 4:16; 23:54-56; 24:1; Acts 17:2; Heb. 4:9-11; Isa. 66:22, 23; Lev. 23:32.)

15. Marriage is one of the God-given institutions dating from the

Garden of Eden, before sin entered the world. Jesus honored the institution of marriage and upheld its sanctity and permanence. The New Testament repeatedly affirms the sacredness of the marriage relationship, and instructs that it is to be entered into with a lifelong commitment to fidelity and moral purity. Sexual intimacies between male and female outside of marriage or between members of the same sex are contrary to the divine plan and are condemned in the Bible as sin. Those who are followers of Jesus will by His grace maintain moral purity within these biblical guidelines concerning sexual relationships. "For this is the will of God, your sanctification: that you abstain from immorality" (1 Thess. 4:3, RSV).

The Christian husband and wife are to love and respect one another as God loves and respects them. They are commanded to love and respect their children, to treat them gently, and to teach them to love and serve God. To this end they are to utilize family worship, attendance at Sabbath School and the other church services, and as much as possible, the schools operated by the church. Likewise children are to fulfill their responsibilities to respect and obey their parents. (Gen. 2:21-24; Deut. 4:6, 7; Matt. 19:3-9; 1 Cor. 6:9-11; Eph. 5:24, 25, 28; Col. 3:18-21; 1 Thess. 4:3-8; Heb. 10:23-35; 13:4; 1 Peter 3:7.)

16. The tithe is holy unto the Lord, and is God's provision for the support of His ministry. Freewill offerings are also part of God's plan for the support of His work throughout the world. (Lev. 27:30-32; Mal. 3:8-12; Num. 18:20-28; Matt. 23:23; Prov. 3:9, 10; 1 Cor. 9:13, 14; 2 Cor. 9:6, 7; Ps. 96:8. See pp. 16, 33, 34, 51, 151-156.)

17. Immortality comes only through the gospel, and is bestowed as a gift from God at Christ's second coming. (1 Cor. 15:21, 22, 51-55; Ps. 146:3, 4; Eccl. 9:5, 6, 10; 1 Tim. 6:15, 16; 2 Tim. 1:10; 1 John 5:11, 12.)

18. The condition of man in death is one of unconsciousness. All men, good and evil alike, remain in the grave from death to the resurrection. (Eccl. 9:5, 6; Ps. 115:17; 146:3, 4; Job 14:10-12, 21, 22; 17:13; John 11:11-14; 1 Thess. 4:13; John 5:28, 29.)

19. The Christian is called unto sanctification, and his life should be characterized by carefulness in deportment and modesty and simplicity in dress. (1 Thess. 3:13; 4:3, 7; 5:23; 1 Peter 2:21; 3:15, 3-5; Isa. 3:16-24; 1 Cor. 10:31; 1 Tim. 2:9, 10. See pp. 16, 166-171.)

20. The Christian should recognize his body as the temple of the Holy Spirit. He will therefore honor God by caring for his body intelligently, partaking in moderation of that which is good and avoiding the use of that which is harmful, abstaining from all unclean foods, from the use, manufacture, or sale of alcoholic beverages, the use, manufacture, or sale of tobacco in any of its forms for human consumption, and from the misuse of,

or trafficking in, narcotics or other drugs. (1 Cor. 3:16, 17; 6:19, 20; 9:25; 10:31; 2 Cor. 7:1; Gal. 5:17-21; 6:7, 8; 1 Peter 2:9-12; 1 Cor. 10:1-11; Lev. 11:1-8. See pp. 16, 33, 34, 185.)

21. The church is to come behind in no gift, and the presence of the gift of prophecy is to be one of the identifying marks of the remnant church. (1 Cor. 1:5-7; 12:1-28; Amos 3:7; Hosea 12:10, 13; Rev. 12:17; 19:10. See pp. 14, 33, 34.)

Seventh-day Adventists recognize that this gift was manifested in the life and ministry of Ellen G. White.

22. The Bible teaches a definite church organization. The members of this organization are under sacred obligation to be subject thereunto, loyally to support it, and to share in its maintenance. They are admonished not to forsake the assembling of themselves together. (Matt. 16:16-18; Eph. 1:10-23; 2:19-22; 1 Cor. 14:33, 40; Titus 1:5-9; Matt. 18:15-18; 1 Cor. 12:12-28; 16:1-3; Heb. 10:25; Acts 4:32-35; 6:1-7.)

23. Baptism by immersion typifies the death, burial, and resurrection of Christ, and openly expresses faith in His saving grace and the renunciation of sin and the world, and is recognized as a condition of entrance into church membership. (Matt. 3:13-17; 28:19; Acts 2:38, 41-47; 8:35-39; 16:32, 33; 22:16; Rom. 6:1-11; Gal. 3:27; Col. 3:1-3. See pp. 30, 33, 34.)

24. The ordinance of the Lord's Supper commemorates the Saviour's death; and participation by members of the body is essential to Christian growth and fellowship. It is to be preceded by the ordinance of foot-washing as a preparation for this solemn service. (Matt. 26:26-29; 1 Cor. 11:23-26; John 6:48-56; 13:1-17; 1 Cor. 11:27-30.)

25. In the Christian life there is complete separation from worldly practices, such as card playing, theater going, dancing, et cetera, which tend to deaden and destroy the spiritual life. (2 Cor. 6:15-18; 1 John 2:15-17; James 4:4; 2 Tim. 2:19-22; Eph. 5:8-11; Col. 3:5-10. See pp. 168-170.)

26. Through the study of the Word God speaks to us, imparting light and strength; and through prayer the soul is united with God. These are Heaven's ordained means for obtaining victory in the conflict with sin and for the development of Christian character. (Ps. 19:7, 8; 119:130; John 6:63; 17:17; 1 Peter 2:2; 1 Thess. 5:17; Luke 18:1; Ps. 55:17; Isa. 50:4.)

27. Every church member is under sacred command from Jesus to use his talents in personal soul-winning work in helping to give the gospel to all the world. When this work is finished Jesus will come. (Matt. 25:14-29; 28:18-20; Rev. 22:17; Isa. 43:10-12; 2 Cor. 5:17-20; Rom. 10:13-15; Matt. 24:14.)

28. In accordance with God's uniform dealing with mankind, warning them of coming events that will vitally affect their destiny, He has sent forth

a proclamation of the approaching return of Christ. This preparatory message is symbolized by the three angels' messages of Revelation 14, and meets its fulfillment in the great Second Advent Movement today. This has brought forth the remnant, or Seventh-day Adventist Church, keeping the commandments of God and the faith of Jesus. (Amos 3:7; Matt. 24:29-34; Rev. 14:6-10; Zeph. 3:13; Micah 4:7, 8; Rev. 14:12; Isa. 26:2; Rev. 22:14.)

Organizations for Holding Church Properties: Trust Services, Wills, and Annuities

Legal Organizations Under the Law

The Seventh-day Adventist Church conducts its evangelistic work and performs its other religious functions as an unincorporated body. It is the general plan not to incorporate or register regular denominational organizations unless required by law. Corporate organizations are established pursuant to governing laws for the management of legal activity, and these operate under rules and bylaws as adopted by each organization. All organizations planning to form legal corporations for operations in North America shall first secure approval from the General Conference Executive Committee. The delegates to the regular conference sessions constitute the delegates to the session of the legal organization.

Title to Church Properties

In order to safeguard denominational property it is necessary to have the title vested in a corporation created by a conference organization according to the laws governing in the locality where the property is located. Title to all local church properties should be held by the conference corporations. When properties are acquired for the use of local churches or conference organizations, the titles should be held by the corporate organizations.

Care of Legal Documents

All legal documents, including insurance policies, church property deeds, abstracts, and trust agreements, should be filed for safekeeping in the office of the corporate organization.

Church Repairs and Upkeep

The church, its related buildings, and their furnishings should always be kept in representative condition. Funds for this purpose should come from the church-expense budget or from special contributions. Under the direction of the church board, this work is generally supervised by the deacons.

Insurance Policies

The church board, through the church treasurer, is under obligation to see that the properties of the denomination, such as the church building, school buildings, and equipment, are kept adequately covered by insurance. Provision for this expense should be made in the church budget. The following procedures are recommended:

1. The local church board, through the treasurer, and in consultation with the treasurer of the conference or corporation, shall be responsible for adequate insurance coverage of assets, including fire, theft, boiler, public liability, and workman's compensation insurance, in harmony with denominational policy.

2. All denominational assets shall be insured with companies of sound financial standing and A-grade general policyholders' rating. Reciprocals and assessable companies are not recommended. Whenever possible, insurance should be purchased through Adventist Risk Management, Incorporated.

3. The conference or corporation treasurer shall be responsible for holding and keeping a complete record of the insurance policies covering the property and assets in the conference and its churches.

a. This record shall include the name and description of the property, the amount of insurance carried, the name of the company with which it is insured, the expiration date of the insurance policy, and other relevant details.

b. Negotiations for the renewal of insurance policies should begin at least 60 days before the expiration date, to avoid unintentional lapse of coverage.

4. It shall be the duty of the conference auditor to review the church, school, or other church property insurance program and report to the governing board or committee any inadequacies in insurance coverages not in harmony with *Working Policy* recommendations.

Wills, Trusts, Annuities, and Life Income Agreements

The spirit of sacrifice and dedication is fundamental to Christian service. Moneys and property which are not given outright to the cause may still be contributed to the work of God through wills, trusts, annuities, and life income agreements.

Laws Must be Strictly Followed

Laws concerning the disposition of one's property, either before or after death, must be strictly followed. If conveyance of real estate is made by deed, the laws of the state or province where the land is located govern the requisites of the deed. Disposing of one's property, whether real or personal, to take effect after death, may be done by will, or the will may be supplemented by a trust agreement. Therefore, a will or a trust agreement is of utmost importance. Christian responsibility is demonstrated when one provides for the future security of one's dependent family, and for meeting future needs of the church.

"Our brethren should feel that a responsibility rests upon them, as faithful servants in the cause of God, to exercise their intellect in regard to this matter, and secure to the Lord His own."—*Testimonies*, vol. 4, p. 479.

Wills

The making of a will calls for good counsel. We are given definite instruction relative to securing proper counsel in the executing of wills, as follows:

"Many families have been dishonestly robbed of all their property and have been subjected to poverty because the work that might have been well done in an hour had been neglected. Those who make their wills should not spare pains or expense to obtain legal advice and to have them drawn up in a manner to stand the test."—*Testimonies*, vol. 3, p. 117.

It is essential that a will be executed in accordance with the statutory requirements of the state, province, or country where the will is made.

Bequests to the Church Organization

Bequests should be made to the legal organization of the local, union, or General Conference, or denominational institutions. In such cases, great care should be exercised to ensure the use of the correct legal title. Church officers should put their members in touch with the conference officers concerning potential bequests and subsequent procedures that the Lord's property, which He has entrusted to His people, may be secured for His work.

Transferring Property Before Death

A donor's wishes for ensuring that moneys and properties will accrue for the Lord's work, for family, or others, prior to his/her death, can be fulfilled through trusts, annuities, and life income agreements.

More detailed information on the advantages of available plans may be obtained, in confidence and without obligation, by consulting with the officers of the legal association of the conference or institution.

Health Care Institutions

The gospel ministry is advanced through health care institutions which are influenced by Christ and His Spirit. Seventh-day Adventists see in the gospel commission, and the example of the Lord and His apostles, the responsibility of followers of Christ to serve the spiritual, mental, and physical needs of humankind through motivated Christian lives and service. Thus from the earliest years of the Adventist movement, health care institutions have been established to help facilitate the total ministry of carrying the gospel to all the world.

General Index

of the General Conference, 1,
27, 28
over funds, 60
positions of, 45
Seventh-day Adventist
Church, *xx, xxi,* 1
tests of fellowship, 186
to solicit help, 158
to speak, 69, 140
Auxiliary organizations of the
church, 93-134

B

Baptism: and Commitment,
Certificate of, 31, 33
as a gospel requirement, 29
by immersion, 13, 30, 33, 34,
212
candidate(s), 29-32, 34, 35, 56,
63, 209
ceremony of, 35
certificate of, 31, 33
children, 29, 76, 132
classes, 31, 35, 76, 132
covenant, 31, 32, 33, 35, 42,
56
deaconesses to assist, 35, 56
deacons to assist, 35, 55, 63
doctrinal beliefs, 209
evangelist's converts, 35
fundamental beliefs, 13, 199
instruction before, 29-31, 209
meaning of, 29, 30
mode of, 29, 30
of former member, 41, 42, 185,
189, 197
prerequisite to membership,
30, 31, 35, 41
public examination before, 30,
31

rebaptism, 41, 42, 185, 189,
197
right hand of fellowship, 35
robes for, 35, 56
school children, 91
service of, 50, 56, 63
symbol of union with Christ,
13
vow, 32
welcome, subject to, 34
who may administer, 50, 52,
137
Baptismal classes, 31, 35, 76, 132
Baptismal covenant, 31
Baptismal service, 50, 55, 56, 63
Baptismal vow, 32
Bazaars, 158
Behavior, Christian, 16
Behavior in church, 67, 68
Beliefs, fundamental, 9-19, 30, 32,
33, 34
Bequests, 217
Beverages, alcoholic, 16, 33,
34, 185, 211
See alcohol, alcoholic
beverages, liquor
Bible, 9, 15, 28, 32, 34, 99, 119,
153, 154, 193, 194, 198,
205, 206, 209, 211, 212
clubs, 96, 120, 132
conference, 105
correspondence schools, 129,
133
courses, 123, 133
evangelism, 123
instructors, 138, 139
pastor's class, 96
principles, 33, 34
prophecy, 33, 34
quizzes, 127
reading plans, 105

responsibility of, for dealing
with sin, 178-185
statistics, reports of, 37
timeliness in disciplinary
process, 185
Church Manual, xix, 1,
Committee, *xxi*
Historical Development, *xix*
Content of, *xxi*
Procedure for Changes, *xxi*
Church meetings. *See* Meetings
Church members. *See* Members
Church membership. *See*
Membership
Church mission offerings. *See*
Mission Offerings
Church missionary funds. *See*
Funds, outreach (missionary)
Church Missionary meetings. *See*
Personal Ministries
Church officers. *See* Officers, of
the local church
Church Officers and Their Duties,
43-65
Church ordinances. *See* Baptism;
Communion services
Church organization. *See*
Organization
Church organizations, bequests to,
217
Church Outreach (Missionary)
Meetings, 80, 90, 91
Church Properties. *See* Properties,
of church
Church records, 57, 58
Church school(s), 84, 108, 109,
110, 128
AJYS, 79, 90, 105
education secretary, 109
expense, 156
financial status of, 91
funds, 60

Home and School Association,
109
objectives, 108
Pathfinder Club, 107
philosophy, 108
principal, 91, 111
teacher, 58, 91
treasurer, 61, 110, 111, 112
subsidy, 157
Church School board, 84, 110
chairperson, 84, 111, 112
duties of officers, 112
functions, North America, 113
meetings, 84, 112
membership, 110, 111
officers, 111
qualifications of members, 112
representing a single church,
111, 112, 128
representing two or more
churches, 111, 129
secretary, 84, 111, 112
term of office, 111
union school board, 111, 112,
128
vacancies, 111
Church, services of. *See* Meetings
Church treasurer. *See* Treasurer,
local church
Churches: dissolving of, 201-204
uniting of, 200, 201
Classes: AJYS, 106
AYS, 105, 106, 128
baptismal, 31, 35, 76, 132
Clerk, local church, 57, 58
corresponds with members, 57,
64
importance of office, 57
keeps records of meetings and
membership, 57, 58
letters of transfer, 35-38, 57
member of church board, 82

Companion (AJY Class), 106
Company, organized, 39, 40
Conference, Use of the Term, *xxii*
    See General Conference
Conference/Mission, 148, 149,
    150
    church, 39, 149
    committee, 150
    constituency, 26, 148, 149
    delegates, 52, 57, 148, 149
    officers, 149
    session, 38, 51, 52, 57, 140,
    148, 149, 200, 204
    See also Union/Conference/
    Mission
Conference/Mission/Field, *xxii*,
    26, 35, 39, 48, 50, 51, 57,
    59, 65, 69, 75, 90, 97, 98,
    100, 104, 110, 113, 116,
    137. 139, 150, 154, 204
    auditor, 60
    church, 38, 39, 40, 199, 202,
    204
    committee, 39, 40, 41, 47, 49,
    50, 61, 111, 125, 136, 137,
    138, 145, 189, 197, 200,
    202, 203, 204
    constituency of, 26, 190, 203
    departments, 51, 90, 93, 97,
    98, 99, 110, 114, 116, 122,
    124, 125, 127, 130, 131,
    132, 134, 136
    funds, 51, 58, 59, 115, 157,
    158, 159
    not to establish tests of
    fellowship, 186
    officers, 43, 81, 154
    policies, 79, 80, 136
    president, 52, 69, 129, 135,
    136, 138, 139, 184, 187,
    199, 200, 202

receiving and removing
    members, 40
    relations, 49, 50, 51, 81,
    135-141, 199, 204
    removing a minister, 140
    reports to, 51, 57, 61, 64, 65,
    125
    secretary, 51, 204
    treasurer, 40, 51, 59, 61, 91,
    147, 159, 204
    use of term, *xxii*
    workers, 39, 135-141, 153,
    154
Conference/Mission/Field church,
    38, 39, 40, 199, 202, 204
Corporations, legal, 215
Corresponding with members, 57,
    64
Cosmetics, 167
Council: Annual, or Autumn, *xxi,*
    xxii, 27
    Health Ministries, 115, 129,
    130
    Pathfinder Club Staff, 106
    Personal Ministries, 62, 91,
    93, 94, 95, 115, 120, 123,
    124, 134
    Sabbath School, 59, 96, 97, 98,
    125, 126, 146
Counseling: family, 117
    marital, 117
    premarital, 117, 173
Courtship, 172
Covenant: baptismal, 31, 33
    marital, 172
Credentials and licenses, 48, 54,
    56, 62, 69, 139, 140, 148
    expired, 140
    ministers without, 141
    of delegates, 57
Crucifixion, memorial of, 75

P

R

Index of Scripture Texts

Index of Extracts From
the Spirit of Prophecy Writings